The Bible Speaks Today

Series Editors: J. A. Motyer (OT)
John R. W. Stott (NT)

Songs from a Strange Land,
The Message of Psalms 42-51, John Goldingay

A Time to Mourn, and a Time to Dance,
The Message of Ecclesiastes, Derek Kidner

The Lord Is King,
The Message of Daniel, Ronald S. Wallace

The Day of the Lion,
The Message of Amos, J. A. Motyer

Christian Counter-Culture,
The Message of the Sermon on the Mount, John R. W. Stott

The Savior of the World,
The Message of Luke's Gospel, Michael Wilcock

Only One Way,
The Message of Galatians, John R. W. Stott

God's New Society,
The Message of Ephesians, John R. W. Stott

Guard the Gospel,
The Message of 2 Timothy, John R. W. Stott

I Saw Heaven Opened,
The Message of Revelation, Michael Wilcock

THE SAVIOR OF
THE WORLD

The Message of Luke's Gospel

Michael Wilcock

InterVarsity Press
Downers Grove
Illinois 60515

InterVarsity Press is the book-publishing division
of Inter-Varsity Christian Fellowship,
a student movement active on campus at hundreds
of universities, colleges and schools of
nursing. For information about local and regional
activities, write IVCF, 233 Langdon St.,
Madison, WI 53703.

Distributed in Canada through Inter-Varsity
Press, Canada, Unit 10, 1875 Leslie Street, Toronto,
Ontario M3B 2M5, Canada.

Unless otherwise stated, quotations from the Bible
are from the Revised Standard Version,
copyrighted 1946, 1952, © 1971, 1973
by the Division of Christian Education,
National Council of the Churches of Christ in
the United States of America, and
used by permission.

ISBN 0-87784-599-9
Library of Congress
Catalog Card Number: 79-2720

Printed in the United States of America

To my Parents
for their
Year of Jubilee
1928–1978

General preface

The Bible speaks today describes a series of both Old and New Testament expositions, which are characterized by a three-fold ideal: to expound the biblical text with accuracy, to relate it to contemporary life, and to be readable.

These books are, therefore, not 'commentaries', for the commentary seeks rather to elucidate the text than to apply it, and tends to be a work rather of reference than of literature. Nor, on the other hand, do they contain the kind of 'sermons' which attempt to be contemporary and readable, without taking Scripture seriously enough.

The contributors to this series will all be united in their conviction that God still speaks through what he has spoken, and that nothing is more necessary for the life, growth and health of churches or of Christians than that they should hear and heed what the Spirit is saying to them through his ancient—yet ever modern—Word.

J. A. MOTYER
J. R. W. STOTT
Series Editors

Contents

CONTENTS

Author's preface

When I embarked on my previous contribution to this series, I had great misgivings about tackling so long and difficult a book as Revelation. The same misgivings have loomed even larger in the case of this present exposition. With regard to difficulty, I think the task of expounding Luke's Gospel is quite as hard as that of expounding John's Revelation, though for the opposite reason: whereas the latter is so unfamiliar, the former is too familiar by half. If there is one thing harder than to chart a region where the foot of man has seldom trod, it is to produce a worthwhile guide book to a place that everyone knows already.

So I can claim no more than to be offering a personal view of what Luke is saying to us. It has been subjected to the criticisms of several discerning friends, in particular those of an articulate (not to say argumentative!) congregation at St Faith's, Maidstone, who recently 'listened to Luke' for the best part of a year, and my thanks are due to them all. But the final responsibility for this book is my own.

Having mentioned the difficulties, I should say something about the matter of length also. The third Gospel, although it has fewer chapters than Matthew or Acts, is actually the longest book in the whole New Testament. Therefore it poses, more acutely than any other which will be dealt with in this series, the problem of selectivity. Godet's old commentary on Luke runs to 903 pages, and Marshall's new one, though produced in a less discursive age, to 928;[1] in an exposition less than a quarter of that size, what is to be put in and what left out?

[1] I. Howard Marshall, *Commentary on the Gospel of Luke* (Paternoster, 1978). Unfortunately this fine work appeared too recently for me to make use of it in my own exposition.

Readers will notice the practical ways in which I have tried to grasp this nettle. For a start, Luke's text is not printed in full, but only quoted, a few verses at a time. It will probably be found helpful, therefore, to have a Bible to hand, and to read the whole of the relevant passage there before turning to the exposition here. For another thing, this book *is* strictly an exposition. It is not a commentary; you will not find systematic comment on each verse and its problems. In fact, while acknowledging the value of detailed Bible study, I have been constantly aware of the danger of not seeing the wood for the trees, and have deliberately tried to stand back and get a view of the landscape as a whole. As a result, I believe I discern in the Gospel a shape, a structure—not the kind *im*posed by a preacher who is determined to find three points all beginning with P, but the kind which is *ex*posed by a careful and prayerful study of what Luke was aiming to 'put across'. Somewhere between two extremes, a fugal complexity on the one hand and a shapeless jumble on the other,[2] is the pattern which Luke had in mind when he constructed his 'orderly account' (1:3). In the pages that follow, I have attempted to find that pattern, to bring out its meaning, and to show, as I understand it, what Luke is about.

Trinity College,   MICHAEL WILCOCK
Bristol

[2] The two opposite tendencies (though not perhaps the extremes!) may be seen in Ellis (pp. 30–37) and Morris (pp. 61–63).

Chief abbreviations

AG   *A Greek-English Lexicon of the New Testament and Other Early Christian Literature* by William F. Arndt and F. Wilbur Gingrich (University of Chicago Press and Cambridge University Press, 1957).

AV   *The Authorized* (King James') *Version* of the Bible (1611).

Caird   *The Gospel of St Luke* by G. B. Caird (Pelican, 1963).

Drury   *Luke* by John Drury (*The J. B. Phillips' Commentaries*, Collins Fontana, 1973).

Ellis   *The Gospel of Luke* edited by E. Earle Ellis (*The New Century Bible*, Nelson, 1966).

Geldenhuys   *Commentary on the Gospel of Luke* by Norval Geldenhuys (Marshall, Morgan and Scott, 1950).

Godet   *Commentary on the Gospel of Luke* by F. L. Godet (T. & T. Clark, 1887).

JB   *The Jerusalem Bible* (Darton, Longman and Todd, 1966).

JBP   *The New Testament in Modern English* by J. B. Phillips (Collins, 1958).

Moffatt   *The New Testament: a New Translation* by James Moffatt (Hodder and Stoughton, revised edition, 1935).

Morris   *The Gospel according to St Luke* by Leon Morris (*Tyndale New Testament Commentaries*, Inter-Varsity Press, 1974).

NEB   *The New English Bible* (New Testament, 1961; 2nd edition 1970; OT 1970).

Plummer   *The Gospel according to St Luke* by Alfred Plummer (*The International Critical Commentary*, T. & T. Clark, fifth edition, 1922).

RSV   *The Revised Standard Version* of the Bible (NT 1946, 2nd edition 1971; OT 1952).

RV   *The Revised Version* of the Bible (1885).

Stonehouse   *The Witness of Luke to Christ* by N. B. Stonehouse (Tyndale Press, 1951).

Weymouth   *The New Testament in Modern Speech* by R. F. Weymouth (James Clarke, 1903).

Introduction

Since I am what some of my friends (regrettably) think of as a 'professional' Christian, many of the books on my shelves are the tools of my profession, and tend to be rather more heavy going than the books which these friends keep on *their* shelves. Such 'professional' books would be even more daunting for a non-professional reader who, instead of dipping in here and there, preferred to start at page 1, because he would find their introductions even more technical than the rest. I hasten to say that I am in no way decrying the value of this sort of writing. It provides the raw material out of which something more readable, though more superficial, can be made. There is no denying, however, that the kind thing to say about most of these introductions is that they are Worthy but Dull.

The book before you is not technical, and it does not—I hope—begin with a Worthy but Dull Introduction. According to the opening sentence of a classic which I had read many times long before I had even heard of the word 'commentary', 'an Introduction is to introduce people'.[1] So without more ado, dear reader, I should like you to meet Doctor Luke.

Many of the things which you will learn about him from the introductions of commentaries—his object in writing his Gospel, his interest in history and in theology and in the relation between the two, his methods, his style, and his characteristics—are touched on as they arise in the main part of this book. The only matter which I shall not mention elsewhere, but to which the commentators devote considerable space, is that of the date when he wrote. I think it likely myself that his two books, the Gospel and the book of Acts, were both produced in the early sixties of the first century. He cannot have

[1] A. A. Milne's *The House at Pooh Corner* (as of course you knew).

completed them sooner, since they include an account of Paul's imprisonment at Rome at the beginning of that decade; and if he had written them later, they could hardly have failed to bear traces of the events of the next few years, especially Nero's persecution of the church in AD 64. But a great variety of suggestions have been made, and no-one really knows for certain.

It is with Luke himself, however, that this introduction is chiefly concerned, the man for whose commemorative day the English reformers provided a wonderfully suggestive prayer:

> Almighty God, who calledst Luke the Physician, whose praise is in the Gospel, to be an Evangelist, and Physician of the soul: May it please thee that, by the wholesome medicines of the doctrine delivered by him, all the diseases of our souls may be healed; through the merits of thy Son Jesus Christ our Lord.[2]

As this collect assumes, the 'Evangelist'—the author of the third Gospel—was indeed Luke, the apostle Paul's friend and travelling companion, whose presence can be detected in those parts of the book of Acts where the writer says that 'we' did such-and-such. This at any rate has been the view most widely held from the earliest times. Secondly, we know from Paul's own testimony in Colossians 4:14 that Luke was a physician. These two identifications (that the evangelist was Luke, and that he was a physician) are generally accepted; but a third statement, that he was also the unnamed person 'whose praise is in the gospel', mentioned by Paul in 2 Corinthians 8:18, is an assumption only. We shall return to this later. First, we meet our author simply as Luke.

1. Luke

It is a fair guess that he was not a Jew but a Gentile. His Greek name might indicate this; although Greek names might be borne by Jews (by Andrew and Philip, for example, among the twelve apostles, rubbing shoulders with two Jacobs, two Simeons, two Judahs, and a Levi!).[3] His command of the Greek language is excellent; although that also might be true of many an educated Jew. The passage which seems to most scholars to show that Luke really was a Gentile is in

---

[2] The 1662 Prayer Book.

[3] These last four names are more familiar to New Testament readers, of course, as James, Simon, Judas, and Matthew.

Colossians 4, where Paul appears to list his Jewish fellow workers in verses 10 and 11, and the rest, including Luke, in verses 12 to 14. Even here, opinion is not unanimous.[4] But what cannot be denied is that this Gospel is thoroughly Gentile in its spirit and outlook.

When you consider this, it is a stirring thought. The so-called 'Gentile mission', the spread of the good news beyond the bounds of the Israelite nation, is a major theme both in the Gospel and in Acts, but the two books are themselves an integral part of that mission, and an instrument of it. In an age when many in the church were still very conscious of their Jewish roots, it is striking that this spacious and beautiful work—its first volume the longest book in the New Testament and the fullest of the four Gospels, and the two volumes together making Luke's contribution to the New Testament bigger than that of any other writer—should have been produced by a Gentile for Gentiles. Had there been coffee tables in the homes of the Roman Empire, they, I think, would have been one destination which Luke would have wanted his books to reach. And this is one reason why they are so relevant today. Most of us, in the western world, are the kind of people to whom Luke was addressing himself. We have so few material needs, but our spiritual need as Gentiles, if we are still both 'separated from Christ' and 'alienated from the commonwealth of Israel',[5] is even greater than that of Jews. The good news, therefore, is even better for us than for them. And we could hardly have it more attractively presented.

One aspect of the Gospel's Gentile outlook is its humanity. It is about man and his needs. True, it centres on a divine Saviour, but he is the Saviour of the *world*. This world view of Luke's has two focal lengths, one close and one distant. First he stands back so as to take in a wide vision of mankind and its world. The commentaries call this his universalism. For example, all four of the Gospels quote, in connection with John the Baptist, the prophecy of Isaiah concerning the voice which cries 'Prepare the way of the Lord'; but only Luke completes the quotation—'All flesh shall see the salvation of God.'[6] This universalism should not be understood to mean that God will save every single individual of the human race, even those who wilfully reject him; such a doctrine runs counter to the basic teaching of the New Testament. Rather, it means that there is no kind of person the gospel cannot reach, no boundary it cannot cross. Luke is

[4] See, *e.g.*, Ellis, pp. 52f.
[5] Eph. 2:12.
[6] Is. 40:3ff.; Mt. 3:3, Mk. 1:3, Lk. 3:4–6, Jn. 1:23.

saying not that *everyone will* be saved, but that *anyone can* be saved, and his view corresponds to Paul's vision of the final abolishing of barriers: in the Christian church 'there is neither Jew nor Greek, there is neither slave nor free, there is neither male nor female; for you are all one in Christ Jesus.'[7] This is one respect in which the gospel is for all.

But then focusing closely, Luke shows on the other hand that 'all' does nevertheless mean 'everyone', provided we understand this is the sense he intends, and that the world is after all made up of individuals. He is depicting many classes of people; but he goes further, and shows us particular persons within those classes. As I have already suggested, the gospel is not only for Jews, but also for Greeks—and for Romans and for Samaritans too. It is not only for males, but also for females—and not simply important women like the wife of Herod's steward, but widows and cripples and prostitutes as well. It is not only for freemen, but also for slaves—and indeed for all whom society despises: for the poor, the weak, and the outcast, for the thief and the quisling. And all of these Luke delights to show as particular individuals. A galaxy of such portraits glitters across his twenty-four chapters. These are real people, and among them the human condition is really to be found. Like the Roman playwright before him, Luke might have said, *'Homo sum; humani nil a me alienum puto.'*[8] Like the English essayist long after him, he might reckon himself a *Citizen of the World.*[9]

And what he writes, he writes in good clear Greek. A thousand years later he would no doubt have used Latin; a thousand years later still, probably English—choosing his language not so much for its literary qualities, as because it is the one which will be most readily understood by the world at large. He is, after all, telling the story of the Saviour of the *world*.

2. The physician

We have seen how Luke's background and culture as a Gentile have fitted him for the writing of a Gospel for the world. Now we turn to his training and his calling, and see the effect which they have had on his work as a Gospel writer.

---

[7] Gal. 3:28.

[8] 'I am a man; I count nothing human indifferent to me.' Terence, *Heauton Timorumenos*, I. i. 25.

[9] Oliver Goldsmith, title of book.

Luke, you see, is a doctor. His business is to heal.

Now Greek is a language of great richness; yet here is a case in which it might seem that English is richer, with a choice of two words where Greek has one.[10] The Greek word is *sōzō*. Is the translator to render it 'heal', or 'save'? For it has to do duty for both ideas.

Yet perhaps it is not a case of the older language being less rich than the newer. Perhaps the Greeks had a truer understanding of the nature of things when they reckoned that to save a man and to heal him were fundamentally the same, and that a single word should convey the double meaning. And perhaps we can see in Luke's eye a keen *professional* interest (to put it no higher) in the story of how there had been born 'in the city of David a *Sōtēr*',[11] a Healer/Saviour, who had come into the world to deliver men both from sickness and from sin. We whose mother tongue is English would have had to make a choice between different translations, and to decide when it was appropriate to call this Man 'Saviour', and when it was more fitting to call him 'Healer'; but the Greeks had a word for it—*a* word, one word—and this word with its layers of meaning fascinated Doctor Luke. *Sōzō* and its related nouns are found much more often in his writings than in those of any of the other evangelists. He is telling of a man who has the power and authority to do the kind of work that he himself has been trained to do, but at depths undreamed-of, and in regions unexplored, and with effects so far-reaching as to confound his own elementary ideas of healing/salvation.[12]

Introductions generally get written last; and as I write this, having worked through his Gospel many times and in great detail, it seems to me clearer than ever that if in the modern fashion he had given it a title, he might well have called it 'The Saviour of the World'. As Luke, the Gentile, he writes about this human world of ours; as the physician, he writes about its divine Healer, the one who can save from all ills and is a Saviour for all men.

3. Whose praise is in the gospel

In 2 Corinthians 8:18 the apostle Paul refers to a certain fellow Christian 'whose praise', according to the Authorized Version, 'is in the gospel', and who has been chosen to travel with him in his

---

[10] In the reverse direction, the one English word 'heal' has three Greek equivalents, *sōzō*, *therapeuō*, and *iaomai*. My point, of course, remains.

[11] Lk. 2:11.

[12] See pp. 66–68, 72f.

missionary journeying. He omits to mention the name of this Christian brother, and commentators down the ages have not been slow to supply it. Barnabas and Silas, Timothy and Mark, and half a dozen others whose names occur in the book of Acts as travelling companions of Paul, have all been suggested. The compilers of the Prayer Book assumed however that Luke was the person referred to, and so the phrase quoted above finds its place in their St Luke's Day collect. In deciding for this interpretation they were following a strong and ancient tradition, the opinion of many scholars, and the direction in which the relevant facts (such as they are) seem to point.

It is only a possibility, of course, and one reason why some may have thought that Paul was here speaking about Luke is in fact a very poor reason. This is that when the apostle speaks of his unnamed brother's 'praise' being 'in the gospel', he means that the said brother was famous for the Gospel, *i.e.* the book, which he had written. It is extremely unlikely, however, that this is what Paul meant. Much more probably the brother is highly regarded for his services to the gospel (JBP, NEB), or for his preaching of the gospel (RSV), in the wider sense of the word.

But even if this verse has no reference to the third book of the New Testament, the fact remains that Luke's praise is indeed in his Gospel. Christopher Wren's epitaph in St Paul's Cathedral—*Si monumentum requiris, circumspice* ('If you seek his monument, look around you')—directs your gaze to a great work of art. Glorious it is; but also inanimate. As you make your way into the Gospel of Luke, the same words might be said of him, except that in this case your attention is turned towards something more than a great work of art. These pages are not only glorious, they are also alive. On account of them, we do not think it at all improper to praise their author, the beloved physician turned evangelist, for the skill and insight with which he has given us this living picture of a living Saviour. Or, still more properly, we praise that Saviour himself, who having healed the soul of this gifted Greek doctor, then engaged his talents in the writing of a book of salvation for the world to read.

The coming of the Saviour

1:1–4

Luke introduces the Gospel

The first four verses of his Gospel form Luke's introduction to it. We shall be giving more detailed attention to them than to any of the following sections; but they are worth such close study, because they are the foundation of all the rest.

It is the commentaries, rather than expositions like this one, which discuss *how* Luke has written his preface—the good classical Greek style of it—and also the person *to whom* Luke is writing: whether he is actual or imaginary, whether Theophilus is his real name or a pseudonym, whether 'Your Excellency' indicates his official rank or is merely a courtesy title, and whether he is a Christian convert or an interested outsider. (None of these questions has a certain answer, except perhaps that 1:4 seems to imply that he is a real person). We shall concentrate rather on *what* Luke claims to be writing. What may we expect to find as we begin to read his Gospel? What, according to this introduction, is it?

We shall find, first, that it is one of many 'Gospels' produced about the same time, each of which claimed to be a narrative of certain facts about Jesus Christ; secondly, that it is Luke's own particular presentation of the facts; and thirdly, that it is a handbook designed to be of real value to all who put themselves in the position of Theophilus, as interested readers. This is what Luke's preface will tell us.

1. His pattern: the gospel in the second-generation church

Inasmuch as many have undertaken to compile a narrative of the things which have been accomplished among us, just as they were delivered to us by those who from the beginning were eyewitnesses and ministers of the word, it seemed good to me also . . . to write . . . (1:1–3a).

23

The first generation of the Christian church was that of the apostles. It comprised many people who had known Jesus personally. They had no need of books to tell them about him, for their memories, minds, and hearts were full of him. Nor did they pass on their knowledge to others in the form of orderly narratives. An early history of the church describes how Peter, for example, 'used to adapt his instructions to the needs [of the moment]',[1] drawing readily on whichever of his vivid recollections of Jesus was most appropriate for the audience to which he happened to be speaking.

The next generation, to which Luke and others like him belonged, was in a different position. In a sense such people could say, 'The words and deeds of Jesus were "accomplished among us"' (1:1), being part of the story of their own times. But since nevertheless those facts had had to be 'delivered' to them (1:2), they—the men of the second generation—were not actual eyewitnesses. The facts had come to them in various forms (accounts of the Lord's death and resurrection, of his sayings, of his miracles, and of other matters concerning him which it was important for Christian converts to know); the reconstruction and study of these early accounts are therefore known as *form*-criticism. For their own benefit, however, and for the benefit of generations yet to come, these men saw the value of having the facts about Jesus woven into a systematic whole. With this object in mind, Mark, for instance, is said to have written down what the apostle Peter used to tell of the 'Jesus story'.[2] Luke claims to have followed the same way.

He tells us that many writers set about this task. Little of their work however has survived,[3] and only the four Gospels included in our New Testament have stood the tests of time and use. Even so, it is worth considering these literary efforts, of which Luke's Gospel is an outstanding example, to see what exactly they were.

a. The sources of the 'Gospels' (1:2)

For convenience we may call them 'Gospels', and although hardly anything of them remains we may yet draw some conclusions about them from the way Luke refers to them here.

[1] Papias, quoted in Eusebius, *Historia Ecclesiae*, III. 39; J. Stevenson, *A New Eusebius* (SPCK, 1960), p. 52.

[2] *Ibid.*

[3] The numerous so-called Gospels, more or less fragmentary, which make up the New Testament Apocrypha, are mostly later productions with a good deal of pious fiction in them. See A. F. Walls, 'New Testament Apocrypha', *New Bible Dictionary* (Inter-Varsity Press, 1962), pp. 879ff.

They all derived from 'those who . . . were eyewitnesses and ministers'. These were not two groups of people, but two descriptions of the same group: men who witnessed, in the double sense of that word—as they had *seen,* so they *spoke.* The following would be a literal translation of what Luke calls them: 'Those who were-eye-witnesses-from-the-beginning and became-ministers-of-the-word'. In fact, of the two books by Luke which we have in our Bible, his Gospel might be summarized by the first phrase, and the book of Acts by the second. The ascension of Jesus is the pivot between the two.[4] From that event Luke's first volume looks back to 'the beginning',[5] and beyond; it tells us what the eyewitnesses had seen. His second volume looks onwards from the ascension and the sending of the Holy Spirit, and tells us what they said and did once they had become ministers of the word.

We have pictured Mark and Luke both engaged in the same kind of work, writing down what they heard from eyewitnesses. Another factor however needs to be borne in mind. There is so close a resemblance between much of Mark's Gospel and much of Luke's (and of Matthew's too, for that matter) that scholars presume some sort of literary connection between the first three Gospels. In the case of Luke, for example, it is usually suggested that he had Mark's Gospel before him as he wrote, and probably other written records, now lost, as well. If this is so, it means that Luke saw nothing incongruous about claiming that his account rested on first-hand testimony, yet incorporating in it much of Mark's second-hand report. The point surely was that the accuracy of all these accounts could still be checked with original eyewitnesses.[6] The commission of the twelve was, in part, that they should act as just such a testimony to apostolic truth,[7] and by that standard all New Testament scripture not actually written by them—even the teachings of Paul[8]—might be judged apostolic, and therefore dominical.

b. The contents of the 'Gospels' (1:1b)
Accordingly, the Gospel narratives consisted of the things which were 'accomplished' by Jesus in the sight of the apostles, and then 'delivered' by them to those who had not themselves seen him.

---

[4] Lk. 24: 51; Acts 1:9. But see p. 209 note 1.
[5] *I.e.* Jesus's baptism, the 'beginning' of his ministry. *Cf.* Jn. 15: 27; Acts 1:21f.
[6] *Cf.* 1 Cor. 15:6.
[7] Jn. 15:27.
[8] Gal. 2:1–10.

25

They were, basically, a set of facts. It is true that no amount of head-knowledge can save a man's soul, and in that sense a mere 'set of facts' does not in itself have any spiritual value. Yet a well-defined series of statements seems to have been precisely what successive generations of the church were to guard and to hand on—'the traditions' about Jesus.[9] They were the things which the 'eyewitnesses' had seen 'accomplished', a settled group of facts which were to be reported 'exactly as' they had been received,[10] and from which a continuous 'narrative' could be composed by arranging them in a certain order (which is the meaning of 'to compile').

These are what we find as the core of the earliest Christian message, when in Acts 2: 22f. we read a set of statements about Jesus. But the context there shows that we have to do with something much more far-reaching than mere academic head-knowledge. For the facts, selected with the interpreting wisdom of the Spirit of God which turns history into theology, are now being *preached*, in the living power of that same Spirit; and the result is that they cut men to the heart and bring them to repentance.[11]

So what had been 'accomplished' is now being 'delivered'; Peter the eyewitness has now become Peter the minister of the word, and that word is proving itself to be 'living and active, sharper than any two-edged sword, piercing to the division of soul and spirit, of joints and marrow, and discerning the thoughts and intentions of the heart.'[12] The apostles 'had discovered among their memories of Jesus that which met the deepest needs of men.'[13]

We can see, then, what these earliest 'Gospels' attempted to be, with greater or less success, and therefore what we may expect Luke's Gospel to be, since it is one of them. We shall find that it is, in fact, a version of the 'Jesus story', an account of actual events. It is not a theory, or an idea, or a philosophy, or even a religion. It is the tale of a thing that really happened. Yet it is not mere history, for it does something to the people to whom it is proclaimed. Those who witnessed the original events found that when the story was preached, it changed men's lives. And those who, like Luke, wrote it up, reckoned that in this form also it would have a similar effect on those who, like Theophilus, would read it.

[9] 2 Thes. 2: 15; *cf.* 1 Cor. 11: 23; 15: 3; 1 Tim. 6: 20; 2 Tim. 1:12–14.
[10] 1: 2a (JB, Moffatt).
[11] Acts 2: 37f.
[12] Heb. 4:12.
[13] Caird, p. 43.

The Victorian heyday of preaching was followed by a long period of reaction, in which the authoritative declaring of facts was at a discount and

> suave politeness, tempering bigot zeal,
> Corrected 'I believe' to 'One does feel'.[14]

It would be pleasant to know that we are now out of that particular wood; but I doubt whether we are. So it is worth reminding ourselves how much store these early Christians set by the plain proclamation of the 'Jesus story'. Whether it was spoken by the first-generation apostles, or written by the second-generation evangelists, they expected it to be effective; and it is so still.

2. His presentation: the Gospel 'according to Luke'

It seemed good to me also, having followed all things closely for some time past, to write an orderly account for you, most excellent Theophilus (1:3).

So far, we have considered the ways in which all these early 'Gospels' were alike; now we consider how Luke's presentation of the facts claims to differ from the others. The earliest title given to the book was simply *Kata Loukan*, 'According to Luke'. Let us then see how, according to him, the events of Jesus's life may best be presented, and note the particular features of his Gospel: thoroughness, accuracy, and order.

a. Thoroughness

In three Greek words Luke indicates how thorough his researches have been in gathering material for his Gospel. He has 'followed' these events, not of course in the sense of observing them, since he was not himself an eyewitness, but in the sense of investigating them. He has followed 'all things' that could possibly be relevant to his theme. And he has done so 'for some time past', or (better, as in RV) 'from the start'; by which he means, as we shall see, not 'from the beginning' of Jesus's ministry (as in 1:2), but 'from the start' of his earthly life, and even earlier. He is like 'a traveller who tries to discover the source of a river, in order that he may descend it again, and follow its entire course.'[15]

---

[14] Ronald Knox, *Absolute and Abitofhell*.
[15] Godet, I, p. 61.

27

b. Accuracy

Luke has surveyed his materials 'closely', says RSV. The word carries the idea of exactness, and so RV and other versions agree with RSV's marginal note in translating it as 'accurately'. He would undoubtedly have checked and re-checked his findings, and in any case a wealth of archaeological discovery over the past hundred years has shown him to have a remarkably correct eye for detail. The writer who never puts a foot wrong in matters which we can verify may well be trusted implicitly in the rest.

His thoroughness and his accuracy combine to show us someone who would have had little patience with certain modern approaches to the gospel story. A shift away from old-fashioned destructive criticism, which was so good at seeing through Scripture that it was in danger eventually of seeing nothing in it, is more than welcome. But Luke would have been chagrined to find it replaced by a 'biblical theology' which distinguishes between truth and fact, and which enthuses over the one while caring little about the other. For him the two are inseparable. The truth of his Gospel is factual truth. Of course this is not to say that a spiritual message may not sometimes be conveyed by means of myth or fable, where the question 'Did it really happen?' is irrelevant. But it is to say that that sort of writing is precisely what Luke is *not* engaged in. He claims to be investigating, thoroughly and accurately, the facts.

c. Order

Some have thought that Luke's 'orderly account' meant a story told in chronological order. None of the Gospels, however, yields any very obvious chronology of the life of Jesus, and Luke's order is much more likely to be a 'logical and artistic arrangement' of some kind.[16] We may take it that with such an arrangement in mind, he must have surveyed the vast wealth of material—'all things' that he had been able to find out about Jesus—and selected from it, as John did in writing his Gospel,[17] the items which would best fit his scheme.

What that scheme is, is not easy to detect at a casual reading. Presumably it is a framework which, like a skeleton, supports the whole structure without making itself obvious. Indeed, this present exposition is to some degree an exercise in anatomy—an attempt to understand the body of the Gospel better by studying its bones.

[16] Geldenhuys, p. 57.
[17] Jn. 20:30f.; 21:25.

Some readers may feel, especially with regard to the central section of the Gospel (9:51 – 19:44), that Luke is unlikely to have had in mind a framework as elaborate as the one I suggest. In this connection three points may be made. The first is that, in the absence of explicit headings and sub-headings provided by Luke himself, no analysis can be anything more than a matter of suggestion. This is all that the present one is meant to be, and it is for the reader to judge whether or not it squares with the contents of Luke's book. Secondly, it is not unnatural that the critical dissection of the Gospel should seem more complex than any scheme which the author may consciously have planned. The same thing happens with the analysis of a novel or a symphony; and the reason is of course that the critic is interested in the subconscious, as well as the conscious, workings of the maker's mind. Thirdly, of the two extremes mentioned in my Preface, complexity on the one hand and shapelessness on the other,[18] I think it is truer to the character of Luke's writing as he himself describes it in this verse—thorough, accurate, and (in particular) orderly—that a suggested analysis should err on the side of complexity.

Here then is a version of the things 'accomplished' and 'delivered' which is claimed by its author to be in several respects an improvement on similar versions produced by his contemporaries. It should whet our appetite, especially if we have become too accustomed to living on spiritual snacks, to know what pains Luke has taken to prepare this feast. It consists basically of the living facts which were common to all the early 'Gospels', but it has been carefully prepared, supplemented with extra courses, and attractively served. We owe it more than a perfunctory nibble.

3. His purpose: the Gospel for Theophilus

. . . that you may know the truth concerning the things of which you have been informed (1:4).

'Poetry', said the French poet Baudelaire, has 'no other aim but itself . . . If the poet has pursued a moral aim, he will have diminished his poetic power; nor will it be incautious to bet that his work is bad.'[19] Not one of the Bible writers would have agreed (and some of them

[18] See above, p. 12.
[19] Baudelaire, 'Further Notes on Edgar Poe', in *Selected Writings on Art and Artists,* tr. P. E. Charvet (Penguin, 1972), pp. 203f.

29

were very fine poets indeed). Baudelaire, with his belief in 'art for art's sake', would for his part have dismissed Luke after reading the first ten lines of the Gospel, for Luke declares unashamedly that his literary work has a 'moral aim': he aims to bring Theophilus to a sure knowledge of the truth of Christianity.

a. What Theophilus has already heard

The 'things' of 1:4 are of a different kind from the 'things' of 1:1; they are in fact 'words'. What Theophilus has heard is something more than the mere events of the days of Jesus. It is a significant choice of those events, which has been preached, with incandescent power, by the apostles. It is a word which changes the lives of men.

Even so, Theophilus apparently still lacks a thorough grasp of the facts, and that is the lack which this Gospel sets out to supply. It is what he needs, whether he is already a convert or still merely an onlooker; for it is not clear how Theophilus stands in relation to the Christian faith ('informed' represents a Greek word which could imply either that he has undergone Christian instruction or that he has heard an unfriendly report).[20] But in either case—if he is on the one hand a new Christian with a rudimentary knowledge of the faith, or on the other hand a non-Christian who is interested enough to learn what it is really about—this Gospel is written especially for such as him.

b. What Luke's Gospel can do for him

The reading of this book, which is written particularly with Theophilus in mind, will enable him to 'know the certainty' (AV, RV) of these things.

Luke places the word 'certainty' emphatically at the end of his long sentence: 'I have written all this, Theophilus, so that you may be *sure.*' Like many men of his day, this man, presumably brought up in a pagan religion which had become increasingly meaningless, may well have felt 'a strong desire for firmly established truth', and 'yearned for trustworthy knowledge concerning religious matters.'[21] And, we may add, like many men of our own day—men for whom both the Christian church under its popular image, and the many beliefs which are offered as alternatives to it, seem very insecure foundations for living. But my Gospel, says Luke, will offer you

[20] Luke uses the word in the former sense in Acts 18:25, and in the latter sense in Acts 21:21, 24.

[21] Geldenhuys, p. 54.

certainty. And in saying this he grasps yet another twentieth-century nettle. For the word is *asphaleia*, which might be translated 'infallibility'—a concept around which long warfare has been waged. Without apology Luke claims it for his Gospel, and its real meaning becomes plain. Read what I have written, he says, and you will see the facts on which Christianity is based; and you will find there something firm and solid and absolutely trustworthy, a sure foundation for faith.

And 'know' also is a special word. It means a deep, thorough knowledge. Luke wants his reader to know the certainty of the gospel not only in his mind but in his heart, so that it becomes part of the fibre of his being. Such knowledge may be yours, says Luke. How? By some mystical experience? By a deep study of philosophy? No: by reading and meditating on the plain facts of the story of Jesus, set out here in my Gospel. *That* is where you may come to know the basic certainties of life.

This, then, is what we look for as we embark on our reading of the Gospel according to Luke. Like many another book of the same kind, most of them now lost, it recounts 'the tradition', the facts about Jesus; though they are not merely facts, but truth which when proclaimed changes the lives of men. This book, moreover, sets them out with a remarkable fullness, accuracy, and meaningful order, and demands our closest attention. Granted this, we may expect it to lay deep in our hearts the infallible basis of spiritual certainty in a world where all else is changing and inconstant. Let us then go to our study of it with a will.

> How firm a foundation, ye saints of the Lord,
> Is laid for your faith in his excellent word;
> What more can he say than to you he hath said,
> You who unto Jesus for refuge have fled?[22]

[22] Richard Keen, *How firm a foundation*.

1:5–80

'His people's hope'

Luke begins his Gospel proper with a sequence of four incidents which lead up to the birth of Jesus. The first takes place in Jerusalem, the second in Nazareth; the other two are set in an unnamed village in the hill country of Judea.

His claim to have followed out the story 'from the very first' (1:3, AV) means, in fact, that he intends to begin not with Jesus's baptism (the start of his ministry,)[1] nor even with his birth (the start of his earthly life), but with something earlier still. For Luke the story begins at the point where after four hundred years of silence the voice of God was heard again by his people Israel,[2] with the announcement, shortly before each was born, of the coming of Jesus and his forerunner John.

There is nothing like this chapter anywhere else in the Gospels, and it may arouse our curiosity in more respects than one.

1. A matter of style and content

There was in the days of Herod, the king of Judaea, a certain priest named Zacharias, of the course of Abia: and his wife was of the daughters of Aaron, and her name was Elisabeth. . . . And it came to pass, that while he executed the priest's office before God in the order of his course, . . . there appeared unto him an angel of the Lord. . . . (1:5, 8, 11, AV).

And the angel answered him, 'I am Gabriel, who stand in the presence of God; and I was sent to speak to you, and to bring you this good news' (1:19).

---

[1] See above, p. 25 n. 5.
[2] See below, p. 54 n. 2.

Bearing in mind the sort of person to whom Luke addresses his book, one wonders whether at the outset his style and his content are not somewhat at odds. The first of the four incidents in this chapter (1:5–25) highlights a curious contrast between what he has to say and how he says it.

a. The style of the passage

The first group of verses just quoted is from AV, rather than RSV, for a purpose. Its seventeenth-century English conveys a little of the picturesqueness of these events. They have about them something supernatural, with their angelic appearances and predictions, and something alien, with their setting in Eastern society and Jewish religion. This is a different world from the cultured paganism of Greece and Rome, and a world still more different from our own. There is something remote, even legendary, about it. It has 'the general tone', suggests Drury, '... of a rich and resonant fairy tale ("once upon a time there were two old people, a man and his wife...").'[3] It is, in the strict sense of the word, *exotic*—'outside' the normal experience of the readers Luke has in mind.

Yet what is the drama that Luke unfolds amid this scenery of a world of far away and long ago?

b. The content of the passage

If the first quotation above gives an idea of the style and atmosphere of Luke's opening chapter, the second pinpoints its subject-matter. The reason for Gabriel's visit is the bringing of good news; and the news is the promised birth of a son to Zechariah and Elizabeth.

But there is more to that than meets the eye. For we are told that the good news was brought in answer to Zechariah's prayer (1:13); yet the promise of John's birth was so unexpected and surprising to Zechariah, that we may question whether his desire for a son was really the prayer that was in his heart on this occasion. Two factors throw a different light on the matter. First, this pious couple was surely among those who, like Simeon and Anna in the next chapter, were looking for the 'consolation of Israel' and the 'redemption of Jerusalem' (2:25, 38). Secondly, the awesome once-in-a-lifetime privilege of serving in the temple must have carried Zechariah's mind beyond the personal tragedy of childlessness to the even more poignant longings of the nation to which he belonged. In short, we may

[3] Drury, p. 22.

take it that his prayer was for the coming of Israel's Saviour; and the 'good news' which the angel brings is not so much that Elizabeth shall bear a son, as that she shall bear a son who is to announce the Saviour's immediate coming.

This good news is the 'evangel' (*euangelion*), the gospel. 1:19 is the first place where the term appears in Luke's book,[4] and the subject is to be one of his main themes. He might well have said himself what he reports Gabriel as saying: 'I was sent . . . to bring you this good news.'

In view of the importance of this, Luke's grand subject, Theophilus might well ask why (like the 'heavenly Child' soon to be 'wrapped in swathing bands') it is first 'to human view displayed'[5] in such unexpected garb. To that matter, the story-book atmosphere in which the good news is announced, we shall return later. But first we must grasp the message itself, as its content and meaning are unfolded in the remaining three incidents which Luke narrates here in chapter 1.

2. The content unfolded

'You will conceive in your womb and bear a son, and you shall call his name Jesus' [= the Lord is salvation] (1:31).

And Mary said,
> *'My soul magnifies the Lord,*
> *and my spirit rejoices in God my Saviour'* (1:46–47).

'You will go before the Lord to prepare his ways,
> *to give knowledge of salvation to his people*
> *in the forgiveness of their sins'* (1:76b–77).

We trace through the rest of this chapter the reason why its subject is so important. We have already seen, in the first incident, how when the angel tells Zechariah that his wife is to bear a son in spite of their old age and her barrenness, the birth of that son is called 'good news' (1:19)—it is 'gospel'. For John is to be the herald of *salvation;* salvation more than anything else is to be the basic theme of Luke's story;

---

[4] *I.e.* the English term 'good news'. The Greek noun *euangelion* does not in fact appear anywhere in Luke's Gospel, and only twice in Acts; the word he uses here is the verb which corresponds to it, *euangelizesthai* ('*to bring* good news').

[5] Nahum Tate, *While shepherds watched their flocks by night.*

and salvation is what makes the news so good. It is the common factor in the three quotations above, one from each of the remaining three incidents which Luke narrates. The meaning of it comes into focus as we look at these more closely.

a. The Bringer of salvation (1:26–38)

Zechariah saw his vision in the temple at Jerusalem. From there we are taken northwards, to Galilee: this second story is located in Nazareth, the home of Joseph and his betrothed wife Mary. The same angel who announced to Zechariah the birth of John now announces to Mary the birth of Jesus.

The stupendous claims which the angel makes for this unborn baby (1:32–33) would have staggered Jewish readers of the Gospel, and we may guess that they would not have been without effect on Theophilus also. For the Son of Mary is a colossal figure. He will be the greatest ruler that not only Israel (1:32b–33a), but the world (1:33b), has ever seen.

The universal authority of Christ is another of Luke's chief themes, and is first introduced here. It is 'an arresting feature of the earlier prophetic testimony', as Stonehouse points out, quoting a series of passages from Isaiah: 'The Lord has bared his holy arm before the eyes of *all the nations* ... *All flesh* shall see it together ... That my salvation may reach *to the end of the earth.*'[6] It will be taken up again in Luke's next chapter, in the words of Simeon, which echo those of Isaiah.[7]

Nevertheless, in this portrait of 'the Saviour of the world' we concentrate for the moment not so much on 'the world' as on 'the Saviour'. What kind of man must this be, to whom in the end 'every knee should bow, ... and every tongue confess that Jesus Christ is Lord'?[8]

For a start, Luke tells us that so great a person is to have no ordinary birth. Mary's virginity is an integral part of the story. Three lines of thought converge to put the doctrine of the virgin birth of Jesus, to my mind, beyond question. The first is the character of Luke. His accuracy as a painstaking historian we have already noted. Myths and legends may be the stock-in-trade of some religious writers, and may in their hands convey much spiritual truth, but these are not what Luke deals in. The second is the character of his ma-

---

[6] Is. 52:10; 40:5; 49:6. Stonehouse, pp. 54f.; our italics.
[7] Lk. 2:29–32. See below, pp. 47–48.
[8] Phil. 2:10–11.

terial. For all his cool objectivity, he does not hesitate to record miracles where he is persuaded that miracles have occurred. If he says Jesus was born of a virgin, it is because he believes that to be a historical fact. The third is the character of the Saviour he is depicting. If the One coming into the world is so sublime a figure, what more appropriate than that the manner of his coming should be miraculous—and that not as a matter of Luke's poetic imagination, but (again) as a matter of fact?

This, then, is the One whom we are first to know by 'his name Jesus' (1:31). And 'Jesus' means 'The Lord is *salvation*'.[9]

b. The scope of salvation (1:39–56)

In the third story the narrative moves again southwards, 'into the hill country, to a city of Judah' (1:39), where Mary goes to visit her cousin Elizabeth. As the two women share their good news, Mary is inspired to utter the great hymn known to generations of Christians as the *Magnificat*. 'My soul magnifies the Lord', she sings; and then, describing him more specifically, 'my spirit rejoices in God my Saviour.'

The saving work for which she praises him is one of total renewal. 'He has shown strength with his arm, he has scattered the proud in the imagination of their hearts, he has put down the mighty from their thrones, and exalted those of low degree; he has filled the hungry with good things, and the rich he has sent empty away' (1:51–53).

How is it (in passing) that although the Saviour is not yet born, Mary's song can declare that the salvation has already come? Perhaps she means two things. One is that in a manner of speaking the old order has indeed been overturned, by the very fact that God's choice has passed over the proud, the mighty, and the rich, and has lighted instead upon her as the future mother of his Son. The other is that with sudden insight she realizes what the end of it all will be, and rejoices that since God has set his saving work in motion, it is already as good as done.

To revert to the previous point, it cannot be denied that this saving work is one of total renewal, and indeed it looks very like social and political revolution. In the last days of British India, Jack Winslow's Christian community there was sometimes visited by CID men because of its known sympathies with Indian nationalism; Wil-

---

[9] It is Matthew, not Luke, who actually spells this out (Mt. 1:21); Luke will make it plain in the course of his narrative.

liam Temple accordingly warned him not to include the *Magnificat* in his services—'it's a most revolutionary canticle!'[10] Now Temple spoke more truly, maybe, than he knew. For in our own day, in many parts of the world, the *Magnificat* and similar scriptures[11] are indeed the 'revolutionary canticles' which inspire, and are held to justify, Christian participation in political liberation movements. This is very upsetting for Christians in those nations which are old enough, or rich enough, to want only to be left in peace to enjoy their accustomed standard of living, and they are tempted therefore to spiritualize the *Magnificat* and say that it must not be used like this. But that is unfair to those of our brothers in the Third World who feel there is no answer to their problems without the overthrow of the political system. The renewal promised in the *Magnificat* really will involve the downfall of the rulers of this world. The question is when, and in what sense, and by what means, this will happen. We had better go on to Luke's next narrative and see how this total salvation is to be brought about.

c. The heart of salvation (1:57–80)

The fourth incident takes place at the same village, a few months later, when the child of the aged couple has eventually come to birth. Like Mary, Zechariah is now inspired to utter a hymn of thanksgiving, the *Benedictus*, in which he praises God for having 'raised up a horn of salvation' (or 'mighty Saviour')[12] 'for us' (1:69). Salvation 'from our enemies' (1:71, 74) is how it may be described; but, as Godet says, 'the very notion of salvation was falsified in Israel, and had to be corrected before salvation could be realized.'[13] The true enemies were not as most Jews thought foreign invaders, but spiritual foes, and it was to be the work of Zechariah's son John 'to give knowledge of salvation to his people *in the forgiveness of their sins*' (1:77). That is where the revolution has to begin. Before there can be a right relationship between man and man, there must be a right relationship between man and God, and the sin which spoils that must be repented of and removed. Thus in due course Luke will quote the apostles' preaching that Jesus is the one whom God has made 'Leader and Saviour, to give repentance to Israel and forgiveness of sins' (Acts 5:31).

[10] Jack Winslow, *The Eyelids of the Dawn* (Hodder & Stoughton, 1954), p. 109.
[11] For example the Nazareth sermon, Lk. 4:16ff.
[12] AG, quoting E. J. Goodspeed.
[13] Godet, p. 114.

We must believe, as clear-thinking Christians in every age have believed, that it is the will and plan of God for all wrong relationships, political as well as spiritual, eventually to be put right. We include therefore in our preaching of salvation the need for the righting of wrong social structures and physical conditions.[14] But we keep at its centre the need for the cleansing of sinful human hearts. That is the primary concern of the people of God.

Here at the outset, therefore, Luke establishes the chief matter of his Gospel, this tremendous project: the saving of the human race. Chapter 1 is 'not so much a prelude to what follows but rather . . . the theme which is to be elaborated in the ensuing "symphony of salvation".'[15] It is the matter which Luke aims to bring to the attention of his readers. He wants to leave them in no doubt that the great need of humanity is that it should, in the fullest sense, be saved.

3. The style explained

Now while he [Zechariah] was serving as priest before God when his division was on duty, according to the custom of the priesthood, it fell to him by lot to enter the temple of the Lord and burn incense. . . . And there appeared to him an angel of the Lord standing on the right side of the altar of incense (1:8, 9, 11).

The message of salvation surely needs to be made as clear as possible, to as many as possible. Luke doubtless knew, and endorsed, the principles of his great friend Paul, whose aim was always 'the open statement of the truth', and who was prepared to 'become all things to all men' so that he might 'by all means save some.'[16] Yet, as we noted earlier, the four stories with which this Gospel introduces his universal message seem to have a quite unsuitably exotic colouring. It is as though one were to arrive at a great international airport, to find all its directions signs posted up in Hebrew only. For notice again the curiosities on which Luke insists.

---

[14] Provided of course that the matter is seen in its proper biblical perspective. See, *e.g.*, my comments on the Christian attitudes to sickness (pp. 66–68) and to poverty and other forms of deprivation (p. 93).

[15] I. Howard Marshall, *Luke: Historian and Theologian* (Paternoster, 1970), p. 97.

[16] 2 Cor. 4:2; 1 Cor. 9:22.

a. Supernatural beliefs

The passage 1:5–10 simply establishes a background for the statement of 1:11. In that verse is described the first great event of the gospel story: that to Zechariah the priest, serving in the Temple, there appeared 'an angel of the Lord'. In each of the first two incidents this angel appears; in each he appears in order to bring a prediction of the future; in each the prediction concerns a miraculous event. Angels, predictions, miracles—? Luke both claims in his introduction, and will subsequently prove, to be a painstaking sober historian. Yet he makes no apology for thus conjuring up supernatural visions at the very start of his narrative.

Indeed, in all four incidents there is an even more far-reaching acknowledgment of the supernatural, in that Zechariah's son is to be filled with the Holy Spirit (1:15). Mary's Son is to be born by the power of the Holy Spirit (1:35), Elizabeth greets Mary with a cry inspired by the Holy Spirit (1:41f.), and Zechariah celebrates John's birth with a prophecy in the Holy Spirit (1:67). Here, unmistakably, is another world breaking into this one.

b. Alien culture.

The commentators tell us that Luke's language from 1:5 onwards has a very Jewish flavour about it, quite different from the civilized Greek of 1:1–4. Having thus plunged into what for his Gentile readers will have seemed a quaintly foreign idiom, he states at once that his story belongs to the 'far away' of the Judaean kingdom of Herod, and the 'long ago' of the religious history of Israel (1:5). His characters are clad in the religion and priesthood of Judaism (1:6, 8), and his scene is set in its temple, before an altar, at a service (1:9–11).[17] The opening speech takes us straight into the world of the Old Testament (1:13–17). And he continues in the same vein throughout the rest of the chapter, and indeed into chapter 2 also.

Luke has created this 'world-of-the-Bible' atmosphere quite deliberately. The title suggested for our present section ('His People's Hope') is to be understood first in this narrow sense. It does not refer to people generally, nor to any ordinary expectations. Luke's first chapter is showing us the faithful few *in Israel,* who were looking forward to the coming of their nation's Saviour, and for whom the promise was about to come true. The 'hope' is of a miraculous breaking-in from heaven; and 'his people', whose hope this is, are strictly God's people the Jews.

[17] For the significance of the setting, see below, pp. 179ff., 215.

And these are two great stumbling-blocks to the acceptance of the gospel of salvation: it involves supernatural beliefs, and it seems to be anchored to a remote and alien culture. On the one hand, it is incredible; and on the other, it is in any case irrelevant. Surely, we might say, Luke is writing for Theophilus, the typical Gentile; and no doubt he is writing similarly for the majority of twentieth-century men—people who may hold a variety of materialistic beliefs, but at any rate are not superstitious and gullible; and who may belong to any one of half a dozen different cultures, but at any rate are not orthodox Jews. Why then does he not play down these unacceptable elements in the story, and stress what will be more palatable to his readers?

The answer is this: Because the apparent 'trappings' are in fact at the heart of the thing, and are not to be evaded. Luke is rather in the position of the United Nations ambassador of some small nation which is the flash-point of a major crisis. What he has to say to the assembled delegates concerns a subject of worldwide importance. But to understand it, they must first understand the local conditions which have given rise to the crisis. In all other respects they may ridicule and ignore his country; but in this respect it is central to the question, and must be taken into account.

If I am concerned about the vital matter of salvation, then whether I like it or not, there is no evading what seem to be the exotic surroundings in which it is brought to my notice. Angels, predictions, miracles, are an intrinsic part of the gospel, because it concerns a supernatural break-in to our world, as unexpected as the message to Zechariah and as staggering as the one to Mary. For such supernaturalism we must be prepared: Christianity is meaningless without it. The Jewishness of the tale is likewise intrinsic to it, because at no other place or time has God ever broken into our world with the full message of salvation, but in these events in first-century Palestine.

Once accepted, however, these principles will form a proper Christian attitude towards two major challenges of our own day. Within the church we find many whose rejection of this or that in the Bible or in biblical theology is based on nothing more objective than an unwillingness to accept the supernatural; but we know that without the supernatural there is no gospel. Surrounding the church we find many who profess religions other than our own—ancient religions, world-religions—and we listen to them courteously, and learn from them humbly; but we know that until they come to Bethlehem and Calvary, they are strangers to the good news of God.

It is the cross of Christ which Thomas Kelly describes in the famous hymn[18] as

> his people's hope, his people's wealth,
> Their everlasting theme.

His words could equally well be applied to the whole scheme of salvation. But if there is to be a salvation for mankind at all, it can be brought about only by the almighty, supernatural, miracle-working God. And he will offer it to men only through the medium of a first-century Jew—Jesus of Nazareth. This man alone, the central figure of Luke's Gospel, is to be the Saviour of the world.

[18] Thomas Kelly, *We sing the praise of him who died.*

2:1–52

The child of good omen

As Luke explained in his introduction, he has 'traced the course of all things from the first' (1:3, RV), and in chapter 2 he sets down the remainder of the stories he has selected concerning the beginning of the gospel.

We remind ourselves of these stories, well-known as they are. One comes from Jesus's earliest days, when he was but a new-born 'babe' (2: 12, 16). In the next, he is a 'child' (2:40) six weeks old. In the last, he is a 'boy' (2:43) approaching his teens. The first is the story of his birth, and of the angel who announced it to the shepherds on the Bethlehem hillside, so that they 'went with haste' to see the baby in the stable. The second tells how he was brought to the temple at Jerusalem for the customary religious service of Purification, and how the aged Simeon there met the holy family and uttered the beautiful words we know as the *Nunc Dimittis*: 'Lord, now lettest thou thy servant depart in peace'. The third describes how when Jesus was twelve he stayed on in Jerusalem, unknown to his parents, after another religious festival; their mild rebuke when they found him was met by a mysterious answer which his mother never forgot, though it was long before she understood it.

We can be fairly certain of the circumstances in which Luke learned of these events. Having come to Jerusalem with Paul just before the latter was arrested,[1] and being on hand to accompany him again when he was eventually sent away from Caesarea on the voyage to Rome,[2] Luke presumably stayed in Palestine for the two-year period of his friend's imprisonment, and without doubt used the opportunity to gather material for his Gospel. Behind chapters 1 and 2 in particular there must surely lie long conversations between him and Mary.

[1] Acts 21: 17ff.   [2] Acts 27:1.

Of all her countless memories of her first-born Son, some were obviously more memorable than others, so that what she kept and pondered (2:19) can only have been a selection. Of the incidents she recounted to Luke, he in turn had to select those which were most suitable for his Gospel. Why, we ask ourselves, should he have chosen these, and not others? And why should he relate them in the way he did? How does this chapter fit into the general scheme of his story, and what does he intend his readers to understand from it?[3]

1. Three stories

For reasons which will become clear, we shall take the angel of the Lord (2:9), the old man Simeon (2:25), and the child Jesus himself (2:43), to be the central figures in the three sections of chapter 2.

a. The angel (2:1–21)

An angel of the Lord appeared to them [the shepherds at Bethlehem], and the glory of the Lord shone around them, and they were filled with fear. And the angel said to them, 'Be not afraid...' (2:9–10).

For many people, the story of Jesus's birth is practically all they know of Christianity. For Luke, however, a mere paragraph of seven verses (his Gospel contains well over 1,000!) is enough to deal with the nativity itself.

This is not to say that his treatment of the great event is in any way skimped. 2:1–7 is a little jewel of economical story-telling, each of its many facets beautifully cut and showing brilliant depths. We could linger over the way Luke brings together the Greco-Roman world of Theophilus (2:1–2) and the Jewish world of 2:4–5, with its religion and supernaturalism;[4] over the sureness with which the histories of these two worlds dovetail in the divine calendar (2:1–6); or over Luke's eye for meaningful detail (*e.g.* 2:7—the 'first-born',[5] 'no place ... in the inn').[6]

---

[3] For a detailed interpretation of this chapter, following similar lines, see Stonehouse, pp. 46–67.

[4] See the exposition of 1:5–80, pp. 32ff. above.

[5] *Cf.* 2:23; Col. 1:15, 18; Heb. 1:6.

[6] *Cf.* 4:29; 19:14; 23:18. 'When Christ first came among us we pushed him into an outhouse; and we have done our best to keep him there ever since' (J. R. H. Moorman, *The Path to Glory: Studies in the Gospel according to St Luke*, SPCK, 1960, p. 19).

Even so, these are scarcely more than the basic facts, and Luke now goes on to take up nearly twice as much space on what is at first sight merely a picturesque addition to the story, the incident of the shepherds' vision of angels and the heavenly message proclaimed to them. It is on this that he seems to concentrate.

Perhaps he hints in 2:15 at his reason for doing so. Something 'has happened', indeed, but it is also something 'which the Lord has made known'; not simply an event, but an event plus a revelation. The event is from one point of view the greatest that ever took place, and the turning-point of history.[7] But it would have no meaning for us unless God revealed that meaning. That is where the angel comes in, for he is (as the word 'angel' implies) the messenger of God. The news which is spread by the shepherds, and which Mary keeps in her heart, is *'the saying which had been told them* concerning this child' (2:17). It is the divine message which the angel brings concerning Jesus.

b. The prophet (2:22–40)

Inspired by the Spirit he [Simeon] came into the temple; and when the parents brought in the child Jesus, . . . he took him up in his arms and blessed God and said, 'Lord, now lettest thou thy servant depart in peace.' (2:27–29).

The key figures in this story are Simeon and Anna. In Luke's description they are 'twinned' characters. Both are old (2:26–29, and 2:36–37). Both are devoutly religious, people who are expecting the 'consolation of Israel' and the 'redemption of Jerusalem' (2:25 and 2:37, 38). Most important, both are prophets. Anna is explicitly given this rare and honoured title (2:36),[8] and when Simeon speaks by the power of the Holy Spirit of God he too is prophesying (2:25ff.).

So we may be sure that Anna's thanksgiving at the sight of the baby Jesus, and what she said about him to her God-fearing friends (2:38), would have been similar to the words of Simeon. It is the latter, however, which Luke chooses to record in full. In doing so, it seems again that he wishes to emphasize what is *said* about Jesus— the divine comment on him; for that, he tells us, is what struck Mary

[7] See C. S. Lewis's fine poem *The Turn of the Tide* (*Poems*, Geoffrey Bles, 1964, pp. 49ff.).

[8] According to Jewish tradition, only 'seven prophetesses have prophesied to Israel . . . Sarah, Miriam, Deborah, Hannah, Abigail, Huldah, and Esther' (quoted by Ellis, p. 83).

and Joseph so forcibly (2:33). This time the word from God comes not through an angel but through a prophet.

c. The Child himself (2:41–52)

The boy Jesus stayed behind in Jerusalem. . . . After three days they found him in the temple, . . . and his mother said to him, 'Son, why have you treated us so? Behold, your father and I have been looking for you anxiously.' And he said to them, 'How is it that you sought me?' (2:43, 46, 48–49).

Here is the story of a visit by the holy family to a festival in Jerusalem. But the visit is not the most important thing. In the sentence of 2:42–43, the only main verb is the last one, so that Luke is writing something like this: 'When he was twelve, and they had gone up, and when the feast was ended, when they were returning, Jesus stayed behind.' The staying behind is what Luke wants to stress. And of that three days' stay among the teachers in the temple, the thing to which he is working up as a climax to his story, the thing which he records in detail as Mary had remembered it in detail, is the boy's answer to her rebuke—'the *saying* which he spoke to them' (2:50).

Like the angel's word and the prophet's word, it is a saying which tells us something about Jesus. Moreover, since it comes from the lips of Jesus himself, the one who is to be Saviour and Christ and Lord,[9] and who is already even at this early age full of wisdom and the favour of God (2:40), it is, like the other two sayings, a divine word. So the central figure in each of the three episodes is one who conveys an important declaration from God concerning the Son of Mary.

2. Three sayings

It seems, then, that what Luke means his readers to see as the main thrust of his narrative here is that a series of sayings—indeed, a series of inspired oracles—accompanies and explains these incidents of the early life of Jesus, and that he (Luke) has selected the stories for that very reason.

A number of considerations suggest this. First, as we have seen, the central figure in each episode is in some sense a mouthpiece for a message from God, one who utters divine words. Secondly, both

[9] See below, p. 47.

these opening chapters of the Gospel are taken up with the thought that after four centuries in which the voice of prophecy has been silent, now at last God speaks again, through 'the tongues of men and of angels'.[10] Thirdly, the things chiefly remembered and recorded in the three stories of chapter 2 are what was 'told' (2:17–20), 'said' (2:33), and 'spoken' (2:50) about Jesus; indeed, the word *rhēma*, though it can mean 'thing' (2:15, 19), actually has the root meaning of 'saying' (2:17), and maybe for that reason Luke deliberately used this word rather than others he might have chosen. Fourthly, the introduction has already told us that he was concerned to record what he had learnt from those who were 'ministers of the *word*', he himself not having first-hand knowledge of that word; so it should not surprise us that, other things being equal, he should especially favour stories which incorporate God-given utterances.

Here, then, there comes amid the 'glory of the Lord' (2:9)[11] an angelic voice; next, 'inspired by the Spirit' (2:27), a prophetic voice; and finally a new thing altogether, the dominical voice itself for the first time in Luke's Gospel, the words of the Word made flesh.

a. What the angel said

'*Be not afraid; for behold, I bring you good news of a great joy which will come to all the people; for to you is born this day in the city of David a Saviour, who is Christ the Lord. And this will be a sign for you: you will find a babe wrapped in swaddling clothes and lying in a manger*' (2:10–12).

The baby's name was given privately before his birth, and publicly afterwards, as 'Jesus' (1:31; 2:21). It was an unexceptional, though splendid, name for a Jewish child; it meant 'The Lord is salvation', and is borne by several persons in the Bible. Usually it tells us less about them themselves than about their parents' faith in the God of Israel. But in the case of this particular child the name had hidden depths; and it was to reveal these that the angel appeared on the first Christmas night. He came to bring 'good news', and the news was precisely this: not only was God indeed at work in salvation, but he was about to accomplish that work once and for all, in and through an actual son of Israel, who might be located that very night 'in the city of David', 'wrapped in swaddling cloths and lying in a manger.'

[10] 1 Cor. 13:1.
[11] The Old Testament *shekinah*; cf. Ex. 16:10; 24:16; Ezk. 1:28. See A. R. C. Leaney, *A Commentary on the Gospel according to St Luke* (A. & C. Black, 1958), p. 94.

So with three further names the angel fills out the meaning of the name 'Jesus' as it applies uniquely to the Son of Mary.[12] First, this child is himself to be *Saviour,* the one who alone can rescue mankind from its predicament of sin, misery, and mortality, and bring the blessings which will meet all possible needs of men. Thus there is no shadow of irony about the 'peace-on-earth' song of the heavenly host (2:14). To this, however, an instructed Jew would have replied: 'But surely that is the role of God only? The very name "Jesus" says so—"The Lord", and no-one else, "is Saviour"—and the whole of Jewish history and scripture repeats it.' Secondly, therefore, the angel explains that Jesus is to be *Christ.* This is the Greek equivalent of the Hebrew 'Messiah', and both mean 'the anointed one, the chosen'. Jesus takes on God's role of saviour because he is the one whom God has authorized and empowered to carry out the work of salvation. But he is even more than that. The third title which the angel gives him is the staggering one of *Lord*; staggering, because already, in little more than a chapter, Luke has used the word nearly twenty times as the regular title (which in fact, among Greek-speaking Jews, it was) for the God of Israel himself.[13] What was implied in the message to Zechariah (1:16f.; *cf.* Mal. 4:5–6), and what the inspired Elizabeth had hinted (1:41–43), is now stated expressly by the angel, with equal divine authority.

All this is focused in Jesus. Through him is to be done God's saving work, for to him is given God's authority, and he is himself God come in the flesh: Jesus, the Christ, the Lord. In him, and nowhere else, is salvation to be found. Can we have enough of him, or say enough of him? Shall we not rather, once we have grasped what the angel is telling us about him, follow the shepherds in seeking him with all haste and then making known the wonderful news?

b. What the prophet said

'*Mine eyes have seen thy salvation which thou hast prepared in the presence of all peoples. . . . This child is set for the fall and rising of many in Israel, and for a sign that is spoken against*' (2:30–31, 34).

[12] This is why I take the naming of the baby in 2:21 not, as some do, with the passage that follows it, but with that which precedes it. The verse completes the first section of the chapter, just as 2:40 and 2:52 complete the second and third sections.

[13] Notice the subtle difference between Simeon's expectation in 2:26 (*Christos Kyriou,* 'the *Lord's* Christ'), and the angel's declaration in 2:11 (*Christos Kyrios,* 'the *Lord* Christ').

47

Simeon, with the Holy Spirit upon him, gives thanks to God in the words of the *Nunc Dimittis* (2:29–32), and warning to Mary in the words that follow (2:34–35). So here again is God-inspired truth concerning the child Jesus, and it amplifies what the angel had said six weeks earlier to the shepherds.

Simeon's thanksgiving to God tells us that the salvation to be found in Jesus is for all men. It is a universal offer. The angel might be thought to have said this already, according to the AV of 2:10 ('to all people'); and, indeed, the fact that his words came first to shepherds, whom respectable religious folk despised,[14] shows how the gospel transcends social and religious barriers. But the wording there should actually be 'to all *the* people' (RV, RSV); in that verse, it is still only the people of Israel who are in view. Jewish privilege, however, is precisely what Simeon here leaves behind. Salvation is for all *peoples*—a light to the Gentiles, as well as glory for Israel.

But Simeon's warning to Mary tells us that the universal offer to salvation does not mean that it will be received by everyone indiscriminately and automatically. It is offered to all; but it has to be considered by each. It is a universal offer, but it brings a personal challenge. There will be those who will speak against this sign of God's love that has been offered to them, for it searches men's hearts, and some will be scandalized by a salvation which can only be achieved by way of the cross (the 'sword' which will pierce Mary's own soul).[15]

There is none to whom the message of the gospel is not directed. Luke, having concentrated this great gift of God in the Lord Jesus Christ alone, now extends it to the whole human race, and to each person in particular, and requires men to ask themselves whether they have yet accepted it or are still rejecting it.

c. What the Child himself said

'*How is it that you sought me? Did you not know that I must be in my Father's house?*' (2:49).

[14] See below, pp. 93, 150 n. 2.

[15] *Cf.* 1 Cor. 1:23f. Simeon's first words to Mary in 2:34 do not in themselves make this point, as is sometimes suggested (*i.e.* that some will fall while others will rise, the gospel being 'to one a fragrance from death to death, to the other a fragrance from life to life', 2 Cor. 2:16). The contrast here is rather between the 'many in Israel' who will *both fall and rise* through the gospel message ('Whoever loses his life for my sake, he will save it,' 9:24), and those who on the other hand will speak against the sign of salvation.

'Thou, O Lord, art our Father', the Jews of old had said.[16] But it is almost certain that they understood by this little more than that it was God who had brought their nation into being; and although the patriarchal communities of the days of Abraham were embedded in their national history as patterns of the family relationship which should exist between God and his people, the idea of his fatherhood was something they had never fully grasped—certainly not in the way that Jesus was going to teach it.[17]

So the first recorded words of Jesus are a statement about himself, and a claim to a relationship between himself and God different from, and deeper than, anything that had ever been known before. Furthermore, it is a relationship into which he is going to bring all others who are prepared to put their faith in God through him. He will teach them to address their prayers regularly to their 'Father' (11:2), and they will learn to use the affectionate, intimate name 'Abba' ('Daddy') which he himself uses.[18] Thus early in his Gospel Luke introduces the great object of the divine plan of salvation, just as John does, in his own way, at the beginning of his story of Jesus: 'To all who received him, who believed in his name, he gave power to become children of God'.[19]

Both these truths—that he is Son of God, and that he has come into the world so that others may become sons of God—are implied in his words in 2:49. For to be 'in my Father's house' really amounts to the same thing as to be 'about my Father's business' (AV): where my Father is, where he centres his activity, there I am always to be found as well. (Again, this is Luke's equivalent of some of the great sayings in John: 'I and the Father are one ... The Son can do nothing of his own accord, but only what he sees the Father doing; for whatever he does, that the Son does likewise ... I always do what is pleasing to him').[20] But the Father's work, as we have seen, is the work of salvation; so this is the work in which the Son also 'must' be engaged. Thus early in his career does Jesus express the compulsion that is upon him to be at one with his Father in the saving of men.

With this Luke rounds off his selection of stories from the very beginning of the life of Jesus. The tale of the birth of a peasant's child might have been no more than a picturesque but unimportant incident had it not been for the omens which surrounded it. Not,

[16] Is. 63:16. [17] *Cf.* Jn. 5:18. [18] Mk. 14:36; Gal. 4:6.
[19] Jn. 1:12. [20] Jn. 10:30; 5:19; 8:29.

however, omens like those of pagan faiths, 'exhalations whizzing in the air',[21] mere portents that mystify. On the contrary, these are by their very nature voices that clarify. For it is one of the glories of the Christian faith that it comes not only by sign but also by speech—by images, indeed, so that the message may be powerful, but also by words, so that it may be plain; and if either method is more important than the other, it must surely be the explaining words. Luke holds no brief, therefore, for those who rate the image *above* the explanation—who reckon (for example) that the ministry of the sacrament is more exalted than the ministry of the word, requiring higher qualifications and greater grace.

As with all signs and sacraments, so with the incarnation itself. The coming of Jesus into the world would mean nothing, were it not accompanied by God's own explanation of it. Accordingly, Luke has told us in the angel's words who Jesus is, and in the prophet's words who may benefit from his message; and now in the words of the Child himself, we learn that to grasp the fullness of this message of salvation we shall need to follow the one who already knows God as his Father, as he prosecutes his Father's plan through the whole gospel story in order to bring us into the same relationship.

[21] Shakespeare, *Julius Caesar*, II. i. 44.

The deeds of the Saviour

3:1 – 4:30
The Son of God

The sonorous list of names in 3:1–2 marks the beginning of something new; it 'has the effect', as Drury says, 'of a ceremonious opening or fanfare'.[1] It indicates that, although in one respect the introduction to the Gospel was the paragraph 1:1–4, from another point of view the whole of the first two chapters has been introductory, while the main story of Jesus starts at this point. Nevertheless the thread of Luke's great subject joins all these chapters together. He is continuing here the account of the good news (3:18), which thirty years earlier had been the angelic message to Zechariah in Jerusalem (1:19) and to the shepherds at Bethlehem (2:10). Here, as there, it is good news of salvation, which is now John's theme (3:6) no less than it had been Mary's in the *Magnificat* (1:47), Zechariah's in the *Benedictus* (1:69), and Simeon's in the *Nunc Dimittis* (2:30).

In the same way, Luke is concerned to show his readers that still, after a thirty-year gap, it is a matter of God speaking to men. There is good news; it is good news of salvation; and the good news of salvation is a divine message come from heaven to earth. That heavenly voice we have heard again and again in chapters 1 and 2. Angels speak, men and women speak under the inspiration of the Holy Spirit, the child Jesus himself speaks. Here now, as the story of the adult life of Jesus opens, the event which Luke sets so impressively in its historical context—placing it in the world scene, in a year when the terms of office of four particular local rulers coincided, and under a particular Jewish high priesthood—is not what we might have expected. It is not that Jesus then began his ministry, nor that he then underwent his baptism; in fact it is, in a sense, nothing to do with Jesus at all. It is that 'in the fifteenth year of the

[1] Drury, p. 44.

53

reign of Tiberius Caesar ... *the word of God came to John*' (3:1–2).[2]
Furthermore, when in due course Jesus does come on the scene, and
is baptized by John, Luke leaves as incidentals what we might have
thought the important matters, and turns the spotlight of his main
verbs on something quite other: 'When all the people were baptized,
and when Jesus also had been baptized and was praying' (these are
just participles which set the scene), what actually *happened* was that
'the heaven was opened ... the Holy Spirit descended ... and *a
voice came from heaven*' (3:21–22).

Luke's God is a God who speaks. He has broken into a world
which, for all the babel of its myriad voices, is perishing for lack of a
life-giving voice from heaven, and he tells us the good news of
salvation; and this salvation is in his Son. The same God speaks
today, on the same subject, to meet the same need. So let us 'hear
what God the Lord will speak, for he will speak peace to his people
... His salvation is at hand.'[3]

1. The voices at the river (3:1–22)

*The word of God came to John the son of Zechariah in the wilderness; and he
went into all the region about the Jordan, preaching ... 'Do not begin to
say to yourselves, "We have Abraham as our father"; for I tell you, God is
able from these stones to raise up children to Abraham*' (3:2, 3, 8).

*A voice came from heaven, 'Thou art my beloved Son; with thee I am well
pleased*' (3:22).

a. The voice of the prophet

John had been sent to 'prepare the way of the Lord' (3:4), and it was
his concern to bring men to an encounter with the coming Christ,
and thus into a relationship with God. It was not by accident,
therefore, that his constant message ('he said', in 3:7, means 'he used
to say') was one of warning, for he was addressing audiences whose
attitude he exposes in 3:8. They were saying to themselves, 'We have
Abraham as our father;' they had grown up with the assumption that

---

[2] 'When John the Baptist appeared, not the oldest man in Palestine could
remember to have spoken even in his earliest childhood with any man who had seen a
prophet ... In these circumstances it was *an occurrence of the first magnitude, more
important far than war or revolution*, when a new prophet actually appeared' (John
Seeley, *Ecce Homo;* quoted by Plummer, p. 7).

[3] Ps. 85:8–9.

since they were descendants of Abraham, and therefore members of the chosen race, they were already in a right relationship with God. This false confidence John had to destroy. It was not enough that he should charm them away from their homes, to come and listen to stirring oratory down by the Jordan. He must touch their hearts, and convince them that not even the greatest spiritual privilege then known—that of being an Israelite—could of itself make an individual right with God and acceptable to him.

John's actions conveyed the same message. For baptism was the rite by which Gentiles would become 'Jews'; those who were already within the Israelite family did not need it. By preaching baptism to the latter (3:3), John 'places Jews in the category of Gentiles. Physical relation to Abraham is of no avail.'[4]

'All the people' who responded to John's preaching 'were baptized' (3:21), for all needed to acknowledge themselves to be in a wrong relation to God. But there was going to be one notable exception.

b. The voice of God

With the crowds coming to be baptized in the Jordan there comes 'Jesus also'. Isaiah had prophesied that the Servant-Son would be 'numbered with the transgressors', and this prophecy 'has its fulfilment', as Luke will remind us, at the time of the passion (22:37; Is. 53:12). But that will be the *ful*filling, the completion, of a process which will have been going on for over thirty years. The Christ will have been filling the place of a man among sinful men throughout the days of his incarnation, and at no point more explicitly than when he accepts baptism along with them.

Yet the very fact that he is willing to number himself among these transgressors emphasizes the difference between himself and them. When he chooses, freely, to be reckoned among sinners, he shows that he is not a sinner himself. 'When Christ came into the world, he said, . . . "I have come to do thy will, O God."'[5] He might truly have claimed that 'a baptism of repentance for the forgiveness of sins' (3:3) was for him unnecessary and inappropriate; but his readiness to undergo it just the same, if that is his Father's will, is the mark of a man unique among men in his total obedience to God. By this consideration he sets aside John's scruples about the propriety of the baptism, as we learn from Matthew's account: 'Thus it is fitting for

---

[4] Ellis, p. 86.
[5] Heb. 10:5–7, quoting Ps. 40:6–8.

us to fulfil all righteousness.'[6] Luke will take up the theme of Jesus's obedience again in 4:1–13, the account of the temptation in the wilderness. For the moment, he is setting forth the grand paradox that Jesus in his baptism declared both his solidarity with, and his distinction from, the rest of humanity.

Having said all this, we should still remember that for Luke there is something even more important than the baptism. 'When Jesus had been baptized'—'it is remarkable', notes Plummer, 'that this, which seems to us to be the main fact, should be expressed thus incidentally by a participle'[7]—'when Jesus had been baptized, . . . a voice came from heaven.' That is the main verb, and the main event. What the voice of God had to say about Jesus was in vivid contrast to what John had had to say to the misguided sons of Abraham. After the people had been baptized—in their case an admission that in spite of their Jewish birth they were out of relationship with God and unacceptable to him—there came God's own declaration concerning Jesus: 'Now this one *is* my beloved Son; with him I *am* well pleased.' Jesus, unlike the rest, is acceptable to God. Like no other, he is from the start in a true relationship to God. He is, in a distinctive sense, the Son of God. God says so.

2. The family tree (3:23–38)

Jesus . . . the son (as was supposed) of Joseph . . . the son of Zerubbabel . . . the son of David . . . the son of Judah . . . the son of Abraham . . . the son of Adam, the son of God (3:23, 27, 31, 33, 34, 38).

The family tree of Jesus hardly looks like a thrilling message from heaven! Yet Luke includes it alongside his account of what I have called 'the voices at the river', for in it God does in fact speak to us. Remembering that in Hebrew the words 'son' and 'father' meant respectively any descendant and any ancestor, however remote,[8] we may quite legitimately short-circuit the whole genealogy; by joining 3:23 with 3:38 we see that this section, like the previous one, is showing us 'Jesus . . . the son of God.' In the course of a long list of unpronounceable names (the terror of lesson-readers—if this passage ever is read in church!) it reveals to us a profound and vital truth about what that title means.

---

[6] Mt. 3:15.   [7] Plummer, p. 98.   [8] *Cf.* 3:8.

a. Jesus the son of Adam

Read immediately after the story of John's baptizing, the family tree presents us with another paradox. It reminds us that Jesus was commonly supposed to be the son of Joseph; that was his legal parentage, a fact which is not affected by the doctrine of the virgin birth. He belonged to the family of the carpenter of Nazareth, 'where he had been brought up' (4:16), a villager among villagers and a Galilean among Galileans. He was also, along with many hundreds of others, a son of Zerubbabel the prince and a son of David the king, a member of the royal house of the tribe of Judah. At a still deeper level, he was by that very fact a son of Abraham, an Israelite, and the genealogy proclaims his solidarity with all other Jews who have ever lived. And Luke (for this is a characteristic interest of his)[9] takes us even further back. Jesus is not simply one with the whole Jewish race: he is one with the whole *human* race, for he is a son of Adam.

Having shown us, as one aspect of the story of the baptism, a Jesus who ranges himself alongside sinful men, Luke now underlines this truth by showing us a Jesus who is indeed one with the rest of humanity, who really belonged to the human race, to a particular nation and tribe, and even to an actual human family in an actual Palestinian village.

But the evangelist takes one step further back still, and in doing so he again sets forth the paradox of how Jesus is both fully, truly, human and yet at the same time different from all other men. For Luke, having shown us Jesus as the son of Adam, does not hesitate to call Adam the son of God; so that Jesus by his very humanity is God's son.

b. Jesus the son of God

'God said, "Let us make man in our image, after our likeness."'[10] And the original man did bear the family likeness—until he fell into sin. All of us are sons of Adam, and Adam was son of God; but the line is not continuous. It was broken at the fall. No other man has ever come into the world bearing the likeness of a son of God, for by Adam's sin every one of his descendants forfeited that sonship.

No other man, that is, except Jesus. The climax of the previous section, the voice at his baptism, made plain that he *is* the Son of God (3:22); and this section likewise points to the unbroken relation-

---

[9] Note the contrast with Matthew's genealogy of Jesus, Mt. 1:1ff.
[10] Gn. 1:26.

ship between him and his heavenly Father. In other words, he is again what Adam once was. He is man as God meant man to be, the image of God, showing the family likeness in perfection. We may picture our present human existence as a pit, in which all of us are trapped, for the sin of Adam has removed any possibility of our climbing out into the upper world. Jesus is *like* us, in that he has come down into the same pit with us. That is the message both of the baptism story and of the family tree, if we leave out their closing verses. But he is *unlike* us, in that while we are here because of a fall in disobedience, he is here because of a descent in obedience,[11] and he has never let go of the rope which joins him to the world above. He is firmly anchored up there, in the unbroken relation of sonship with his Father. That is why his humanity is distinctive. That is why it is only by clinging to him that we can ever be lifted out of the pit. That is the message of the last words of the baptism story (3:22) and of the family tree (3:38).

3. The devil (4:1–13)

The devil said to him, 'If you are the Son of God . . .' And Jesus answered him, 'It is written . . .' (4:3–4).

'Immediately,' to use one of Mark's favourite words,[12] the story of Jesus's temptation follows; and it is not hard to see why, when we remember that chapter 3 has shown us Jesus as the Son of God in the special sense of his being the perfect Man. These thirteen verses are going to show the practical meaning of Jesus's perfect manhood.

a. The temptations

It has been pointed out earlier how much Luke is concerned with a God who speaks. But this God uses some unexpected mouthpieces. Even less likely than the genealogy of chapter 3 is the tempter of chapter 4. Nevertheless the devil's words do contain truth, and they elicit from Jesus further truth, about the subject we are considering.

The devil takes up the precise point established by chapter 3, and makes it the basis of his challenge. 'So you are the Son of God? Very well: if that is true, then prove it.' In three ways Jesus may demonstrate, to the devil's satisfaction, that he is in fact what the voices at the river, and the family tree, have said that he is. Surely it is the

---

[11] Phil. 2:6–8.   [12] Mk. 1:12.

right of God's Son to have the provision of all his needs; he needs food, he has the power to make it—let him do so (4:3). Surely it is his right to receive power over all nations, and to become King of kings; and since the world is in Satan's hands, it is from him that Jesus can receive it—with the sly proviso that he acknowledge Satan as his lord (4:5–7). Surely it is his right to claim protection against all dangers; and his Father has actually promised it, so let him put that promise to the test (4:9–11).

The answers we may expect from Jesus, therefore, will deal with a threefold challenge as to whether he is or is not the Son of God, as he is claimed to be.

b. The answers

It is an obvious, and not unhelpful, lesson to us that in dealing with the devil's temptations Jesus turns each time to Scripture. But we have to look more closely to see the point which is really being made here. Jesus quoted Scripture, it is true; but the devil can do that too (4:10–11). What is more important is to ask ourselves which scripture Jesus quoted, and why. When we think that question through, we shall find that the answer sheds great light on the whole meaning of this episode, and on its connections with what has gone before.

For each of Jesus's answers to the devil is a quotation from the Book of Deuteronomy.[13] The word 'deuteronomy' means 'the second law'; the book is a re-statement of the divine law given through Moses. And it is the law which God gave *for man to live by*. The answers of Jesus are in effect as follows. 'You suggest that feeding my body may take precedence over obeying my God. But God has told men'—*men*—'that they shall not live by bread alone; therefore *I* shall not do so. You offer me universal power, at the price of worshipping you. But God has told *men* that they are not to worship any but him; therefore *I* shall not worship you. You propose that I should test his promises to suit my own convenience. But he has told *men* that they are not to test him in this way; therefore *I* shall not do so.'

What is he doing? He is deliberately emptying himself of his power and glory—'Do you think that I cannot appeal to my Father, and he will at once send me more than twelve legions of angels?'[14]—and putting himself in the position of a *man*, under the authority of the law of God. 'Being found in human form he hum-

---

[13] Dt. 8:3; 6:13; 6:16.
[14] Mt. 26:53.

bled himself and became *obedient'*. [15] He is in fact going right back to the beginning, back to square one: he is the new Adam. In Eden, the head of the human race was confronted by the tempter, disobeyed God's word, and set the whole of mankind off on the wrong track. Now comes the second Adam, and alone in the wilderness he in his turn confronts the tempter. The difference is that he will win. He will be the totally obedient Man, Man as he was meant to be, Man who is altogether righteous, Man who never loses his relationship with God through sin. He overcomes Satan by his undeviating obedience to the will of God, an obedience which, as Philippians 2:8 goes on to tell us, he pursues inexorably even 'unto death, even death on a cross'. It is no wonder that Milton, having described 'Man's first disobedience' in *Paradise Lost,* chose as his subject for *Paradise Regained* the story of Jesus's temptation.

This is not, of course, the crucial conflict, where the victory will be won. That will come, as the word 'crucial' implies, at the cross. The passion of Christ, three years hence, is the 'opportune time' to which Satan looks forward—his 'hour, and the power of darkness' (4:13; 22:53)—and the crisis in which he will be broken at the very moment of his triumph. But the confrontation here in the wilderness is the first occasion in history that a son of Adam has raised an effective defence against Satan. For him, the writing is on the wall. For humanity, the possibility of a new start comes electrifyingly into view.

4. The folks at home (4:14–30)

All spoke well of him, and wondered at the gracious words which proceeded out of his mouth; and they said, 'Is not this Joseph's son?' (4:22)

The return to Galilee which Luke records here seems to have taken place a considerable time after the temptation in the wilderness. [16] But he omits the various events of Jesus's early ministry which John describes, and goes straight on to the incident in the synagogue at

---

[15] Phil. 2:8. It is clearly in this sense that Luke would have understood the 'emptying', the *kenōsis,* of Phil. 2:7. The theory that kenosis affected the *teaching* of Jesus, so that it was possible for him to make mistakes, is based on an assumption—namely, that to be truly human is to be fallible. This assumption has yet to be proved. Luke's picture of the 'true Man' points, if anywhere, in the opposite direction: sinful man errs, sinless man does not—his knowledge may indeed be partial, but what he does know is accurate. See above. p. 31.

[16] See Jn. 2:12–13, 23; 3:22–24; 4:1–3, 45; Mt. 4:12; Mk. 1:14.

Nazareth, which will make very clear some of the implications of what he has been saying about the Son of God.

Jesus 'came to Nazareth, where he had been brought up; and he went to the synagogue, as his custom was, on the sabbath day' (4:16). He was becoming widely known as a preacher (4:15), so it was quite natural that he should be asked to read the Scripture, and that he should then sit down again to give a short sermon on it (4:20).

It is doubtful if any of the worshippers, his own kith and kin, really appreciated what he was saying, when he took the splendid and moving declaration which the Old Testament puts into the mouth of God's chosen Servant, [17] and told them that even as they were listening to it, it was coming true: that he himself was the Servant long foretold. The revolutionary nature of this passage has been touched upon earlier;[18] and it is not on that that Luke dwells, but on the next words of Jesus, which arise from the reaction of his hearers. They were impressed, certainly, as we see in the first part of 4:22; but the depth of their failure to understand him is obvious from the rest of the verse. They knew him so well, this 'local boy made good'! And, we may imagine, with many a knowing nudge and delighted smile they turned to one another and said, '*Is not this Joseph's son?*'

And the answer is No, no, a million times no! As the voices at the river had declared, as the family tree had revealed, as the devil himself had admitted, this is the Son of *God*! And what it means for him to be not the son of Joseph, but the Son of *God,* the new Adam, the founder of a new mankind, he goes on immediately to make plain.

Their vision can see him only in the setting of their own village; they have heard rumours of his doings twenty miles away at Capernaum, but what really matters is that he should perform a miracle or two here at Nazareth (4:23). Now listen, says Jesus: I have come with the good news of salvation not for Nazareth only, but for all Galilee, and indeed for all Israel; and—although this will scandalize

---

[17] Is. 61:1–2.

[18] The reference is on p. 37; but see the whole passage on the scope (1:39–56) and the heart (1:57–80) of salvation, on pp. 36–38. As I have indicated there; and shall do again in commenting on 'the poor' (7:1–10, 11–17, 36–50) on pp. 92–94, it is not legitimate to take the 'revolution' and 'liberation' sayings of Jesus as a political manifesto. To claim that they justify the attempt to set up by force one system of government instead of another, is to misinterpret them radically by taking them quite out of their context.

you—if Israel turns out to be as blinkered and narrow-minded as you are, then she will forfeit it, while the rest of the world receives it. Your own history warns you of the possibility of Gentiles being blessed while Jews are rejected (4:25–27).

Salvation is, in other words, not restricted to the sons of Abraham, let alone the villagers of Nazareth; it is for every son of *Adam,* for Jesus has come to save not just Jewry, but humanity. As this Gospel has already indicated and will stress increasingly, he is to be the Saviour of the *world.*

This is a message which, as they grasped it, changed the attitude of the people of Nazareth from admiration to fury. Luke here puts in a narrative what John puts in a statement, 'He came to his own home, and his own people received him not'; and as Drury points out, looking on to the closing paragraphs of Luke's second volume, 'his own people do not want to know about him to the bitter end'.[19]

But by the same token it is a message for which the majority of us may be profoundly thankful. For 'to all who received him, who believed in his name, he gave power to become children of God.'[20] It means that the perfect righteousness of the new Man can be extended to *every* other man, however sinful, who will receive it in repentance and faith. He does not need to be a Jew; he does not need to belong to the same tribe, or the same culture, or even the same century, as Jesus; he does not need to be religious or clever or influential. The mere fact that he is a sinful *man* means that Jesus came to save him, and to make him also a son of God.

Even I, therefore, can bring every one of my sins to him, and know that in respect of all of them he has faced the same kind of temptation and emerged victorious: he is 'one who in every respect has been tempted as we are, yet without sin'.[21] At every point at which I have failed, he has achieved a righteousness which will cover my sin. On that righteousness, and not on my sin, God will look; he will 'only look on me as found in him'—in Jesus. As I claim the perfect obedience of the Son of God, the second Adam, for my own, it is to

---

[19] Jn. 1:11; Acts 28:23–28; Drury, p. 57. In Acts 22:21–22, even more clearly than in the passage Drury quotes, Luke draws a parallel between the experience of Jesus at this time and the experience of his apostles afterwards: '"He said to me, 'Depart; for I will send you far away to the Gentiles.'" Up to this word they listened to him; then they lifted up their voices and said, "Away with such a fellow from the earth! For he ought not to live."'

[20] Jn. 1:12.

[21] Heb. 4:15.

me that God will say 'Thou art my beloved Son; with thee I am well pleased.'

And what is thus good news for me, whoever I may be, is good news equally for me to pass on to my neighbour, whoever *he* may be.

4:31 – 5:39
'His word was with authority'

If there are two things which stand out more than any others in the opening chapters of Luke's Gospel, they are his developing portrait of its central figure, and his record of how God has spoken. His two great concerns are a Man and a message. From one point of view the Man is the son of Mary, a truly human being who is nevertheless surrounded by marvellous omens declaring his divinity (chapters 1 and 2); from another point of view he is presented as the 'Son of God', yet in such a way that that title seems to stress his perfect manhood (chapters 3 and 4). The message is the good news from God proclaimed through Gabriel (1:19), through the Christmas angel (2:10), and through John (3:18), the 'word' which will in due course be handed on to the generation of Luke and Theophilus (1:2).

Here, in chapter 4, begins the record of the three years of preaching, teaching, healing, and disciple-training which is known as the ministry of Jesus; and as it begins, the Man and the message converge—Jesus of Nazareth declares, '*I* must *preach the good news* ... for I was sent for this purpose' (4:43).[1]

Luke leaves us in no doubt as to what is happening as Jesus embarks on his preaching ministry: 'The people pressed upon him *to hear the word of God*' (5:1). It is fashionable in some circles, as I have remarked earlier,[2] to play down the importance of preaching in the church. It is claimed that the gospel is conveyed much less effectively by what we say, than by what we do and what we are. There is no avoiding the fact, however, that in these opening scenes of the minis-

---

[1] It is, we notice, 'the good news *of the kingdom of God*'. Some take 'the kingdom' to be a theme of highest importance in Luke's mind. This however is the first time he refers to it explicitly, and for the moment he does not develop it. But see below, pp. 89ff., 169ff.

[2] See above, p. 27.

try of Jesus the way God's message 'comes across' is by *words:* one man speaks, other men hear. Let us then see what happens as the word, the message, is proclaimed by its supreme expositor.

1. A word of power (4:31 – 5:28)

Luke gives us a sequence of stories, no doubt drawn for the most part (though not altogether) from Mark, which might all be illustrations of what God had said through the Old Testament prophet: 'My word ... that goes forth from my mouth ... shall accomplish that which I purpose, and prosper in the thing for which I sent it.'[3] So when the Son of God speaks, things happen. The various effects are presented here in a spectrum, ranging like the seven colours of the rainbow from long-wave red to the most penetrating violet; and reactions to the word of Jesus today will correspond to one or another of those which Luke depicts here. With this in mind, we watch the word in action.

a. *Tickling men's ears*

Reports of him went out into every place in the surrounding region (4:37).

So it had been at the time of his earliest preaching tour, before the one Luke is describing (4:14–15, 23), and so it would continue to be (5:15). And it is something, after all, that people should at least have heard *about* Jesus, even if they have not actually heard him speak to them. Even a secondhand report of him is better than nothing at all. At any rate they are no longer sunk in the ignorance of utter heathendom.

There is in this a challenge to the churches of the western world, where the great majority of people have in some way or other heard 'reports of him'. The folk-religion which survives from past generations more Christian than our own may be little more than superstition; the image of Christ purveyed by the mass media of the present may sometimes be highly unsatisfactory; but the churches can at least try to correct such knowledge, by ensuring that the Jesus known through them, at any rate, is the genuine Jesus of the New Testament. The way they live and preach and worship must be, as far as they can make it so, an embodiment of his word.

---

[3] Is. 55:11.

Even so, merely to have heard about Jesus is a hopelessly superficial grasp of the message. No-one should rest content, or be allowed to rest content, with it. Those whose acquaintance with Jesus is based on nothing more than rumour, or inherited assumptions, or what they read in the papers about the doings of his church, deserve a more penetrating presentation of his word.

b. Gripping men's minds

He was teaching them on the sabbath; and they were astonished at his teaching, for his word was with authority (4:31–32).

It is worth noting that, before this particular visit to Capernaum begins to produce sensational miracles, Jesus has already astonished the people by nothing more extraordinary than a sermon. The first thing that happens, once the message has got beyond being a mere secondhand report, is that men's minds are gripped by it. Jesus makes them *think*.

Admittedly, lesser preachers than he can easily make the message too intellectual. A professor of theology, preaching in a village church, is said to have been struck by a sudden thought in the midst of his sermon, and to have exclaimed to his rustic hearers: 'But perhaps at this point some of you may be suspecting me of Eutychianism.' (They weren't!) However aware we may be of that danger, we must not fly to the opposite extreme and imagine that when properly presented the gospel is childishly simple. Jesus never insulted his hearers' intelligence in that way. He made every allowance for men's limitations, certainly, and never broke the bruised reed or quenched the smoking flax;[4] but even so he expected earnest listeners to give his word the attention of their total mind.

Once it is heard with the ear and grasped by the mind, we shall find that word at work in more far-reaching ways.

c. Healing men's bodies

A man who had the spirit of an unclean demon . . . cried out with a loud voice . . . But Jesus rebuked him, saying, 'Be silent, and come out of him!' And when the demon had thrown him down in the midst, he came out of him (4:33, 35).

---

[4] Is. 42:3, AV.

*Simon's mother-in-law was ill with a high fever . . . And he stood over her
and rebuked the fever, and it left her* (4:38–39).

In the ancient world ills of the first kind were called, out of mere
ignorance, demon-possession; in fact they were probably epilepsy and
similar disorders. Such at least was the view of a more recent and
more sophisticated ignorance! With today's widespread interest in
the occult, he would be a rash man who would now simply deny the
older diagnosis. Perhaps the men of the Bible were right after all
when they spoke of two distinct and equally real afflictions, 'diseases
. . . and demons also' (4:40–41).

Jesus, who came 'to destroy the works of the devil',[5] dealt with
both the cases quoted as though they were (one directly and the other
indirectly) satanic evils, for he 'rebuked' both;[6] and, as ever, his word
was effective. The general question which arises from the whole
account of his healing ministry is, of course, 'Does he do the same
today?'

My own view (and it is no more than that, in a matter where there
are such divergent views) is this. Luke presents throughout this
whole section a Jesus who utters words of power, and in these particular instances a Jesus who is the Healer of men's ills. And Jesus is
the same today: 'Thy touch has still its ancient power; No word from
Thee can fruitless fall'.[7] But his methods are his own, and not the
over-simplified ones his patients would sometimes prescribe for him.

I would therefore make a broad distinction between two methods
of healing: not the obvious distinction between the miraculous and
the medical, but one which lies deeper than that. Where his object is
to be known as the Healer, he works immediately; such cures are, as
it were, for the shop-window—the kind of success story which establishes the reputation of a great surgeon or physician. I see no reason
why in some circumstances today Jesus may not choose to work in
this way and for this purpose. But where he is already known, he may
well say to his trusting patient: 'I could of course give you immediate
relief; but I would rather take the opportunity to do something more
far-reaching, which will be to your greater benefit in the long run.
You will find it more protracted and perhaps more painful, and you
may not understand what I am doing, because I may be treating
disorders of which you yourself are unaware.' He will then set to

---

[5] 1 Jn. 3:8.   [6] *Cf.* 13:16.
[7] Henry Twells, *At even, ere the sun was set.*

work to deal with the needs of the whole person, rather than with the obvious need only. He may aim at a calming of spirit, or a strengthening of courage, or a clarifying of vision, as more important objectives than what we would call healing. Indeed the latter may not be experienced at all in this life, but only at the final 'saving and raising' of the sick, when their mortal nature puts on immortality.[8] For I think it is no accident that each of these two words in James 5 has a double meaning, making them applicable equally to this life and to the next: $s\bar{o}z\bar{o}$, to heal, or to save; $egeir\bar{o}$, to raise from sickness, or to raise from death. The 'prayer of faith' cannot fail to bring about this result, one way or the other. But the faith in which such prayer is prayed must be, not faith *that* Jesus will heal in some particular way (*i.e.* the way we should advise him to do it!), but faith *in* Jesus the Healer, who will choose his own timing and method. Then even today his word of power in this respect will amaze onlookers (4:36) and bring others to seek him (4:40).

d. Affecting men's situations

He said to Simon, 'Put out into the deep and let down your nets for a catch.' And Simon answered, 'Master, we toiled all night and took nothing! But at your word I will let down the nets.' And when they had done this, they enclosed a great shoal of fish (5:4–6).

Religion is a curse!—when, that is, it means the admitting of God into one department of life, while every other door is labelled 'Secular' and bolted against him. Such religion Jesus now repudiates with the next of his words of power.

As long as Simon's boat is being used for a pulpit, the owner has no objection to Jesus's saying in it what he likes. But when it reverts to being a fishing-boat, it is Simon's once more, and Jesus no longer has a say in how it is to be used. Fishing is Simon's job. In the same way, people will listen to Jesus, will consider what he says, and will even ask him to 'make them better' when they are sick; but for him to do as he does in this fourth episode, and to interfere in their job, their home, their leisure, that is another thing altogether. Those matters have nothing, surely, to do with 'religion'.

So Jesus, the carpenter turned preacher, tells Simon, the fisherman, how to fish. We may guess the tone of Simon's answer (5:5), and imagine the expression on his face! Might there have been some

[8] Jas. 5:15; 1 Cor. 15:53.

Jewish proverb that flitted across his mind, equivalent to the English one about grandmothers and eggs? Yet the word of power shows that Jesus knows even more about Simon's job than Simon does himself, and it has a very material effect on the brothers' situation (5:6–7).

Many would have to admit that it is at this point that the word of Jesus comes home to them—literally, because it invades the privacy of their own workaday life, instead of staying respectably in a Sunday church service where it belongs. To learn from Jesus that they should be acknowledging his Father's *daily* gifts of sun and rain, food and clothing, life and breath;[9] his own lordship over *all* creation;[10] and his Holy Spirit's work of sanctifying *every* part of their being,[11]— this is a new and convicting thought, and perhaps the beginning of the gospel's effective entrance into their hearts. And for us to whom it is no new thought, but a reminder, it may sometimes be equally necessary and equally convicting.

e. Mending men's relationships

A man full of leprosy . . . fell on his face and besought him, 'Lord, if you will, you can make me clean.' And he stretched out his hand, and touched him, saying, 'I will; be clean.' And immediately the leprosy left him (5:12–13).

It is not hard to see why Luke continues with a story about the healing of a leper. For it is not merely another healing. Because the disease is what the Bible calls leprosy,[12] more is involved than restoration to physical health. The leper was not just ill; he was outcast. He had not simply lost his health; he had lost his family, his friends, his home, his livelihood. No-one would, indeed no-one was allowed to, associate with him. So we can imagine how with the tingling of his revitalized flesh this man felt a thrill of emotion as Jesus 'stretched out his hand, and *touched* him'. For it was literally a renewed contact with his fellow man, perhaps the first for many years; and it signalized a coming reunion with family and friends, a reintegration with the society from which the disease had cut him

---

[9] Mt. 5:45; 6:31f.; Acts 14:17; 17:25.

[10] Phil. 2:10f.; Col. 1:18.

[11] 1 Thes. 5:23; 1 Pet. 1:2.

[12] The term which in most English versions is translated 'leprosy' in fact covers a variety of skin complaints. It was not to leprosy in particular, in the modern sense of the word, that the old Jewish law attached the social penalties mentioned here.

off. It was to bring about a mending of all those broken relationships.

This too the word of Jesus can achieve, and in our tormented world we do not have to look far to see the need for it. Not only do we see 'nation . . . rise against nation, and kingdom against kingdom' (21:10), but there are antagonisms and divisions all down the scale, between colours, creeds, classes, between management and labour, husband and wife, old and young. Even within the Christian community, wᵉ find all too often estrangement between brother and brother. But oñe of the great key words of the gospel is 'reconciliation'; and as we are reconciled to God, so we are reconciled among ourselves, and the church whose members are no longer 'lepers' to one another, but united in fellowship and love, is a most powerful testimony to the power of the living God.[13] No wonder that at this point Luke again notes that 'so much the more the report went abroad concerning him', and the crowds came flocking (5:15).

f. Saving men's souls

Men were bringing on a bed a man who was paralyzed. . . . And when he saw their faith he said, 'Man, your sins are forgiven you' (5:18, 20).

Another healing? No; as with the leprosy, something more than healing. Luke's sixth episode shows the word of Jesus penetrating yet deeper into the need of man. We are indeed practically at the core of the matter now. Another healing was what they expected (and in due course they obtained it); but though the minds and bodies of men, their daily life and their human relationships, are all important in the eyes of Jesus, the fact remains that salvation consists primarily 'in the forgiveness of their sins', as the Holy Spirit had inspired Zechariah to prophesy (1:77). I need to be right in myself, and right with my neighbour. But above all I need to be right with God. There is an immense accumulation of guilt before God which my proud self-centredness has piled up over the years; how can that possibly be dealt with?

With whatever more obvious 'paralysis' I may come to Jesus, this is the real deep need which his eye perceives and to which his word of power is addressed. And when he speaks, it is dealt with finally, for ever: 'Man, your sins are forgiven you.'

[13] Jn. 13:35; 1 Jn. 4:8, 12.

It was with that message that John had heralded his coming (3:3), and it would be with the same message that his disciples would later be sent out into all the world (24:47): the message of forgiveness—salvation from sin.

g. Claiming men's hearts

He went out, and saw a tax collector, named Levi, sitting at the tax office; and he said to him, 'Follow me.' And he left everything, and rose and followed him (5:27–28).

With these verses we reach the violet end of the spectrum, where the power is most penetrating. We have already seen how Simon and his friends had 'left everything and followed him' (5:11), but the power of the word to claim the hearts of men is seen most clearly here, where the command is so bald and unprepared, and the ties which might have bound Levi to his old life are so strong.

If the sixth example, the paralytic's sins forgiven, showed Jesus as the Saviour from sin, this seventh one shows him as the Lord of life. All that has gone before is summed up in this vignette of two verses: the lordship of Jesus over a man's mind and body, his relationships and his way of life—and then what underlies it all, the cleansing of his soul's sin and the claiming of his heart's allegiance.

The conversion of Levi leads on immediately, both in the narrative (5:29) and in Luke's train of thought, to two final words of Jesus, which are not words of power like those we have heard so far, but words of explanation. He tells us in them what has really been happening when, with the seven different kinds of effect that we have noticed, 'he spoke, and it came to be; he commanded, and it stood forth.'[14]

2. A word of explanation (5:29–39)

Admiration had followed Jesus from the start (4:15); but the opposition which Luke notes after Jesus's first preaching in Nazareth (4:28f.) makes itself felt again part way through our passage (5:17ff.), as the Pharisees, the strict religious party of Judaism, begin to see that the dynamic word of the new rabbi is not saying quite what they would like it to say.

[14] Ps. 33:9.

The party given by Levi to celebrate his acceptance of the 'Jesus message' accordingly becomes the occasion for some of the Pharisees to take Jesus to task. The practical effects of his preaching seem so different from what they would consider 'true religion'; to be one of his followers seems to entail carelessness about keeping proper company (5:30) and proper religious observances (5:33).

Jesus's answer explains what is really happening when a man receives this message of his, which seems so destructive of traditional Jewish religion. Something comes about which makes Pharisaic ideas of holiness—holiness by keeping aloof from doubtful characters, or by rigorous fasting—quite irrelevant. The effect of his word he illustrates in two ways: it is a cure, and it is a change.

a. The word brings a cure

'Those who are well have no need of a physician, but those who are sick' (5:31).

The reason why he mixes with sinners is simple, and he gives a simple but powerful picture to explain it. There is the healthy man, there is the sick man, and there is the doctor; meaning (says Jesus) the righteous, the sinful, and Me. I mix with sinners because they have a need and I have a cure. The more painfully they feel their need, the more unreservedly they will put themselves in my hands. Their basic disease is sin, which leads to death; my message of salvation is its only remedy. A familiar saying in John's Gospel puts the same truth succinctly: 'He who hears my word and believes him who sent me, has eternal life'.[15]

That is one way of looking at these introductory stories. They show the authoritative word of Jesus 'curing' men at every level, the more superficial levels of physical and mental health, and the deepest one, that of spiritual health.

It is worth reiterating a point suggested earlier: namely, that this idea (a spiritual cure brought about by the word of Jesus) would have appealed greatly to Luke in his professional capacity as a doctor.[16] And, although he nowhere says so, we can hardly doubt his own conviction that the same treatment can be equally effective in the

[15] Jn. 5:24. Notice incidentally the subtle claim to deity in Lk. 5:31–32 (Jesus sets himself apart from all other men, the 'healthy' as well as the 'sick'); also that in Lk. 5:20–21 (Jesus forgives sins, a thing only God can do).

[16] See above, p. 19.

hands of later practitioners—that he himself, for example, can prescribe this word-medicine in written form for the spiritual needs of Theophilus, and expect it to produce results.[17]

Our Lord's use of this medical metaphor, and the fact that, as Luke's own practice shows, it continues to be valid, oblige us to think of the church's own evangelistic responsibility in the same terms. On the one hand, there really are men and women (and multitudes of them, as these crowded pages of Luke's book suggest) who are spiritually sick and dying for want of the healing word. We cannot assume, as many do, that people in general are basically 'all right', or that at any rate they will be in the end. On the other hand, the gospel is still 'the power of God for salvation to every one who has faith',[18] and we therefore have in our own hands the very thing which can cure these sin-sick souls, the 'balm in Gilead' which makes the sinner whole. With our experience of the remedy comes the confidence that it will work for them also; and with our possession of it comes the responsibility to make it available to them.

b. The word brings a change

'No one tears a piece from a new garment and puts it upon an old garment ... No one puts new wine into old wineskins ... No one after drinking old wine desires new' (5:36, 37, 39).

Think of Jesus as a doctor, and his preaching means a cure for spiritual ills; think of him now as a bridegroom (5:34), and his preaching means that a special occasion has arrived, a day for time off, celebration, and best clothes, when the atmosphere of the workaday world is altogether changed. This change he indicates in three little pictures.

There will be some who are prepared to take bits and pieces of his new message, and to stitch them into the fabric of their own old ideas where that has become threadbare. But what sensible housewife would cut up a new dress to make patches for an old one? My word, says Jesus, is meant as a total replacement, not as a source of useful patches.

There will be other people who want not some of the new and some of the old, but *all* the new—provided they can keep the old as well. That, however, simply will not work. If you are prepared to

---

[17] See above, pp. 29ff.
[18] Rom. 1:16.

receive the new wine of Jesus's message in its fullness, the brittle wineskins of your old beliefs will not be able to hold it. You must expect to forfeit them altogether.

There will be yet others, of course, who are not prepared even to taste the new wine. It is not that 'the old is *better*' (5:39, AV, wrongly); no—'the prejudiced person will not even try the new, or admit that it has *any* merits.'[19] He will not bother to compare the two, because the old is good enough. That is refusal to accept the very possibility of change.

For change is what the acceptance of the word will certainly involve; a new day is dawning as the bridegroom arrives. And cure is what the physician will bring with him for those who are willing to listen to him. This is what will happen as a man opens his ears to the word of Jesus and lets its power begin to work in him.

[19] Plummer, p. 165.

6:1–49
Israel reborn

'The Son of man is lord of the sabbath' (6:5).

He called his disciples, and chose from them twelve, whom he named apostles (6:13).

'I say to you that hear, Love your enemies, do good to those who hate you . . .' (6:27).

Luke now brings us to a point of crisis in the story of the Saviour of the world. A theme which has begun to make itself heard in the course of chapter 5 now comes to the fore and dominates the whole of this chapter.

At the beginning of his ministry Jesus had been universally popular (4:15). But all over Galilee and Judea the news of him had aroused an interest not only among the common people but also among the religious leaders (5:17). The latter viewed him with a more critical eye, and began to see strange, and indeed dangerous, tendencies in what he said and did (5:21, 30, 33). The little parables which Luke records at the end of chapter 5 show Jesus explaining the kind of difference between him and the Pharisees which was coming into the open. His teaching, when compared with traditional Jewish belief, was like a new garment which will replace an old, or new wine which will burst old wineskins (5:36–37).

So far from trying to placate the opposition, he seems deliberately to aggravate it. In chapter 6 he throws down the gauntlet to the fault-finding Pharisees. He precipitates a crisis, by making clear how different his teaching is from theirs, and by challenging men to come to *him,* and to hear and obey *his* words (6:46–47).

The first incidents which Luke recounts in describing this crisis

(6:1–11) both happened on sabbath days. Religious rules about what constituted 'work', and was therefore forbidden on the sabbath, had been developed so ludicrously that the action of Jesus's disciples in 6:1 was officially reckoned to be a combination of reaping, threshing, and the preparing of food, and therefore 'not lawful' (6:2) on three counts; while the healing of a withered hand, since the patient's life was not at stake (which would have made a doctor's 'work' permissible), was also grounds for an accusation of law-breaking (6:7). Jesus had healed before on the sabbath (4:31–35), but the Pharisees had not then begun to take notice of his doings. Even so, now that they are present and eager to find fault he still makes no attempt either to avoid or to soothe their enmity. Instead he deliberately says, in effect, 'It may be your kind of sabbath to leave men hungry and disabled. My kind of sabbath is different.'

Omitting for a moment the next paragraph and moving on to 6:20–49, we find a lengthy discourse which might have seemed more in place in the long central section of the Gospel, where Luke gathers together most of the teaching of Jesus (9:51– 19:44). Presumably it has been separated from the rest and inserted here in chapter 6 for a purpose. It describes the way in which the true followers of Jesus will live. It is, in fact, Luke's counterpart of the 'sermon on the mount', more familiar perhaps as chapters 5, 6, and 7 of Matthew's Gospel. It is interesting to note that where Matthew relates how Jesus explained, practically in so many words, that this was his 'fulfilled' version of the old Jewish law,[1] Luke omits most of that explanation. No doubt this is because the context in which he includes the sermon makes it sufficiently plain that Jesus is here putting forth a new kind of law which he intends shall replace the old one.

In the light of this, it is not hard to see the point of the short middle section of the chapter, the choosing of the twelve apostles (6:12–19). One would not want to base the interpretation of these verses simply on the suggestion that the number twelve may be symbolic of the nation of Israel; nevertheless, given the circumstances (the replacement of the Jewish sabbath rules by a new kind of sabbath, and the replacement of the old law by a new one), the point of what Jesus was doing when 'he called his disciples'—by this time 'a great crowd' (6:17)—and 'chose from them twelve, whom he named apostles' (6:13), can scarcely have been lost on those who were present. The twelve sons of Jacob, from whom the whole Israelite

[1] Mt. 5:17–48.

nation had grown, were to be replaced by these twelve apostles, who would stand at the head of a whole new people of God.

To the defenders of the old established religion of Judaism Jesus throws out this challenge. He is bringing in a new thing, before which their beliefs and structures will have to give way. Yet he does not cut himself off completely from the old. He does not say 'No more sabbaths, no more people of God, no more law.' There is a continuity. The new religion has its roots in the old; and we may trace the beginnings of Christianity right back to the beginnings of Judaism—and indeed still further, as we shall see.

1. Christianity as old as Judaism

There must be a crisis, a change, and a choice between the old and the new. But the day in which men are fed, good is done, and life is saved, is still called a sabbath; there will still be a people of God, with leaders of his choosing at their head; a law still goes forth from him, for men to follow. Old cloth or new cloth, but still cloth; old wine or new wine, but still wine. It is a matter not of replacing religion by philosophy or politics, but of replacing Pharisaic religion by Christian religion. Jesus can speak of his own new teaching still in terms of the old, for he is not abolishing, but fulfilling.[2]

a. The sabbath

The keeping of the sabbath day was included among the ten commandments, but it had an importance all its own, as we can see from the way Jesus gives it separate consideration here. The sabbath ('Six days you shall labour, and do all your work; but the seventh day is a sabbath to the Lord your God; in it you shall not do any work')[3] stands as an example of the whole framework of life of God's people in Old Testament times. Not only the calendar of their days and years, but also the geography of their land, is pressed into service as a way of describing the framework of the Christian's life. Thus we find the land of Israel,[4] its capital city Jerusalem, or Zion,[5] and its great temple,[6] all providing a vocabulary with which to describe Christian truths, just as the gospel age is referred to as 'the acceptable year of the Lord' (4:19), and a central experience in the Christian life is spoken of in terms of a sabbath day.[7]

[2] Mt. 5:17. [3] Ex. 20:9–10.
[4] Heb. 4:1–10. [5] Heb. 12:22.
[6] 1 Cor. 3:16. [7] Heb. 4:9.

b. The twelve

It is a mistake to visualize the disciples of Jesus as being just a dozen close friends with perhaps one or two others tagging along, for Luke refers to the 'great crowd of his disciples' (6:17) from whom the twelve were selected. They are the leaders of a numerous party.

With regard to the apostles, the way their names are listed varies from Gospel to Gospel; so it seems, as Caird observes, that 'to the early Church the number was more important than the names',[8] for as we have seen they are the 'founding fathers' of the Christian church as the twelve sons of Jacob were the founders of the nation of Israel. 'The apostles constitute the "twelve-tribe" framework upon which the Israel of the new age is to be formed.'[9] Naturally, therefore, the symbolism is concentrated on the number of them, and names and order are comparatively unimportant.

The church of which they are leaders is similarly referred to again and again in the New Testament in terms taken from the Old Testament story of Israel. Jesus's statement that the apostles are to rule the twelve tribes of Israel (22:30) is illuminated by Paul when he describes them as those upon whom, and by whom, the Christian church is built.[10] Accordingly, the church can be described as 'the Israel of God', the 'chosen race ... royal priesthood ... holy nation ... God's own people': indeed, 'if you are Christ's, then you are Abraham's offspring'.[11]

c. The law

If the terminology of the 'twelve tribes' can be applied to the New Testament people of God, and that of the 'sabbath' to the framework of the Christian life, then equally the way of life of the Christian church—its character and behaviour—can be spoken of in terms of the Old Testament 'law'. Perhaps Jesus even chose the setting for his sermon with this in mind, for he spent time alone on the hilltop with

[8] Caird, p. 101.
[9] Ellis, p. 110.
[10] Eph. 2:20; 4:11–12.
[11] Gal. 6:16; 1 Pet. 2:9; Gal. 3:29. Caroline Glyn's retelling of the story of Jesus, *In Him was Life* (Gollancz, 1975), is fictional, but full of rare insight. Seeing through the eyes of one of the Gospel characters, she says: 'It came home to me that he had *twelve* disciples—precisely twelve—and I saw with a shiver of fear, as though I had indeed seen them raised from their graves, Israel himself and his twelve sons, the fathers of the twelve tribes ... those long-ago patriarchs walking through the land again. ... So I've come to know him as the new Jacob, God's favourite and beloved, the bearer of his promises, the father of a new people' (p. 72).

the second, or Jewish, sabbath, is quite foreign to the spirit of the New Testament.

b. The twelve

Like the sabbath, the idea of the community of God's people which is represented by the twelve apostles and those who are their spiritual descendants goes back long before the beginnings of Israel. It is true that Jesus was renewing the structures of the Israelite nation, the twelve tribes which stemmed from the sons of Jacob. But it was not with Jacob, nor with his grandfather Abraham, that the idea had begun.

For this also we return to the story of creation, and find that when God made mankind, 'male and female he created them . . . and God said to them, "Be fruitful and multiply."'[25] From the start man was made to be a social creature, to live in a family, a community, where all belong together, inter-related and inter-dependent.

Like the original sabbath of fellowship with God, this fellowship between men also was spoilt almost as soon as it had begun, and the very first two men who are recorded as being born into the world became a murderer and his victim.[26] Centuries pass, in which self-centredness, independence, and mutual hatred become quite as marked a feature of human life as the loving, caring, family sense which had been meant to characterize it. Eventually God intervenes again and brings into being a new family. Abraham, his son, his grandson, and his twelve great-grandsons are the founders of a nation which is to show the world once more what a close-knit family God intended humanity to be.

Yet by the time of Jesus the divine inscription on that coinage also has become defaced. Pride of race has made Israel exclusive, clannish, and unloving. So Jesus tells his Jewish enemies: 'The kingdom of God will be taken away from you and given to a nation producing the fruits of it.'[27] He sets up a new people of God, under the leadership of his new twelve, with the object of showing for the third time how relationship with himself brings men into right relationships with one another. The family of Adam failed; the family of Abraham failed; and now it is up to the church of Jesus Christ to demonstrate what the common life of men ought to be like. 'By this all men will

[25] Gn. 1:27–28.
[26] Gn. 4:1–8.
[27] Mt. 21:43.

God, just as the great lawgiver Moses had done, and then came down from the height, again like Moses, to deliver God's 'law' to his people (6:12–17; Ex. 34:29–32).

It is not the same law; but it can still be thought of as law. It is 'a new commandment . . ., that you love one another'; it is 'the royal law'.[12]

It makes for a great enriching of our Christian lives when we learn to apply the story of Israel to them. Israel's salvation from Egypt becomes a powerful picture of our own salvation from sin; her experiences guide us, her virtues challenge us, her failures warn us; her prophets and priests, her judges and kings, all of them (in so far as they live up to their high calling) show us something of the Lord Jesus. We begin to find as we sing the psalms of the Jewish church that we can 'make them always speak the common Sense of a Christian'.[13] We begin to see how much meaning there is in the work of the Christian hymn-writers who have grasped this truth before us, who speak 'Glorious things of . . . Zion' and 'The God of Abraham praise'. We begin, perhaps, to pity those who think the Old Testament largely irrelevant, and so deprive themselves of these blessings.

2. Christianity even older than Judaism

There is something even more profound that we can learn from the way that Jesus adopts Old Testament patterns, 'fulfilling' them with Christian meaning. For these principles of his teaching, in some ways radically different from traditional Judaism yet in others still so like it, did not originate in the times of Moses or of Abraham. Even at its primitive best, the Jewish race and its religion enshrined something yet more primitive and basic.

a. The sabbath

It may not be without significance that the fourth commandment, alone among the ten, begins with the word 'Remember'. This could of course mean 'Bear in mind from now on'; but it could equally well mean 'Bring to mind something you know already', for like many

[12] Jn. 13:34; Jas. 2:8.
[13] Isaac Watts, in the Preface to his *Psalms of David Imitated in New Testament Language* (1719), quoted in B. L. Manning's splendid book *The Hymns of Wesley and Watts* (Epworth, 1942), p. 80.

other religious observances the sabbath day existed long before it was given a particular religious status. The writer to the Hebrews points out just how far back in history the sabbath goes: 'He has somewhere spoken of the seventh day in this way, "And God rested on the seventh day from all his works."'[14] The quotation comes, in fact, from the account in Genesis 2:2 of the original creation of the world.

One implication of the Genesis story is that a sabbath day's rest, one day in seven, is a pattern which has been built into creation and into human life from the start. It is not merely a Jewish or a Christian observance; whatever a man's religion, his constitution as a human being needs a rhythm of this kind.

But the reference in Hebrews, and the words of Jesus in Luke 6, reveal a more far-reaching principle. Although, as Jesus says on another occasion, there is a sense in which 'My Father is working still',[15] it is also true in a different sense that 'his works were finished from the foundation of the world'.[16] Genesis 1 describes the creation of the world as the occupation of God's 'working week'; his last accomplishment, on the sixth day, was the making of man. Mankind was born, therefore, as God's 'weekend' began. Had the plan proceeded as it should have done, the whole of human history would have been spent in the joyous 'sabbath rest for the people of God'.[17]

In the event, that ideal was spoilt when man fell into sin, and one of the explicit results of the fall was that he found his days were not, as previously, pleasantly occupied,[18] but burdened now with wearisome toil.[19] So, after thousands of years during which the original vision had receded into the background, and men had forgotten that God's plan for their lives was meant to be the constant enjoyment of a 'weekend' with him, he made them aware of it once more by reflecting it in the religion he gave to the nation of Israel in the time of Moses.

The sabbath day became a very important feature of Jewish religion, and when their vision was clearest the Jews understood that the weekly day of rest was a 'ritual anticipation of the advent of the messianic age'[20]—a kind of picture, in the form of a religious observance, of what the whole of life would once again be like when God's Messiah came into the world to set things right—and therefore a thing of delight.[21] But it was easy for that truth to become obscured, and for the sabbath to be hedged around with so many 'Thou shalt

nots' that instead of a delight it became a misery. It i
situation that Jesus comes, in Luke 6:1–11, to renew onc
vision of what the sabbath really is.

This calls in question some of the traditional views abo
observance, the kind which lend colour to the ill-natured
when the fourth commandment says 'Thou shalt not work
days', it really means 'Thou shalt not play on Sundays'. V
indeed 'remember the sabbath day', but not as if we were
ing the law-bound religion of Moses, which ruled tha
activities were wrong on the sabbath but right on any oth
you apply such rules to the Christian Sunday, you are
'days, and months, and season, and years! I am afraid I have
over you in vain', says Paul.[22] Of the four sabbaths of Scrip
are perpetuating the very one which was meant to be only te

For consider these four. The last of them is the celestial
which God's people will enjoy in heaven,

> where keep the saints, with harp and song,
> An endless sabbath morning.[23]

Of the three which belong to this world, the first is the
sabbath, which we 'remember' by insisting—against the pres
commerce, the lure of overtime, the vagaries of shift-wo
(sometimes) the demon of a guilt-complex—on the need of
to have one day's rest in seven. When most of us are free on t
day of the week, we are certainly glad to make use of it for fell
and worship, but that is a matter of convenience, not of obli
the rest from work is the important thing about this first sa
The third sabbath is the Christian one—the *perpetual* rest, th
delight, which God's people enjoy with him now. Their life
filled with praise, they can say:

> So shall no part of day or night
> From sacredness be free;
> But all my life, in every step,
> Be fellowship with Thee.[24]

A sabbatarianism which falls between the first and the third
makes rules for Sunday observance as if we were back in the d

---

[14] Heb. 4:4. [15] Jn. 5:17. [16] Heb. 4:3.
[17] Heb. 4:9. [18] Gn. 2:15. [19] Gn. 3:17–19.
[20] E. C. Hoskyns, quoted by Ellis, p. 110. [21] Is. 58:13f.

[22] Gal. 4:10f.; *cf.* Col. 2:16f.
[23] Elizabeth Barrett Browning, *Sabbath Morning at Sea*.
[24] Horatius Bonar, *Fill Thou my life, O Lord my God*.

know that you are my disciples, if you have love for one another.'[28]

In three respects, even the tiny sketch of 6:13 hints at what the community of the people of God is like in both Old and New Testament times, and what, therefore, it should be like today, if it is to fulfil its calling. We are shown its members, the disciples; its leaders, the twelve; and its creator, the Lord.

Its membership is unexpectedly ill-defined. The word 'disciples' simply means 'learners'; and though some learn much, others learn practically nothing. The community is in fact a thoroughly mixed bag. Whatever may be the marks of official membership, they do not guarantee real membership. As Matthew tells of weeds which look confusingly like wheat,[29] and John tells of 'believers' who eventually try to kill Jesus,[30] so Luke will draw the same lesson from the parable of the sower,[31] and will elaborate it a long passage showing Jesus as the Divider.[32] Nine hundred years earlier, many who by birth 'belonged' to Israel nevertheless rebelled against the house and faith of David.[33] Three hundred years earlier still, many who, by baptism in the cloud and in the sea, 'belonged' to Moses, were nevertheless overthrown in the wilderness.[34] There was division within the family of Isaac,[35] and before that, division within the family of Abraham,[36] though in each case both sons 'belonged' to the covenant people not only by birth but also by circumcision. And at the beginning of history Scripture gives us a stark prototype of the divided community in the story of Cain and Abel.[37] Nor does the community alter in this respect even after it has been remade by Jesus and filled with the Spirit. Its official membership is loose enough to include Ananias and Sapphira, Demas and Diotrephes; and Simon Magus has already been baptized as a believer when it transpires that his heart is 'not right before God'.[38] Scripture therefore seems to give little precedent for the idea of a pure church, with a definable membership and a restricted and delayed admission.

Yet paradoxically, if there is one thing more than another which

[28] Jn. 13:35.   [29] Mt. 13:24–30, 36–43.   [30] Jn. 8.31, 59.
[31] Lk. 8:4ff.; see below, pp. 94f.
[32] Lk. 12:13 – 13:21; see below, pp. 133–141.
[33] 1 Ki. 12.   [34] 1 Cor. 10:1–5.
[35] 'Jacob I loved, but Esau I hated': Rom. 9:13, quoting Mal. 1:2–3.
[36] 'The son of the slave', Ishmael, 'shall not inherit with the son of the free woman', Isaac; Gal. 4:30, quoting Gn. 21:10.
[37] Gn. 4:1–16.
[38] Acts 5:1–11; 2 Tim. 4:10; 3 Jn. 9–10; Acts 8:9–24.

this chapter stresses, it is the distinctiveness of the people of God. They are meant to be clearly different from the world around them. And the mark which distinguishes them as members of the church is their acceptance of the leadership God has given them. They give their allegiance first to Jesus, then to the apostles to whom Jesus bequeaths his authority. This principle also can be traced back to the beginning of Bible history. The original creation is meant to function under the authority of Adam,[39] the family of Abraham lives under his patriarchal sway, as the word implies (patriarch = father/ruler, or family-ruler), the nation of Israel is governed by Moses and the laws he administers, and in the same way the new Israel will be under the apostolic rule of the twelve.[40] As we have just noted, the teaching of the apostles is not used in New Testament times as a detailed basis for the screening of those who want to be admitted to the church. But it is certainly applied to those who, once admitted, make it plain that they deserve to be expelled.[41] Today the emphasis seems often to be curiously reversed, with more rigour shown towards candidates who are outside and want to come in, than to heretics who are inside and ought to be put out. But however it may be applied, this is the criterion: the truth brought by Jesus and taught by his apostles. By their adherence to this—to the gospel given by a revelation of Christ, the deposit entrusted to the men of the New Testament, the faith once for all delivered to the saints[42]—the true disciples may be distinguished from the false.

Behind all this is an even more profound truth concerning both the church's members and its leaders, and therefore determining the nature of the church. The disciples were attracted, and the apostles appointed, *by the Lord*. The church would not exist had he not brought it into being. He was, and is, calling out a people for his name,[43] just as he did in the days of Abraham and Moses. An even more dramatic parallel, and one to which Scripture draws our wondering attention, is that he was and is bringing into being an entire new creation, just as he did in the days of Adam. J. B. Phillips's translation of Colossians 1:17–18 makes this superbly clear: 'He is both the first principle and the upholding principle of the whole scheme of creation. And now he is the head of the body which is the Church. Life from nothing began through him, and life from the

[39] Gn. 1:26, 28; Ps. 8:6–8.
[40] Lk. 22:30.
[41] 1 Cor. 5; 14:37–38; Gal. 1:6–9; 2 Jn. 10–11.
[42] Gal. 1:12; 2 Tim. 1:12, 14; Jude 3.   [43] Acts 15:14.

dead began through him, and he is, therefore, justly called the Lord of all.'

A community with these rules of membership and leadership, and called thus into existence, is what the church should be seen to be even in our own day. We need to accept that the visible church will inevitably be a mixed multitude.[44] At the same time, we should strive to reform it constantly in line with the apostolic teaching which is still our final authority. And our confidence regarding it must ultimately be placed not in our own ability to maintain or purify or extend it, but in the sovereign power of the Lord its creator, who will not let the powers of death prevail against it.[45]

c. The law

In the same way, Jesus is doing more in 6:20-49 than simply putting forth a new law of his own to fulfil and replace the law of Moses. God had a law for man from the very beginning. The first words spoken to Adam after he has been created concern what he is to do, what his is not to do, and what he may do.[46] Thus long before the time of Moses God was telling man how to live, and explaining that his greatest happiness lay in obedience to this law.

It need hardly be said that the law was immediately broken, and the way of submission replaced by the way of self-indulgence.[47] In this case also, the years rolled by; the law was brought back into prominence in the form of a religious system given by God through Moses to the Israelite nation; this religious law in turn ceased to be a testimony to the way God wanted man to live, and became a matter of bondag3 to rules; and the coming of Jesus renewed it once again in the form of the sermon on the mount, the way of life which brings real blessedness (6:20ff.).

That way is the underlying theme of the great central section of Luke's Gospel, and will be dealt with at length there.[48] Even so we should at least note here what is new about this law: it sets new standards of behaviour, which have to do with inward character rather than with outward observance. This is not to say that they are matters of theory rather than of practice. In four thoroughly practical

[44] Ex. 12:38.   [45] Mt. 16:18.
[46] Gn. 1:28f.; 2:16f.   [47] Gn. 3:1-6.
[48] See below, pp. 117ff.; also such passages as the exposition of the term 'poor' (and thus of the first beatitude, Lk. 6.20) on pp. 92-94. Indeed, to Matthew's version of the sermon an entire volume in this series is devoted: John R. W. Stott's *Christian Counter-Culture* (Inter-Varsity Press, 1978).

ways the new Israel will show its respect for the new law.

In the life of God's people will be seen first of all a remarkable *reversal of values* (6:20–26). They will prize what the world calls pitiable, and suspect what the world thinks desirable. Values which are taken for granted by other men are questioned by them, and are considered in the searching light of spiritual truth, hidden reality, and a future life.

Thus they are to see as God sees; and they are, secondly, to act as God acts. They will therefore follow not merely the call of duty, but the call of *love* (6:27–38). They will seek to do not simply what is right, but what is good. And they will act in this way not only towards those who deserve it but also towards those who do not. Such open-heartedness does not in fact go unrewarded—but the very essence of it is that that must never be their motive for practising it!

The third quality they must show is *integrity* (6:39–45). What they say, what they do, what they are, must be all of a piece. The rules you apply to your brother you must apply also to yourself. The standards you commend with your lips you must also honour in your life. Indeed the attempt to have it both ways is in any case hopeless: it is not that you must not, but that you actually cannot, produce the right kind of fruit if you are the wrong kind of tree. The attempt to do so is hypocrisy, the opposite of integrity, and there is no sin about which Jesus spoke more scathingly.

Although the demands of the new law are so much higher than those of the old, they may be summed up by the same word, and that is *obedience* (6:46–49): obedience to the law, but even more than that, obedience to the Lord who gives it. And who is this Lord? In this respect also we see that we have here something new; for the obedience which under the old law was due to the God of Israel is now claimed, with no hint that the claim is inappropriate, let alone blasphemous, by Jesus. It is another of the pointers to his deity with which the Gospels abound.[49] For their final authority his people look 'beyond this world of time and sense'. Neither the rules of men, nor the mere acknowledgment of the rule of Christ, is an adequate basis for the building of their lives. They dig deeper, and ground their building in an actual personal acceptance of Christ as Lord, with all that that implies. Only from a foundation laid as deep as this can they begin to scale the height of the law's demands.

---

[49] See already in this exposition, for example, the comments on 1:26–38 (pp. 35f.), 2:11 (p. 47), 3:1–4:30 (pp. 53), 5:20–21, 31–32 (p. 72 n. 15).

Chapter 6 thus shows us the new sabbath of peace with God, the new apostolic community of the church, and the new way of life for the Christian. Each one replaces a spoilt version of itself by going back to the original. Each one is a preview of the splendid reality which will be seen in its fullness only in the next world. But although we cannot hope to see that fullness in this world, there is no evading the challenge that Jesus expects us to get as near to it as we can—daily rejoicing in our Father, loving towards our brethren, and holy within ourselves.

7:1 – 8:21
Good news

'The poor have good news preached to them' (7:22).

He went on through cities and villages, preaching and bringing the good news of the kingdom of God (8:1).

Luke continues with another group of stories, some about happenings in the ministry of Jesus, some dealing with his teachings. What are we to make of them? Are they simply the next beads on the string, or is there a pattern in the mind of Luke, and a corresponding pattern in the ministry of Jesus?

It so happens that questions of the same kind were in the thoughts of John the Baptist; and to these, in the passage 7:18–23, we turn first. It was not immediately obvious to John, any more than it may be to modern readers of Luke's report, what exactly was going on. The mysterious 'Coming One' referred to in 7:19–20, whose forerunner John knew himself to be, would surely have identified himself by activity rather different from that for which Jesus was becoming noted. John had expected him to bring wrath, destruction, fire, judgment (3:7–9, 15–17); but of such things there seemed little sign in the deeds and words of Jesus. Even John's arrest and imprisonment—of all King Herod's misdeeds the worst yet, for it was an attempt to silence the good news[1]—had provoked no counterblast of judgment from the powers of the kingdom of God.

Jesus answers John by pointing to what is in fact happening: 'The blind receive their sight, the lame walk, lepers are cleansed, and the deaf hear, the dead are raised up, the poor have good news preached to them' (7:22). John expects the Coming One to come as Judge;

[1] 3:18–20.

Jesus replies that he must first come as Saviour. He is not yet coming to announce doom; for the present he is still bringing good news. We have already seen how, inaugurating his ministry in the synagogue at Nazareth (4:18f.), he quotes Isaiah 61:1–2 only as far as the commission 'to proclaim the year of the Lord's favour'; it is not yet time for him to complete the quotation, and announce 'the day of vengeance of our God'.

So far as the Jewish nation was concerned, the day of opportunity came and went. The spectacular ending to the whole affair, the burning up of fruitless trees and useless chaff, did not arrive quite as soon as the fiery John seems to have expected, and the patient Jesus gave the tree of Judaism three more years to disprove its barrenness (13:6–9). But barren it was, and the tree had to fall. For the world at large, however, the judgment envisaged by John is delayed even yet, and still Jesus is proclaiming the good news, as other New Testament writers reiterate: 'Now is the acceptable time; behold, now is the day of salvation;' 'The Holy Spirit says, "Today, when you hear his voice, do not harden your hearts."'[2]

The good news is the keynote of this section, as Luke indicates by quoting Jesus's answer to John in 7:22, and we find that the various incidents he relates here do in fact harmonize with it. He has mentioned it often already (1:19, 2:10, *etc.*). What we shall note now, illustrated in detail, is first its substance, then its recipients—to be ungrammatical but plain, what it is about and who it is for. Both questions were answered at the beginning of Jesus's ministry: it is 'the good news *of the kingdom of God*', Jesus explained (4:43), and 'he has anointed me to preach good news *to the poor*' (4:18). Both answers are combined in the opening words of the sermon on the mount:[3] 'Blessed are *you poor*', the recipients of the good news, 'for yours is *the kingdom of God*', the substance of it (6:20). And in our present passage both occur yet again, in the verses quoted at the head of this section (7:22; 8:1).

1. The good news is about the kingdom

He went on through cities and villages, preaching and bringing the good news of the kingdom of God (8:1).

---

[2] 2 Cor. 6:2; Heb. 3:7f.

[3] Luke's version is often referred to as the sermon on the plain, to distinguish it from Matthew's. I use the other term simply because it is more familiar.

The theme of the kingdom of God was introduced as far back as 4:43. We postponed consideration of it then, because that was what Luke did. Now however he treats it in detail. What does it mean, to say that the substance of the good news is the kingdom of God? The incidents he relates help us to understand this by showing both what was good about it, and what was new.

a. Something good

First Luke tells of Jesus's encounter with a Roman centurion at Capernaum (7:1–10). The officer's slave 'was sick and at the point of death' (7:2); but Jesus performs a miracle at a distance, and at the end of the story we find 'the slave well' (7:10). Matthew's version, it may be noted, mentions the deed itself—'the servant was healed';[4] Doctor Luke prefers to describe the subsequent condition of the man, namely his health. To such a condition the power of Jesus restores the sufferer when it overcomes his sickness.

Then we read of the raising of the widow's son at Nain (7:11–17). Jesus halts the tragic procession to the grave (what a wealth of symbolism there is in that picture) and again by his word of power a miracle takes place. The 'man who had died' (7:12) thereupon 'sat up, and began to speak' (7:15). Of the three recorded instances of Jesus's raising the dead, John has the story of Lazarus, while the other three Gospels all have the story of Jairus's daughter. Only Luke adds this extra one, putting it here in chapter 7 as if to illustrate just how good the good news is—it brings salvation not only into the realm of disease but into that of death itself.

To the next eighteen verses, chiefly concerned with Jesus's teaching, we have referred already and shall return shortly. They are followed by the incident in the home of Simon the Pharisee (7:36–50), in which Jesus's power deals with the profoundest need of all. In telling us of the woman who intrudes into Simon's dinner party, Luke says three times over that she is a sinner (7:37, 39, 47), and three times over that Jesus is the forgiver of sins (7:47, 48, 49). The tiny parable about the two debtors (7:41–42) is so much a part of the incident that its meaning, unlike that of some parables, is unmistakable. The woman's love and gratitude is evidence of how great her 'debt' has been, and how correspondingly great the Lord's forgiveness is. The formal religion of the Pharisees had no real answer to the problem of sin, and could only respond with disapproval and con-

[4] Mt. 8:13.

demnation. But Jesus could actually do away with sin, and in this deepest sense bring salvation and peace (7:50).

There is more to be said about each of these stories. For the moment we concentrate on the goodness of the news that Jesus brings to the people concerned. What is so good about it is that it tells of One who can not only analyse or comment on these great enemies of mankind, sickness and death and sin, but actually overcome them. That is why this news of salvation (for that is how Luke basically conceives it) is also rightly described as news of the *kingdom*. [5] For the evils that spoil human life are the work of Satan, in whose power, as we saw in 4:5–6, lie all the kingdoms of the world. During his temptation in the wilderness, Jesus was offered that power on Satan's terms. But when finally 'the kingdom of the world has become the kingdom of our Lord and of his Christ'[6] it will be because he has won it on his own terms. In 11:14–23 Jesus is going to use a case of demon-possession, the most blatant work of the devil, to explain the head-on collision which is taking place between the kingdom of Satan and the kingdom of God. But already, here in Chapter 7, he is showing that his kingly power is present in all its majesty, to overcome the 'ruler of this world',[7] and to bring in an order of things in which the old curse is replaced by a new blessing, misery by joy, and despair by hope.

If today's preachers of the good news follow the example of Luke, they too will not be content with mere analysis or comment. They will be proclaiming as a fact that the power of that kingdom really does get to grips with these basic evils, and in each case ushers in the opposite good. They will be remembering, as they do so, cases known to them where this power is joyously at work, if not in identical ways yet certainly in equivalent ways. And they will be expecting equivalent results from their preaching.

b. Something new

Between the second and third of the incidents just mentioned are three paragraphs referring to John the Baptist. One (7:18–23) has been touched on at the beginning of our exposition of this section. The others (7:24–30 and 31–35) reveal the newness of the good news of the kingdom, first with respect to John himself, and then with respect to those who listened to him and to Jesus.

John was a very great man indeed (7:26–28a), the greatest man of

[5] See pp. 169ff.   [6] Rev. 11:15.   [7] Jn. 12:31; 16:11.

his age. But that age has come to an end with the coming of the kingdom of God. A new thing has arisen with the advent of King Jesus. And the humblest person who knows the kingly rule of Jesus in his life has entered a greater experience than even John ever knew (7:28b). 'Turning to the disciples he said privately, "Blessed are the eyes which see what you see! For I tell you that many prophets and kings desired to see what you see, and to hear what you hear, and did not hear it"' (10:23–24).

The news was new also with respect to the Jews of that time, who had heard the messages of both John and Jesus. The children's games mentioned in 7:32 illustrate the fact that these hearers complained equally when John refused to play 'Weddings' and when Jesus refused to play 'Funerals'. When they 'piped', and asked for a message that was undemanding and cheerful, John fasted and talked about sin; he was too gloomy, they wanted something brighter. But when they 'wailed', and expected from the rabbi of Nazareth a solemn discussion on morals and religion, Jesus went to parties and talked about salvation; he was too exhilarating, they wanted something more proper. For the news of the kingdom is always new, unexpected, upsetting. It will not fit in with men's preconceived ideas, nor pander to their prejudices. It digs far deeper than their shallow understanding of the evils of Satan's kingdom, and soars far higher than their low view of the glories of God's kingdom.

2. The good news is for the poor

He answered them, 'Go and tell John what you have seen and heard: ... the poor have the good news preached to them' (7:22).

The events of our present passage are not the first which Luke has recounted of this sort. But there is a special emphasis here on the kind of person who will benefit from the good news of the kingdom. It is noticeable both in Jesus's deeds, the incidents already considered in 7:1–10, 11–17, and 36–50, and also in his words, in 8:4–21.

a. Explained in Jesus's deeds

'The poor' figure in Mary's song, the *Magnificat,* at the beginning of Jesus's life story (1:52–53), and in his sermon at Nazareth, at the beginning of his ministry (4:18). They are the object of his special concern and of his work of liberation. The three stories in this section which have earlier suggested to us how good the good news is also illustrate for us what is meant by 'the poor' to whom it is addressed.

Both problems and people are significant. First, the problems to be coped with are sickness, as with the centurion and his slave; death and bereavement, as with the widow of Nain; and sin, as with the woman at Simon's dinner party. If Luke chose these examples deliberately, as one presumes he did (1:1–4), then it is not poverty in the economic sense which is in the forefront of his mind. Of the three cases only that of the widow is likely to be affected by this, and even in her case it is only one of the problems she is facing. But what *is* noteworthy in all three incidents is that each describes a need which God alone can meet; and when we think of the people concerned, we realize that their 'poverty' consists precisely in this—that in the eyes of Jesus's contemporaries such people have no resources to meet those needs, because they have no claim on God: the centurion is a mere Gentile, the widow a mere female, the woman at the party a mere sinner. They are outside the circle of privilege. For God to help them at all they have to receive his help *gratis.*

Poverty in the economic sense, and with it all other kinds of deprivation, are a separate issue. The grounds on which Christians combat such evils are the justice and love of God and the equality and dignity of man. The methods they use should be three out of the four available. By these four I mean philanthropy, using goodwill to alleviate the symptoms; social action, using law to deal with the causes; political revolution, using force to change the system; and spiritual infiltration, using the gospel to renew the hearts of men. We are to work at all these levels except the third, since that one, by breaking the rules, creates more problems than it solves.

But all the same the 'poverty' referred to by Jesus is of another sort. It is a theme which is first cousin to the 'universal gospel' theme (the Saviour of the *world*),[8] and it has been woven into the composition of Luke's Gospel from the start. All those to whom the good news was made known in chapters 1 and 2, in Jerusalem or Nazareth or Bethlehem, were unassuming folk with no spiritual pretensions. The same theme is brought to the forefront here in Chapter 7, and is crystallized in 7:29–30. 'When they heard this all the people and the tax collectors justified God'; they were not reckoned to be nearly religious enough to have a claim on him, yet here he was offering them salvation as a gift! On the other hand 'the Pharisees and the lawyers rejected the purpose of God for themselves'; they were so very

[8] See above, p. 48.

religious that they reckoned they did have such a claim, and when they found that salvation was a gift and not a right, they were offended, and refused it.

Good news *for the poor* is, in other words, a message of *grace*. As these verses tell us, the acceptance or rejection of this message when Jesus proclaimed it simply confirmed his hearers' acceptance or rejection of John's message earlier. For John's preaching of repentance and Jesus's offer to salvation belong together. John, in prison in Doubting Castle, may be encouraged: his ministry is being fulfilled, not betrayed, by the One who comes after him.

b. Explained in Jesus's words

The parable of the sower, which Matthew includes in a sequence of seven in his thirteenth chapter, stands alone here in Luke (8:4–15). According to Mark's account, it is a parable of fundamental importance: 'Do you not understand this parable? How then will you understand all the parables?'[9] Luke condenses it, and inserts it here as part of his conclusion to this section on the good news. Then he ends the section with Jesus's words about his relatives, when they attempted to reach him through the crowds that thronged him (8:16–21). He defines those who in the spiritual sense are truly 'related' to him.

In both episodes, the subject is the good news. 'The parable is this: the seed is the word of God' (8:11); 'My mother and my brothers are those who hear the word of God and do it' (8:21). The word of God is of course the message Jesus has come to bring. And in both episodes the question is, Are his hearers the sort of people who are prepared to receive it?

For the 'parable of the sower' is merely a title hallowed by use; in fact less is said about the sower than about anything else in the story. It would be truer to call it the parable of the seed, as I have just suggested. But more truly still, it is the parable of the soils, representing those who hear the good news. Are they ready for the sowing, or are there factors in their lives—hardness, shallowness, preoccupations—which prevent the message from taking root effectively?

In the same way, the passage which closes this section asks whether they take heed how they hear (8:18). Is there a relationship of receptiveness and obedience which unites them to Jesus, or do they presume on some other kind of relationship which they imagine

[9] Mk. 4:13.

exists between him and them, and which is less humbling?

The subject of the good news is the kingly rule of God in Jesus Christ, a rule which will bring untold blessings to those who are ready to receive it. But they must be ready. The good news is for the poor—for those who recognize their poverty, their need. They must give up their own ideas on how to cope with their problems, and accept the answer which the good news brings to them—abide by it and live on it.

8:22–56

Lord of the new Israel

Four miracle-stories follow. Jesus calms a storm on the Lake of Galilee (8:22–25), exorcizes the demons from a possessed man (8:26–39), heals a woman of her haemorrhage, and raises a child from death (8:40–56). Luke is skilled in the art of word-painting, and he displays this series of incidents before us like a row of pictures of the miraculous power of Jesus.

To regard Luke thus as an artist, at any rate in this chapter and some of those that have gone before it, is to gain insight into what he is aiming to do as he depicts these incidents.

1. Luke the artist

The best-known name in the world of modern art is probably that of Picasso. To those who know next to nothing about art, his work no doubt seems to be a collection of pictures which are all equally peculiar. But once you begin to study them, you find that in fact there is a progression in them. Pictures produced between certain dates belong to his Blue Period, others to his Pink Period, and so on, and in a gallery they might well be arranged in groups accordingly.

This is what we find with Luke's word-pictures when we begin to study them. His stories about Jesus are not a heap of miscellaneous items jumbled together. He has grouped some of the miracles here in chapter 8, others in chapter 7, others again in chapters 4 and 5: an early 'period', a middle 'period', and here the latest 'period', though there will of course be more to follow.

We shall consider first the pictures in this room in the gallery, then compare them with those of the 'early period', and then try to see the relationship between all three groups just mentioned.

a. 'Eighth-chapter' pictures: a group

One day he got into a boat . . . They arrived at the country of the Gerasenes . . . He got into the boat and returned . . . When Jesus returned . . . As he went . . . While he was still speaking (8:22, 26, 37, 40, 42, 49).

We have seen that Luke's story of Jesus is by no means a straight-forward account of things in the order in which they happened. The order of his Gospel is not chronological, but logical. He has a plan in which he is prepared to rearrange events so as to bring out their true meaning.

But in this chapter he is for once grouping together a series of events which actually did happen, it seems, in sequence. Follow through the verses quoted above, and you can see how the four stories are linked, not only in the way that Luke has written them up, but in their actual order of occurrence. A comparison between Luke 8 and the corresponding passages in Matthew (8 and 9) and Mark (4 and 5) will show that it is the other two evangelists who have rearranged the incidents to suit their own purposes, while it is Luke for whom the original sequences of events best expresses what he wants to say about Jesus.

It is not only that Luke groups these stories together, then. Apparently Jesus himself performed these four miracles in quick succession. They clearly belong in the same group.

b. 'Fourth-and-fifth-chapter' pictures and 'eighth-chapter' pictures: a contrast

Great multitudes gathered to hear and to be healed (5:15).

When he came to the house, he permitted no one to enter with him, except Peter and John and James, and the father and mother of the child (8:51).

Comparing the miracle-stories of the 'latest period' with those of the 'early period', we notice obvious similarities. In each case there is a series of striking examples of the power of Jesus over the power of evil, whether in the minds, bodies, or circumstances of men.

But there are differences; and one respect in which the earlier group gives a different impression from the later one is epitomized in the verses quoted above. In chapters 4 and 5 most of Luke's pictures are crowded canvasses; in chapter 8, most of the scenes depict a few figures only. Consider the following: in the 'early period', Jesus heals a demoniac in a synagogue full of worshippers (4:31–37), heals many sick folk at Simon's house (4:40), is prevented from finding solitude (4:42) and is mobbed by the people (5:1), finds great multitudes gathering after his curing of a leper (5:15), and performs another cure in a house so crowded that the sick man has to be lowered through the roof (5:17–19). In the 'latest period', by contrast, he is alone on the lake with no more than a boatload of his disciples (8:22), heals the Gerasene demoniac in the presence of the same few friends (8:26ff.), and raises Jairus's daughter from death in the presence of only five other persons (8:51).

Exceptions to this might be pointed out (*e.g.* 5:12–14; 8:42b). But it is an unmistakable impression; and when we ask ourselves why it should be so, chapter 6 provides an answer.

For between the two groups of miracles an event of great importance has occurred. Jesus has instituted a new kind of sabbath (6:1–11), appointed twelve new leaders for the people of God (6:12–16), and given the new law (6:17–49). We are beginning to see the new Israel appear. From among the people in general, Jesus is 'calling out' his own people, the church.[1] So it is not surprising that whereas the first miracles were performed before the general public, these later miracles are more especially for the benefit of his own disciples. Those were for the world at large; these are for the church.

c. 'Fourth-and-fifth-chapter', 'seventh-chapter', and 'eighth-chapter' pictures: a sequence

'The Son of man has authority on earth' (5:24).

He went on . . . bringing the good news of the kingdom of God (8:1).

They went and woke him, saying, 'Master, Master' (8:24).

Now we come to compare all three groups of miracle-stories that Luke has so far presented to us, as it were the 'early', 'middle', and 'latest' periods in the picture-gallery.

In the first group Jesus uses of himself the title which was to become his favourite, 'Son of man' (5:24). It means Man with a capital M, real Man, God's Man. We have already seen this status claimed for him in the genealogy of 3:23–38 and the temptations of

---

[1] *Ekklēsia* (church) means precisely that—'called out'.

4:1–13, as part of the meaning of another great title, 'Son of God'. For the first time in human history we are seeing Man as God meant him to be, with authority over the world and the devil.[2] No wonder that when this sort of greatness was demonstrated before the eyes of men in general, 'they were all amazed' (4:36). There was such a contrast between normal human experience and what this Man was doing. The difference between him and them was made very plain.

The miracles of the second group illustrate the 'good news' Jesus brings. It is good news for the poor (7:22) and good news of the kingdom (8:1). Jesus the Man, whose manhood contrasts so strongly with that of mankind at large, is here Jesus the King, who out of his wealth and power offers blessings to any who are 'poor' enough to receive them—the Gentile, the widow, the prostitute (7:1–17, 36–50); those who are prepared to receive, listen, and obey (8:4–21). We might say that while the early miracles brought conviction to the careless outsider, those of the 'middle period' brought blessing to the concerned enquirer.

And those of this 'latest period' bring challenge to the committed follower. For the peerless Man and the generous King is also the 'Master' among his disciples (8:22, 24). They have been convicted of the hopeless gulf that yawns between themselves and him, they have humbly and gratefully accepted his offer of salvation, and now they are his committed followers. They find themselves literally all in the same boat! It is for them, his own people, his own disciples, that Jesus performs this group of miracles.

2. Luke the preacher

The word-pictures of 8:22–56 have a message, then, for Jesus's disciples; which means that they have a message for the church. Luke, who is concerned not only to paint pictures but to preach sermons, intends that these four miracles should speak particularly to those who have attached themselves to Jesus and are trying to learn from him as a group of his people.

If this is so, and the events of this passage took place especially for the benefit of the church, what lessons are we, as members of the church, meant to learn from them?

In general, we may notice that all of them concern the evil that is in the world, especially as it affects the ordinary life of men. For this

[2] Gn. 1:26, 28; Ps. 8; and the comment on 4:1–13 (pp. 58ff.).

99

aspect of evil we might use the old-fashioned word 'tribulation', which is comprehensive enough to cover a near-shipwreck, a meeting with a madman, a hopeless illness, and a harrowing bereavement. It might be asked why, as he begins his course of instruction for those who are now his committed followers, Jesus places at the head of his syllabus this subject of tribulation, rather than (say) the fatherhood of God, or the demands of the law, or the nature of the church. One answer would be that in this chapter he is doing wonderful works, rather than speaking wonderful words; and since the chief point of most of his miracles is to show how he overcomes evil, the facing of tribulation is a subject which naturally arises at this point, while the others may be more readily taught by word of mouth. But there is a deeper answer. For Luke, Jesus is above all things the Saviour of the world. It is therefore of the first importance to understand that title. From what does he save us? Why, from evil! But in what sense does he save us from it? Are we exempted from it? If not, how do we cope with it? What in practice does 'salvation' mean, in a world where evil is obviously still so strong? Questions of this sort spring directly from Luke's main theme.

In particular, we are to learn three things concerning this matter of tribulation: the necessity of it, the conquest of it, and the purpose of it.

a. The necessity of tribulation in the Christian life
It is a pernicious error to suppose that the Christian life brings freedom from trouble. When Jesus says that 'If the Son makes you free, you will be free indeed',[3] he is certainly not promising exemption from the normal ills of life. The man who accepts Christ imagining that from then onwards trouble will no longer come his way is heading for disaster. For it is sure to come; and when it does, he will be pitched into doubt or even despair.

No, Jesus does not promise a trouble-free life. It is not that tribulation *may* come, nor even that it *will* come, but that it *must* come. In the very next chapter we shall find him spelling this out: 'The Son of man *must* suffer ... If any man would come after me, let him deny himself and take up his cross daily and follow me' (9:22–23). The apostolic church teaches the same severe truth: 'To enter the kingdom of God we *must* pass through many hardships' (Acts 14:22, NEB). That is why the heading of this section is not 'The possibility',

[3] Jn. 8:36.

nor even 'The inevitability', but 'The necessity of tribulation in the Christian life'.

For we cannot avoid the fact that Jesus was altogether in control of the whole chain of events in this passage. *He* took his disciples across the lake, where a storm was going to burst upon them, to the other shore, where a demoniac was going to meet them; *he* took them back to Capernaum, drew their attention to the sick woman in the crowd, and at Jairus's house closeted three of them with himself and the dead child. They have become his own special friends, and members of the kingdom of God—do they perhaps imagine that henceforth they will escape the grimness of life? Instead, Jesus forces them to confront a storm, a demoniac, an invalid, and a corpse. He is saying, as it were, 'Though you enjoy my salvation, you still live in a world where evil is rampant. How will you face it?'

The storm on the lake is an example, of course, of all the adverse circumstances which may come our way—not excluding actual storms, as many a Christian traveller has found.[4] The demoniac of Gerasa exemplifies all the evil that afflicts the minds and personalities of men, again not excluding, even in our own day, literal demon-possession. The woman's haemorrhage represents any kind of physical illness or weakness; and the death of Jairus's daughter reminds us of the 'last enemy' that lies in wait for every one of us. Peter, without doubt a witness of all four incidents, sums up this lesson in his first letter: 'Beloved, do not be surprised at the fiery ordeal which comes upon you to prove you, as though something strange were happening to you' (1 Pet. 4:12). Although he is speaking particularly of the fires of persecution, he could have said the same with regard to any kind of tribulation. Christians *must* learn to confront trouble.

b. The conquest of tribulation in the Christian life
But even plainer in this group of stories is the fact that though tribulation must be expected, it can also be overcome. The stories are told for the sake of their happy endings.

Is it stressing the obvious to point out *who* overcomes the problem in each case? But perhaps the church does need reminding, especially when it has become established and organized, and has set up its machinery for coping with trouble, that it is *Jesus* who puts forth his power in the conquest of evil; and it may be a good thing for us to notice that the nearest the disciples got to even co-operating with

---

[4] The apostle Paul among the first and most notable (Acts 27; 2 Cor. 11:25).

him, let alone doing the job themselves, was a cry for help (8:24).

So to the question 'Who can overcome tribulation?' the answer is 'Jesus only'; and that enables us to answer also the question of *how,* in quite practical terms, it is to be overcome. If Jesus is the overcomer, then the first necessity for those facing trouble is that they should have him with them, or rather that they should be with him. In the case of these disciples, he was present to their sight; in our case, he must be present to our faith—both in the individual heart ('Whoever would draw near to God must believe that he exists and that he rewards those who seek him')[5] and in the loving friendship of fellow-believers ('Where two or three are gathered in my name, there am I in the midst of them').[6] But for us as for them the principle is the same, and that is that apart from him we can do nothing.[7] We need to know that he is present, in both senses of the word: he is *here,* and he is *now.*

Secondly, we must believe him to be Lord of the past also. Long before we reached our present situation, he had already planned our journey to Gerasa and our return to Capernaum, seeing in advance the evils which would confront us, the dismay they would cause, the victories he would win, and the lessons we should learn. Because he is the Author of the story, and therefore is not himself bound by the time sequence along which his brain-children must move, all the great 'beforehand' words of theology add their special lustre to his name: foreknowledge, predestination, grace. Here we are, wherever 'here' may be; but not without his knowing that we should come here, nor without his knowing how he would bring glory and blessing out of our being here.

This brings us at once to the third practical step: that we grasp the fact that he *will* bring good out of evil. He is Lord not only of the past and the present, but also of the future. Naturally, where our own future is concerned this is altogether a matter of faith. But that faith has a firm basis in what we know of our predecessors' 'futures': the kind of Christians, for example, that emerged in the end from the harrowing experiences recorded by Luke here in chapter 8. What the Lord had in store for them we shall see in a moment, when we come to consider the purpose of tribulation in the Christian life. But that the outcome of their troubles was in his capable hands, and that our own future is no less secure, there can be doubt.

[5] Heb. 11:6.
[6] Mt. 18:20.
[7] Jn. 15:5.

In this way Jesus teaches us how we for our part may cope with tribulation. As to the question of how he for his part deals with it, we should understand that his methods here are only examples, just as the troubles themselves are only examples. There are other kinds of problem, and there are also other ways of dealing with the problems. Reading the story of the early church, we find that where demon-possession is concerned, practically every case which is mentioned is also cured; but we find also that, with regard to illness, there were some notable cases in which the divine answer was *not* miraculous healing,[8] while as for the raising of corpses, most first-century Christians who died seem to have stayed dead! And the one great storm described in detail in the New Testament raged for fourteen days on end, till it had shipwrecked Paul on Malta (Acts 27).

Jesus may not give the kind of victory we expect. But he will always overcome trouble in some way if we ask him. His answer in trying circumstances may be relief; but it may equally be endurance. His answer in illness may be health; but it may be courage instead. He may plan rescue from death's door, or permit bereavement and give new hope with it. But 'in all these things we are more than conquerors through him who loved us' (Rom. 8:37).

c. The purpose of tribulation in the Christian life

We have to look on into the next chapters to find out why the disciples of Jesus needed to learn these lessons. For there we see a splendid and challenging sight. 'He called the twelve together and gave them power and authority over all demons and to cure diseases, and he sent them out' (9:1–2); 'After this the Lord appointed seventy others, and sent them' (10:1). It was in preparation for the church's own gospel outreach that it had to have its own private course of lessons from the miracles of its Lord.

With what message do Christ's disciples go forth—not simply on their lips, but in their lives? What does their corporate witness show to the world?

The church is not a company of people who enjoy a trouble-free life. It never experiences such a thing itself, and has no right to offer it to others. Neither, on the other hand, should it be a community which is inundated with troubles and has no more ability than anyone else to cope with them. No; the miracle which the church of Jesus Christ should both embody and proclaim is *the power to cope with*

---

[8] 2 Cor. 12:7ff.; 1 Tim. 5:23; 2 Tim. 4:20.

the evils of life. The disciples of Christ are neither free *from* tribulation, nor helpless *in* tribulation, but victorious *over* tribulation. We turn again to the words of Luke's great friend Paul, to summarize this lesson—the purpose of trouble in the Christian life:

'Blessed be the God and Father of our Lord Jesus Christ, the Father of mercies and God of all comfort, who comforts us in all our affliction, so that we may be able to comfort those who are in any affliction, with the comfort with which we ourselves are comforted by God.'[9]

[9] 2 Cor. 1:3–4.

9:1–50

Mission of the new Israel

This section ends the first main division of Luke's Gospel, and with it certain things which have been emerging in his first eight chapters come clearly into focus. It is as though the picture he has been sketching is now complete, at least in outline.

In some respects, however, it is noticeably unfinished. To this fact we shall turn our attention when we come to the latter part of the section.

1. A picture clear in outline (9:1–36)

The first thirty-six verses of the chapter before us comprise six paragraphs. Their contents may be summed up and set out as follows.

(1) The twelve are sent on a missionary tour (9:1–6).
(2) King Herod asks who Jesus is (9:7–9).
(3) Five thousand people are miraculously fed (9:10–17).
(4) At Caesarea Philippi, the twelve are asked who Jesus is (9:18–22).
(5) The disciples are called to follow the way of the cross (9:23–27).
(6) Jesus is transfigured, and the heavenly voice declares who he is (9:28–36).

So the picture which here stands before us, complete and definite, is a double one. In the first, third, and fifth paragraphs we are shown the Lord's people; in the second, fourth, and sixth, the Lord himself.

The new Israel began to emerge from the old Israel in chapter 6. There we saw Jesus replacing the outworn Jewish system with a new religion and a new nation of his own. His people are to be known as his 'church', those who are 'called out' from the kingdom of Satan, as their predecessors were called first out of heathendom and then out of slavery.[1] The miracles of chapter 8 were especially concerned with the instruction of these 'new Israelites'.

Those chapters, describing who and what his people are, had been preceded by chapters in which Luke was sketching who the Lord himself is. Men asked the question (4:22; 5:21), supernatural voices from both heaven and hell answered it (3:22; 4:41). By these voices, and by his own words and deeds at the beginning of his ministry, were demonstrated both the deity and the manhood of Jesus the Son of God.

By the time we reach 9:36, both these outlines have been made as clear to us as they really need to be. We know what the church is, and who the Lord is. The six episodes of this present passage are put together[2] in such a way as to make the picture plain once and for all.

a. The Lord's people

He sent them out to preach the kingdom of God and to heal (9:2).

He said to them, 'You give them something to eat.' . . . And taking the five loaves and the two fish he . . . gave them to the disciples to set before the crowd (9:13, 16).

'If any man would come after me, let him deny himself and take up his cross daily and follow me' (9:23).

The first paragraph of the chapter (9:1–6) describes a 'mission' on which the twelve apostles were sent out. Some time before, Jesus had spoken of himself as a missionary: 'I must preach the good news of the kingdom of God . . . for I was sent for that purpose' (4:43). Now the twelve—representing, as we have seen, the new Israel or 'people of God'—are commissioned for the same kind of work. Evangelizing, or bringing good news, is his primary task; it is to be theirs also. They live in a world sorely in need of the good news of the kingdom of God, and the spreading of that news is one of the

[1] See above, p. 98, n. 1.
[2] Between the feeding of the five thousand (Lk. 9:10–17 = Mk. 6:30–44 = Mt. 14:13–21) and Peter's confession (Lk. 9:18ff. = Mk. 8:27ff. = Mt. 16:13ff.) Mark and Matthew both include a string of incidents which Luke leaves out. The omission is presumably intended to tighten the structure of Luke's narrative, and to underline the connections he wants his readers to see in the group of stories in chapter 9.

purposes for which he has 'called them out' to be a group of people dedicated to following him.

By-passing for the moment the second paragraph, we go on to the third (9:10–17), which is the familiar story of the feeding of the five thousand. Again it concerns the twelve; though the whole crowd also may be taken to represent the people of God, for the incident is meant to recall the occasion centuries earlier when Israel had been in another 'desert place' (9:12, AV), and had been fed miraculously by 'bread from heaven' which God gave them by the hand of Moses.[3] The theme of a great feast to which their generous God would welcome all his people is a recurrent one in Scripture.[4] The five thousand are those who accept the Lord's invitation, and he will feed them. But to the twelve he says, '*You* give them something to eat' (9:13); and when he miraculously increases the loaves and fish, it is to the twelve that he gives the work of distributing them. The needs of the Lord's people are being met by the ministry of the Lord's people.

The words of the fifth paragraph (9:23–27), though addressed 'to all', nevertheless do not apply to all, for they specify what is required in those who will be Jesus's disciples: 'If any man *would come after me* . . .'. Here also, then, it is of his own people that he is speaking. For the third time, the way he treads is to be the way they must tread; having foretold his own suffering and death (9:22), he goes on immediately to warn that his people must likewise deny themselves, take up their cross, and go the same way that he is going (9:23). The life must be lost before it can be saved (9:24); the suffering must come before the glory. For an exceptional few, there is a glimpse of glory before death,[5] but as a general rule the order is reversed: 'through many tribulations we must enter the kingdom of God'.[6] First the cross, then the crown.

---

[3] Jn. 6:31–32; Ex. 16:4ff. It is John's account (Jn. 6:1–59) which makes explicit the connection between the two miracles.

[4] 1 Ki. 19:4ff.; Ps. 23:5; Is. 25:6; Lk. 14:15ff.; Rev. 19:9.

[5] The sight of the kingdom of God, which Jesus says some of his hearers will be given before they die (9:27), has been interpreted in various ways. Plummer lists no less than seven! The transfiguration seems an obvious possibility, since the Gospels link it so closely with this saying. On the other hand, it may seem odd that something predicted to happen 'before you die' should take place the very next week, and some therefore refer the saying to a later event such as the resurrection, or the ascension, or (remembering Mk. 9:1, 'the kingdom of God come *with power*') Pentecost. The connection between this saying and what precedes it seems clearest if, whatever it refers to, it is taken as an exception to the rule 'First suffering, then glory'.

[6] Acts 14:22.

In this way the permanent characteristics of the church of Christ are spelled out. The outline is very clear and simple. The mission of 9:1–6 is a whirlwind tour, 'in haste, carrying not an ounce of superfluous equipment, relying entirely on hospitality, and wasting no time upon the inhospitable and unreceptive';[7] but it imprints on the brain of the church that one of its chief functions is to evangelize. The feeding of the five thousand (9:10–17) is only one miracle among many, but it is obviously of the greatest importance (the only miracle related in all four Gospels), and leaves the church in no doubt of its responsibility to care for its own members; even after the crowd has been fed, there remain twelve baskets full, 'one from each apostle, symbolizing perhaps the continuing miraculous sustenance of the new Israel of God'.[8] The first prediction of the passion of Jesus must have been almost too much for the disciples to take in, but the necessity of their following him in this also is made quite unmistakable (9:23–27): the shadow of the cross looms over them as well as over him.

By this basic outline the shape of our own churches must be judged. How much of the activity of the Christian communities to which we belong falls under the condemnation of being deficient in one respect, overblown in another, when compared with the kind of community the Lord here calls his disciples to be? With regard to the world, we try to impress it with our success or our social importance, when our great concern should be to evangelize it. Within the church, we strive for bureaucratic efficiency and economic security, when our real aim should be its growth into spiritual maturity. As for the cross, we do indeed bear it publicly—as a necessary feature of our church buildings, or as an ornament round our neck, or (more importantly) as the heart of the message we preach. But that is not enough. We are meant to be bearing it to a daily crucifixion at our own personal Calvary.[9] Like the 'Falling Tower' of the old Tarot mythology, the true Christian community is perpetually dying, yet ever being built up; and thus embodying the double principle of death and resurrection, it demonstrates before the world the gospel of its Lord.

b. The Lord himself

Herod said, '. . . Who is this about whom I hear such things?' (9:9).

---

[7] Caird, p. 126.   [8] Ellis, p. 139.   [9] Gal. 2:20; 6:14.

Peter answered, 'The Christ of God' (9:20).

A voice came out of the cloud, saying, 'This is my Son, my Chosen; listen to him!' (9:35).

Each of the episodes concerning the Lord's people, the first, third, and fifth of Luke's stories in this chapter, is followed by an incident which relates to the Lord himself, in which questions are asked and statements made about his identity. On the basis of what has happened so far, the record of the first eight chapters of the Gospel, who exactly is this Jesus? Popular rumour suggests that he may be John the Baptist, risen from the dead; or Elijah, reappearing after eight centuries; or some other resurrected prophet of a former time. But who really is he? What should we understand him to be, after all we have read so far? Such questions, and their answers, are the gist of the second, fourth, and sixth paragraphs.

In 9:7–9 we hear the opinion of King Herod. What he knows is that John is dead—he himself had him executed. What he does not know is who this new prophet can be; he is 'perplexed'—'utterly at a loss'.[10] His attitude is that of the majority of the people. They are still intrigued by Jesus, and in a way eager to see him, as Herod is (9:9); but the fact that even after all that has taken place they can still say 'Who is this?' belies the genuineness of their desire really to learn from him. The response of those who genuinely want to know him will, by this time, be more like Peter's than Herod's. In 9:18–22 the same rumours are referred to—Jesus is thought to be a resurrected John, or Elijah, or another prophet. The same question is asked— Who actually is he? But the answer of those who 'press on to know the Lord'[11] is quite different from that of Herod: Jesus is 'The Christ of God'.

Luke's account of the transfiguration (9:28–36) also makes a statement on the matter, and this is the final statement, for it is made by the voice of God. 'This is my Son, my Chosen; listen to him!' Enough information has been given by this time for people to have reached this conclusion themselves; as they have been given a clear outline of what the church is, so they have been given a clear outline of who the Lord is. Herod represents all those, the majority, who hear of Jesus and discuss him but will not follow him. Theirs is

[10] Plummer, p. 241, on 9:7.
[11] Ho. 6:3.

an attitude common at all levels of society, but especially among thinking, articulate people. It is not sufficient, however, that this subject should make the brain stir and the tongue wag. It is meant to move the will to action. Peter represents the minority who are moved to follow Jesus: to them his identity is revealed.

The terms in which the divine voice identifies Jesus on the mount of transfiguration ('This is my Son, my Chosen; listen to him!') are of the greatest interest. According to them, Jesus combines in himself three of the great figures of the Old Testament faith.

The command 'Listen to him!' recalls Deuteronomy 18. 'The Lord your God will raise up for you a prophet like me', says Moses; 'him you shall heed.'[12] 'Son' brings to mind the 'royal psalms', where it is the king of Israel who is spoken of as God's son, and his kingship is chiefly seen in providing for and protecting his people: 'He has pity on the weak and the needy, and saves the lives of the needy'.[13] 'Chosen' means the chosen Servant of the Lord, in the later chapters of Isaiah,[14] whose service for God is of such a kind that it leads him to suffering and death.[15]

In this striking way we see that the marks which according to 9:1–6, 10–17, and 23–27 will characterize the church, if it is being true to Christ, are indeed his own distinguishing marks. For he is the Prophet who is to be heard and heeded: that is why the church, if it is to carry on his work, is to be a preaching church. He is the royal Son, who with his wealth and power provides for all the needs of his people: that is why his church must exercise the same ministry and be a community in which members are likewise concerned with one another's needs, caring and nourishing and building up. He is the Chosen, the Servant, who treads the path of suffering: that is why all those who wish to be his disciples must similarly take up the cross and deny themselves.

The message, the family, the cross—is this how we see the life of the church to which we belong? Does it follow the example of its evangelizing, caring, suffering Lord? And when it proclaims Christ, is he seen to be that kind of a Lord? By the time we reach 9:36, Luke's picture of Christ and his church is quite clear, and we must measure our own understanding of these things by it.

[12] Dt. 18:15.
[13] Ps. 72:13; cf. Ps. 2:6–7.
[14] E.g. Is. 42:1.
[15] Is. 52:13 – 53:12.

2. A picture still unfinished (9:37–50)

Although clear, it is however still only an outline. The picture is as yet unfinished. We may wonder why Luke inserts the next ten chapters, the great central division of his Gospel, since by this point the issues are plain. The ministry in Galilee has come to an end; some have accepted the call of Christ, but the majority, though still 'marvelling at everything he did' (9:43), show by their wilful ignorance of who he really is that they have in effect rejected him. Why then does Jesus not move straight to the climax of his ministry, and precipitate the crisis which will bring him to Calvary? What remains to be done, and why does at least a year[16] need to be devoted to the doing of it?

The reason why the Gospel narrative, like the Israelites' journey through Sinai, comes within sight of its goal only to be turned away into a lengthy detour before it actually gets there, is brought out by the four incidents which Luke relates immediately after the story of the transfiguration. Each one sheds an unfavourable light on Jesus's disciples, and makes plain how deficient they were, even now, in one respect or another.

a. In faith (9:37–43)

'Look upon my son, for he is my only child; and behold, a spirit seizes him ... And I begged your disciples to cast it out, but they could not.' Jesus answered, 'O faithless and perverse generation, how long am I to be with you and bear with you?' (9·38–41).

Commentators differ as to whose lack of faith is being rebuked by Jesus; but in the context of the other stories in this section, which all reflect on the disciples' failure in one way or another, this episode seems to gain most point if we take it that they are the faithless ones. So much had they seen of the healing, cleansing power of Jesus, and so much had they, indeed, experienced of it themselves only recently, in the mission of 9:1–6, that their failure on this occasion highlights all the more just how immature they were, and how much they still had to learn. For all Peter's confession of who Jesus was, the disciples still lacked a practising faith in him as the Prophet of salvation.

---

[16] Compare Jn. 6:4 and 12:1. The feeding of the five thousand takes place at one Passover, the crucifixion at another (the next one?).

Such faith is poles apart from that of the White Queen in *Alice*, [17] who was able to believe six impossible things before breakfast. For it has seen that the victories of the kingdom are *not* impossible: that is its very basis. It counts its blessings and sees no reason why they should not be multiplied. It calls Christians of little faith to study the history of God's people, and indeed to reflect on their own experience, to remind themselves of what the Lord can do.

b. *In understanding* (9:44–45)

'Let these words sink into your ears; for the Son of man is to be delivered into the hands of men.' But they did not understand this saying (9:44–45).

Granted that the cross was a scandalous, offensive thing, against which they instinctively rebelled,[18] this was even so the second time Jesus had told them about it, and would be by no means the last.[19] Yet in spite of his obvious willingness to teach them, they were reluctant to ask him (9:45), and did not really begin to understand the cross till after the resurrection (24:25f.).

Of course there were reasons for this. But they are no excuse for dull-wittedness among the people of God today. The way to sharpen one's wits is to use them. Christians who understand are those who have not been content with going through the motions of Christian discipleship, but who have applied themselves to asking and listening and thinking.

c. *In humility* (9:46–48)

An argument arose among them as to which of them was the greatest (9:46).

It seems incredible that a band of grown men, still more of Christian disciples, could argue openly over their own relative importance. It is shown up for the childishness that it is when Jesus takes an actual child and places him before them as a standing rebuke to their lack of humility. It is quite clear that they have scarcely begun to learn what it means to follow either the Servant on the path of self-denial or the King in his concern for the welfare of others.

This immaturity also is a recurrent blight on the life of the church. Not that I am out for personal glory, of course—but I do think

[17] Lewis Carroll, *Through the Looking Glass*, ch.5.
[18] *Cf.* Mt. 16:22.
[19] *Cf.* 9:22, and the sequence in Mark (8:31; 9:9, 12, 31; 10:33f., 45).

people ought to recognize my *status*, since I am after all the Rev. (or Dr, or Sir, or whatever). Or if I can laugh at that temptation, I may feel a more genuine superiority because of my *function*, and the important Christian activity I am involved in. Or, more subtly, I may be tempted to what one might call pride of *affiliation*, when I stick up not for myself but for my group or organization. In each case, though, there is a lack of the humility which enables the Christian to look 'not only to his own interests, but also to the interests of others';[20] and it is a lack which bedevils again and again the growth of unity among the people of God.

d. In tolerance (9:49–50)

'Master, we saw a man casting out demons in your name, and we forbade him, because he does not follow with us' (9:49).

If we think of John as the author of the five New Testament books bearing his name, we can see in his complaint to Jesus here all the zeal for truth, but none of the insight and love, which those writings show to be his later. The zealous among God's people—especially perhaps those who, like John here, are concerned for the purity of the church—stand in particular need of a breadth of sympathy and a depth of vision which will temper their native zeal. To adapt Reinhold Niebuhr's famous prayer, they must ask for the serenity to accept what does not need to be challenged, the courage to challenge what does, and the wisdom to know the difference.

A wiser response than John's excited denunciation would have been that of the Jewish teacher Gamaliel, which Luke quotes in his second book: 'If this plan or this undertaking is of men, it will fail; but if it is of God, you will not be able to overthrow them.'[21]

What then can Jesus do with a group of disciples still so unbelieving, slow-witted, swollen-headed, and narrow-minded, except take them with him on another year's course of teaching? In this way Luke rounds off his first main section, and introduces the long middle section of the Gospel (9:51 – 19:44). It is sometimes called 'The Journey to Jerusalem', but within the loose framework of a sort of travel diary it is more exactly a course of instruction for the disciples. It will show us, to borrow the title of A. B. Bruce's book, *The Training of the Twelve*.

[20] Phil. 2:4.   [21] Acts 5:38f.

We may well search our own hearts, in the light of all we have learnt so far, to see just how much we have really taken in concerning who the Lord is, and what we, his people, ought to be. And when we have admitted how little we, like the disciples, have really grasped about him and about ourselves, we shall appreciate all the more his forbearance and love in giving us repeated opportunities for learning more of his Word, and make the fullest use of what he gives us.

The words of the Saviour

9:51 – 10:42
The way

With 9:51 Luke begins not merely a new section, but the middle third of his Gospel. This is clear first from a comparison between his account on the one hand and Matthew's and Mark's on the other, since up to this point all three run generally parallel, but from here on they diverge. It is clear also from a reading of this Gospel itself, for it has consisted so far chiefly of the deeds of Jesus, whereas henceforth there is to be a concentration on his words. Perhaps this was in Luke's mind when he wrote at the start of his second volume: 'In the first book . . . I have dealt with all that Jesus began to *do* and *teach*.'[1]

Jesus as Teacher, then, is the central figure of this central section of the Gospel. And the learners, the disciples, have certainly shown their need of his teaching, as we have seen in the closing passage of the previous section (9:37-50). The final verses of that passage provide a direct lead in to the new subject. They speak about following Jesus (9:49); and Luke immediately goes on to explain how, and whither, Jesus is to be followed (9:51-56).

9:51 and 53 give the keynote. Jesus has 'set his face to go to Jerusalem'. That is the way he is to go. 'The Way', therefore, is our title. Luke's whole middle section, from 9:51 to 19:44, is set in the framework of an actual journey (as he reminds us from time to time, though the details given are so sketchy as to suggest that we are not meant to try to plot its geography or chronology);[2] its overall subject is Jesus's teaching about his 'way', the way to be a Christian; and it begins, in our present passage, with some instruction particularly on

[1] Acts 1:1.
[2] 10:38; 13:22; 17:11; 18:31,35; 19:1,11,28ff. Drury (p. 55) remarks on the appropriateness of 'the symbol of life as a journey', and compares Bunyan's use of it in *The Pilgrim's Progress*.

that subject. From 9:51 to 10:16, we learn what 'the way' is; from 10:17 to 10:42, we learn what it is not.

1. What the way is (9:51 – 10:16)

We have already noticed the incident in Samaria with which Luke begins this section (9:51–56). The motive of the Samaritan villagers in not welcoming Jesus might have been hostility to him as a Jew, or (less likely) the assumption that he would not want to linger anyway; James and John took it to be the former, and were quick to defend their Master's honour. The defence was as misguided as the opposition, and Jesus dismissed both. What mattered at this stage was that he was soon 'to be received up'—to die, rise, and ascend—and to that destiny he was now on his way.

At the end of chapter 9 Luke groups together three incidents concerning people who are interested in Jesus's way, and the reiterated thought is 'Follow . . . follow . . . follow' (9:57, 59, 61). Then at the beginning of chapter 10, those who have come to follow him are now 'sent . . . on ahead of him' (10:1). This is what is meant by involvement in the way of Jesus: to come after him (9:57–62), and to go before him (10:1–16)—to be his followers, and to be his heralds.

a. The way to be his followers (9:57–62)

To the first would-be follower, Jesus points out that the security of hearth and home which one expects in normal life has to take second place where commitment to the Son of man is concerned. To the next, who simply wanted, it seems, to fulfil the normal custom of looking after his parents until their death, and would then reckon himself free to follow, Jesus gives the same harsh answer. Similarly to the third: the normal courtesies of family affection must give way to the overriding demands of the kingdom of God.

The uncompromising words of 9:62 are sometimes taken as a warning that those who have entered the kingdom may yet forfeit their place in it. It is not however his followers' final salvation which is uppermost in Jesus's mind here. He is simply pointing out that, once they begin to plough, the only way to drive a straight furrow—one that is 'fit for the kingdom'—is to keep looking ahead, and not back. It is he himself who is 'ahead of them',[3] and on whom

[3] Mk. 10:32.

their eyes must be fixed. Going his way takes precedence over everything else.

Now we are not to misunderstand this. Ordinary security, accepted customs, home ties, are still the norm. Jesus approves of them, since they are part and parcel of the social life of mankind as his Father created it, and that is normally the way his followers are led to live. But the crucial question, and the one he is asking here, concerns what happens at the *parting* of the ways. 'Suppose I were to lead you towards work in which your income would be lower, your prospects (humanly speaking) more uncertain, and your accustomed standard of living non-existent? Or suppose I were to ask you to do something for me which according to most people of your class and background is simply 'not done'? Or suppose I were to summon you to my service with such a peremptory call that your nearest and dearest would have to be left without an explanation? Would you even then come my way?'

Regularly God tests the earnestness of men's hearts by bringing them to this fork in the road. When it becomes necessary to choose between two ways, which do we follow? Comfort or convention or custom—or Christ? The test from the very outset (see, for example, 5:27) has been 'Follow *me*'.

b. The way to be his heralds (10:1–16)

Those who come to follow Jesus and to learn from him are then sent out ahead of him, to introduce him to others. The seventy were to go 'into every town and place where he himself was about to come'.

To those who are thus to be his heralds, Jesus speaks in terms of toil (10:2), danger (10:3), single-mindedness (10:4), and forthright proclamation of the good news of the kingdom (10:5–12). The toil is the toil of harvesters; when the offer of salvation is finally closed, this will be angels' work,[4] but so long as the offer remains open, the bringing of converts into the granary of the Lord is the responsibility of his disciples. The danger from spiritual 'wolves' is something to be especially aware of, we note, when the 'lambs' are going out on evangelistic work. The single-mindedness arises from the fact that for the work in hand they will have to forgo both comfort and leisure. And the actual heralding, outlined in the second part of the paragraph, must be as clear and urgent as they can make it. We begin to

---

[4] Mt. 13:30, 39.

see how in practice the lesser preoccupations of 9:57–62 are discarded, as Jesus sets the tone of dedication to the supreme task of introducing him to men.

Here is a challenge; and many might feel that while 'following' is within their capabilities, 'heralding' is only for those who are specially gifted. But the passage contains more than one hint that every Christian is expected to do both. In the first place there is probably symbolic meaning in the number of disciples sent out.[5] Already Jesus had commissioned twelve out of his many disciples to be leaders of the new people of God,[6] and if this number were meant to correspond to the twelve sons of Jacob, the other one would be significant in a similar way: seventy was the total number both of the members of Jacob's family when he went down into Egypt, and of the representative elders of the Israelites when they eventually journeyed out of Egypt.[7] We might distinguish the two symbolic numbers by saying that 12 = the patriarchs of Israel = the apostles; while 70 = the people of Israel = the church in general.

In addition, the marching orders for the seventy are by their very nature applicable to every Christian. Exceptional people are not required. It is the message they carry, and the driving power that carries them, which are exceptional. The message is a matter of life and death: the last judgment is in view, heaven and hell, eternal bliss or woe, which will be determined by the acceptance or rejection of the divine message (10:12–16). The driving power is the Lord himself: the harvest is his, the whole scheme is under his control, and three times in as many verses he takes the responsibility for sending out the workers (10:1–3). No Christian can excuse himself from this service by pleading, as Moses did, his own inadequacy. For the Lord replies: 'Who has made man's mouth? Who makes him dumb, or deaf, or seeing, or blind? Is it not I, the Lord? Now therefore go, and I will be with your mouth and teach you what you shall speak.'[8]

In the event, it may sometimes be the mouth of Moses' eloquent brother which is used rather than his own.[9] Moses the diffident does, even so, become a 'prophet' and speak for his Lord,[10] and he longs that all the Lord's people should do the same.[11] His hope has been fulfilled in our New Testament days, now that the Spirit has been

---

[5] Some commentators prefer the alternative reading 'seventy-two', instead of 'seventy', and suggest ways in which that figure also may be appropriately symbolic.

[6] See above, pp. 76ff., 82ff.   [7] Gn. 46:27; Nu. 11:16ff.

[8] Ex. 4:11–12.   [9] Ex. 4:14–16.

[10] Dt. 18:15.   [11] Nu. 11:29.

poured out on all flesh, [12] and all who are saved can not only believe in the heart but also confess with the mouth—whether eloquently or not—that Jesus is Lord. [13]

From two points of view, then, the way is described. Jesus calls men to come after him, to be his followers, disciples, learners; and as they learn of him, so he sends them out ahead of him, to be his heralds, his messengers, and his servants. In both respects the way must be one of utter devotion to his cause.

2. What the way is not (10:17–37)

This kind of devotion, however, is often misunderstood. In spite of what has just been said about relying on Jesus's power, and not our own, when we go out to serve him, we still tend to assume that 'commitment' means 'achievement'; as if being followers and heralds of Jesus were something we had to accomplish, instead of something we had simply to *be*.

But is not the way of Jesus a matter of what we do, as well as of what we are?

Of course it is. But the misunderstanding, and its clarification, are explained in the next paragraphs.

a. Explained to insiders (10:17–24)

'The seventy returned with joy' (10:17); they had had a successful mission. But was this response to the good news something which had been brought about by *their* efforts? Or was their own grasp of it in the first place something achieved by *their* studies?

On the contrary, they realize what we have already noted—that their power to exorcize demons is only in the name of Jesus; and he makes this quite explicit—'I have *given* you authority' (10:17–20). *He* is making them into messengers who can proclaim his message effectively. It is much less important that they should rush out doing the things they believe he wants, than that they should let him make of them the kind of people who inevitably will do such things.

In the same way, their grasp of the message is not due primarily to the exercise of their own minds (10:21–24). Jesus thanks his Father for having 'hidden these things from the wise and understanding and *revealed* them to babes'. In these two short sections it is certainly not

[12] Acts 2:17–18.
[13] Rom. 10:9.

being suggested that God's people can be passive and unthinking, while he manipulates their bodies like puppets and programmes their minds like computers. Of course both in body and mind they are active in his service, now in this evangelistic rehearsal as later in the full-dress mission of the church. But their passionate, devoted, activity springs from abilities which he has given, not which they have evolved, and from understanding which he has revealed, not which they have attained. Indeed, the thing which above all else makes Christ's people what they are, is the fact that every one of them can say, 'It is no longer I who live, but Christ who lives in me.'[14] Thus the account of the return of the seventy reaches forward in time, and captures the essence of the new age of the Spirit which is to begin at Pentecost: the supernatural indwelling power of Christ among and within his people. Well may they and he rejoice together (10:17, 21) at this divine seal on the wonders that are to come.

b. Explained to an outsider (10:25–37)

There follows the famous story of the good Samaritan.

Thousands of people, Christians and non-Christians, set this before themselves as the ideal of neighbourly love. Christ's people in particular value it as his own illustration of his second great commandment: second, that is, to loving their God, they are also to love their fellow man, and the parable describes such a love. The Samaritan is one who sees the need of another, and having the resources to meet it, does so, without prejudice and regardless of circumstances. This is, in one sense, the Christian way of life.

But like all the parables of Jesus, the story of the good Samaritan has hidden depths, and one clue to them is the lawyer's original question. He had asked, not about a way *of* life, but about a way *to* life—'What shall I do to inherit eternal life?' (10:25)—and the distinction is all-important.

Jesus answers with what is called an *argumentum ad hominem*, an 'argument to the man'. His questioner is a specialist in Jewish religious law; so Jesus replies 'to the man' on the man's own terms— 'What is written in the law? How do you read?' (10:26). The lawyer asks what he must *do* to inherit eternal life; so Jesus replies first that he must *do* what the two great commandments tell him, and then that he must *do* as the Samaritan did (10:28, 37). He wants to know the way to life; so Jesus says, 'Do this, and you will live' (10:28).

[14] Gal. 2:20.

122

But where eternal life is concerned, if there is one thing more than another about which the whole of Scripture speaks with one voice, it is that 'no human being will be justified in his sight by works of the law'.[15] It is theoretically true that 'the man who practises the right-eousness which is based on the law shall live by it';[16] the trouble is that no-one ever succeeds in doing so. If the lawyer thinks eternal life can be obtained by doing what the law demands, he will have to learn how extreme those demands are.

And in this lies the barbed point of the story of the good Samari-tan. For the thing is impossible. We are so used to thinking of the victim and his rescuer as 'neighbours', that we forget this was Jesus's scandalous twist to the story; he deliberately wove it around the representatives of two groups of people whom his hearers knew to be not good neighbours at all, but inveterate enemies. As well visualize the Ethiopian changing his skin or the leopard his spots, as imagine a Samaritan helping a Jew. But nothing less will do. 'An Irish Repub-lican fell among thieves, and an Ulster Orangeman came and helped him; a white colonialist fell among thieves, and a black freedom fighter came to his aid; that is what God's law requires of you.'

The lawyer was right in one thing, at any rate. Eternal life is something to be inherited. And to receive an inheritance, you have to *be* an heir. No amount of *doing* will make you into one. Keeping the law is a way of life; it is not a way to life. It is only when by God's grace we have become the right sort of people—his people, by the new birth—that we begin to do the right sort of things.

The way of Jesus is one of devotion and dedication, both in following him and in heralding him. But the way is not, on that account, a matter of assiduous 'religion' and frenzied service, of busy-ness and incessant good works. It means not achievement, but commitment; not activities, but attitudes; not quantity, but quality.

The last episode of this section sums it up (10:38–42). It was 'on their way' that Jesus and his friends were passing through the village of Martha and Mary, and he was invited to visit the two sisters; and the incident in their home crystallizes what has gone before. 'Mary . . . sat at the Lord's feet and listened to his teaching': that is what the way is. 'But Martha was distracted with much serving': that is what the way is not.

[15] Rom. 3:20.
[16] Rom. 10:5.

As Jesus says to Martha, 'One thing is needful'; and whatever that debatable phrase may mean, it shows, alongside the gentle rebuke to her for getting her priorities wrong, a recognition that practical service does have its place and is truly acceptable to the Lord. But Mary has the nub of the matter. 'The way' means to be with Jesus, to learn of him, and to know him. As we saw in the opening episode (9:51–56), it means to be prepared to accompany him even 'to Jerusalem', to the cross, where our old self-life dies. All the striving after spiritual achievement must die—all the supposition that eternal life is obtained, and God is pleased, by our much doing. When Jesus expects us to follow him all the way, he means not a frenzy of religious activity undertaken in our own strength, but the total abandonment of ourselves to him, for him to work in us both to will and to work for his good pleasure.[17]

[17] Phil. 2:13.

11:1 – 12:12
The gift of the Spirit

The banner that flew over the gathering of the people of God on the first Whitsunday bore the text of a prediction: 'This is what was spoken by the prophet Joel: "And in the last days it shall be, God declares, that I will pour out my Spirit upon all flesh." '[1] The prophecy came true on that day, has been true ever since, and will be true till the end of time. The age of the Holy Spirit dawned then, and is the age in which we live.

Before that day, the Spirit had been at work in the world, and had from time to time 'clothed himself' with chosen individuals,[2] a prophet here, a king there. But that generation was to be given a new vision of the work of the Spirit. 'Blessed are the eyes which see what you see! For I tell you that many prophets and kings desired to see what you see, and did not see it' (10:23–24). What was then seen for the first time in history was the pouring out of spiritual blessing on *all* who would receive it, as the whole people of God and every individual member of it were put in possession of the gift of the Spirit.

In the first twelve verses of chapter 11, however, God the Holy Spirit is nowhere mentioned, and it may be asked why I have introduced my exposition of this section by two paragraphs all about him. For the subject of these opening verses is prayer, not the Spirit. In them, we see first the *importance* of prayer (11:1–2): Jesus used to pray, his disciples asked him to teach them to do the same, and he responded to this formal request with explicit instruction, thus setting his seal on the importance of the matter. Secondly, we are shown the *substance* of prayer (11:2–4). The 'Lord's prayer', even in this briefer version (the fuller one is in Matthew 6:9–13), is a model, not

[1] Acts 2:16–17.   [2] See Jdg. 6:34, RV mg.

in the sense that these are the actual words with which we should pray, but in the sense that these are the lines along which we should pray. Thirdly, there is a parable dealing with the *practice* of prayer (11:5–10), and fourthly, two mini-parables illustrating the *basis* of prayer (11:11–13). The former (the story of the friend's importunate request for loaves at midnight) teaches us to pray persistently, not *because* God *will not* answer otherwise, but *as if* he *would not*. In other words, it is about the practice of prayer, or our part in it. It does not illustrate God's side of the matter. The basis of prayer, or God's part in it, is the subject of the sayings about the father who naturally will not give his son a serpent or a scorpion if the boy has asked for a fish or an egg. At the receiving end of our importunate prayer is a Father who does not need to be importuned, but is only too eager to give the best of answers.

Now it is in this connection—what the Father gives in answer to prayer—that the Holy Spirit is first mentioned (11:13). Setting the passage in its context, we see how Luke is leading from chapter 10 into chapter 11. The former described 'the way' of Jesus, the way to God. It is the way of single-minded devotion to him; a matter not of achievement, doing all that we can *for* him, but of attitude, bringing all that we are *under* him. When we seek thus single-mindedly to yield ourselves to him (that was the subject of our last section, 9:51– 10:42), what happens? We find that this great Lord is also our heavenly Father, who meets our seeking with his giving. When we ask, seek, and knock, he gives the answer we need (11:9–10). As the response of a human father to his son's need is not one of cynical disregard (11:11–12), neither is God's response to our need anything less than the provision of what Matthew calls 'good things',[3] and what Luke can sum up as the gift of the Spirit (11:13).

Luke has already in the opening verses of chapter 11 condensed this truth into even smaller compass. He places here his version of the Lord's Prayer as a hinge between the two chapters. To pray, 'Hallowed be thy name. Thy kingdom come' (11:2), is to hand over the sovereignty to God: that is chapter 10. To be able to continue, 'Give us each day our daily bread . . . forgive us our sins . . . lead us not into temptation' (11:3–4), is to find that he then supplies all our need: that is what follows in chapter 11. The old life is shed, abandoned to him; then the new is received, and may be characterized as the new life in the Holy Spirit.

[3] Mt. 7:11.

126

The episodes that follow unfold what is meant by this inbreaking of the power of the Spirit.

1. Spiritual revolution (11:14–32)

What Jesus has to say concerning the revolution brought about by the Spirit arises from an incident (11:14ff.) in which a demon-possessed man is exorcized. The miracle provokes two objections, and Jesus replies to each in turn (11:15 answered by 17–28; 11:16 by 29–32).

The first objection concerns what he is doing. His opponents have already made up their minds that he cannot have divine power, so his exorcizing of demons must itself be demonic. To this he replies that, on the contrary, his exorcisms show the power of the Spirit of God at work. They are indeed divine acts of salvation.

The second objection concerns who he must be, to be doing such things. The healings themselves are not reckoned to be sufficient proof that he is a man with divine authority; the objectors want more—an unmistakable 'sign from heaven'. To this he replies that in him alone will they find both salvation and the sign which authenticates the salvation. He is the Saviour.

a. Salvation (11:17–28)

We know that the kingdom of God has come, because salvation has come; and we know that salvation has come, because in this case (in other cases it will express itself in other ways) we see it healing a demon-possessed man (11:20).

And this salvation is the work of the Spirit. Matthew's version of the words of Jesus here shows that the 'finger of God' means the 'Spirit of God'.[4] Perhaps because his whole passage is about the work of the Spirit, Luke records instead this striking metaphor 'finger'. But the Spirit it is. And the salvation which the Spirit brings is very like the kind of thing which has happened often in history, a political coup or 'palace revolution'. This is what has happened in the exorcizing of the demon-possessed man: the evil power is the 'strong man' who 'guards his own palace', but the divine power is the one who is 'stronger than he', and brings off a successful coup (11:21–22).

It is worth noting that for Jesus, as Luke quotes him, the exorcism of demons is a reality; for he appeals to this as a vindication of his

---

[4] Mt. 12:28.

central message—'You may be sure that the kingdom of God has come, by the fact that I can employ his divine power to cast out demons'—and it would be rather curious if he were to rest such a crucial argument on an erroneous belief. That would indeed be a broken reed.

But although it seems that Jesus recognizes exorcism as being in itself a reality, nevertheless here he uses it only as an example of what is true right across the board when the salvation of God breaks into the world. In every case there has to be a revolution. Anyone who needs to be saved, in whatever sense, is being kept under guard in the palace of the 'strong man'. Luke will later quote his friend Paul, in Acts 26:18, as claiming that his mission is to rescue men 'from the power of Satan to God.' Such is the condition of the unsaved, even if they are far less obviously in the grip of the evil power than was the demoniac man.

Furthermore, in no case will there be any lasting value in mere reform, as Jesus goes on to explain. First he describes an evil spirit leaving the person in whom it has been living (11:24ff.). Some think Jesus is here referring to the work of Jewish exorcists; he does not specify, however, because his main point is to show how useless (indeed dangerous) is the expulsion of an evil power, by whatever means, if no corresponding good power comes in to bar the door against its return. And this is always true, whether it is by exorcism or by sheer determination that men try to rid themselves of the evil within them.

Secondly (11:27–28) he seizes upon the exclamation of a woman in the crowd: 'Blessed is the womb that bore you, and the breasts that you sucked!' Bengel's comment, *Bene sentit, sed muliebriter loquitur*,[5] might be unfairly translated 'A nice thought, but how like a woman!' His point really is that there was a good sentiment ('Jesus is a wonderful person') expressed as only a woman would express it ('How blessed to be his mother')—none the worse for that, since Mary herself had said the same in 1:48; and this gave Jesus the opportunity to say that true blessedness does indeed consist in relationship to him, though not the mother-son relationship. It belongs to those into whose hearts he has come with his message of salvation, so that there is no longer any place there for the ousted spirit of evil: 'Blessed rather are those who hear the word of God and keep it!'

[5] Quoted by Plummer, p. 305.

Salvation, then, means more than reformation; it means revolution. Nature abhors a vacuum. Not only must the strong man be overcome; the stronger man must have total victory and take possession of the palace.

This leads Jesus to speak next of himself. He is the stronger man, the one who brings this salvation. He is the Saviour.

b. The Saviour (11:29–32)

Such a revolution, the calling of men 'out of darkness into his marvellous light,' a rescue like that effected long ago—then also by the 'finger of God'—at the time of the exodus,[6] is the work of the Holy Spirit in bringing salvation. But now where exactly is that salvation to be found? To whom do we look to find it?

For those who seek the truth sincerely, there are many pointers towards the one in whom salvation is to be found. Such, for example, are the seven great 'signs', or miracles, recounted in John's Gospel.[7] But for an evil generation there is only one sign to indicate where the truth is to be found. That, says Jesus, is the sign of the prophet Jonah (11:29). The pattern of events in the book of Jonah corresponds to that in the story of the Son of man. Jonah is thrown into the sea and swallowed by the fish, returns three days later to the land of the living, and proclaims God's message to the men of Nineveh; and the career of Jesus shows the same kind of sequence—death, burial, resurrection, proclamation.

The difference between Jonah's sign to Nineveh and Jesus's sign to his own generation is that in the latter there is 'something greater than Jonah' (11:32). Not some*one* greater, you notice: Jesus is not, strictly speaking, comparing *himself* with Jonah. It is the whole thing which is greater, deeper, more *real*. Jonah experienced a kind of death, a kind of burial, and a kind of resurrection, and he went to Nineveh with only an embryonic version of the good news—good, but limited. But in Jesus something greater is happening. The Holy Spirit has broken into the world in power, and by means of a real death, a real burial, and a real resurrection, he is able to offer to the world real salvation, at the deepest possible level. That which the story of Jonah illustrated and foreshadowed is made actual in the person of Jesus.

And it is to Jesus, always, that the Holy Spirit points. 'He will bear witness to *me*.'[8] Jesus is the Saviour.

[6] 1 Pet. 2:9; Ex. 8:19.   [7] *E.g.* Jn. 2:11.   [8] Jn. 15:26.

At Pentecost the age of the Holy Spirit began. Ever since then he has been offering salvation to men—the revolution in which the rule of evil is ousted by the rule of God. That is what he, the 'finger of God', does. And this salvation is located in Jesus, and in him only. He is the Saviour. It is to him that the 'finger of God' points.

2. Spiritual transformation (11:33 – 12:12)

The other side of the Spirit's work is introduced by Luke with a group of sayings about light. Jesus is speaking of the individual man in whom the Spirit has brought about the revolution spoken of above. Just as a lamp is lit, not in order to be hidden, but purposely to illuminate a whole room, so a sound eye means the enlightening of the whole person; in other words, the ability to see things clearly should affect the whole way you act and live (11:33–36).

So once the Spirit has revolutionized a man, or 'cleared his vision', he then sets about transforming him, or bringing his general way of life into line with the way he now sees things. Having lit the lamp, he now lifts it up to shed its rays into every corner of the room.

Luke proceeds to recount conversations of Jesus on this subject, first with Pharisees and then with his own disciples.

a. Outward religion (11:37–54)

Here Jesus is speaking not only to, but also about, Pharisees (11:37, 39). He is not afraid to tell them that their religion, although it is the major preoccupation of their lives, is in fact a hollow sham. They have never allowed the Spirit to bring about the revolution in them and therefore there is no transformation either. They 'cleanse the outside of the cup and of the dish, but inside' they 'are full of extortion and wickedness'; and because there is no change in their real character, he denounces against them the six woes of 11:42–52. Luke spells out the evil of their unrenewed hearts, but it is Matthew who records Jesus's direct and repeated accusation: they are 'hypocrites'.[9] They are acting a part, which is what the word means. Their religious life is simply a role they play; it bears no relation to the kind of person they really are when off-stage. Their religion is no more than an outward show.

---

[9] Mt. 23:13, 15, 23, 25, 27, 29.

b. Inward renewal (12:1–12)

Having spoken to Pharisees about themselves, Jesus now turns to his disciples, and talks to them about themselves. In the former, there had been no revolution, so there was no transformation either. In the latter, by contrast, there has been a revolution; so now there must be a transformation too.

He reminds them first that a day will come when the inner life of men will be exposed. This is what the Pharisees have not understood (12:1–3); everything they do has been contaminated with the leaven of hypocrisy, so that provided the outward appearance is all right, the inward state does not matter. But they are wrong, says Jesus. What you are like inside matters very much, and will one day 'be proclaimed upon the housetops.'

The important thing, therefore, is to consider the welfare of your soul rather than of your body. Be prepared, not for the judgment of any earthly tribunal, but for the judgment of the One who 'has power to cast into hell', Almighty God. Let it be your preoccupation to be, through and through, the kind of person of whom he will approve when that day comes (12:4–5).

If this is your aim, then the revolution will be followed by the transformation of your character into one of trust in God and courage before men (12:6–12). And, once again, it is the Spirit who will accomplish this. His is the power in both respects.

One verse towards the end of this present section has often caused much heart-searching. 'Every one who speaks a word against the Son of man will be forgiven; but he who blasphemes against the Holy Spirit will not be forgiven' (12:10). The first half of the verse has its problems,[10] but it is the second half which is the real stumbling block. What is this 'blasphemy against the Spirit' which can never be forgiven?

There are certain things which even God finds impossible. When we understand that, we begin to understand the nature of this sin which he cannot forgive. For it is impossible for him to lie, or to

[10] If we take it (some commentators do not) that in 12:10 Jesus did use the words 'Son of man', and did mean himself, then we have to explain what might seem to be a contradiction between 12:9 and 12:10a. This passage has been much debated. But those who either acknowledge or deny Jesus (12:8–9) are presumably those to whom the Spirit has revealed who he is; so the denial of the Son in 12:9 corresponds to the blasphemy against the Spirit in 12:10b. Simply to 'speak against him' (12:10a), on the other hand, may mean to do so without understanding who he is.

deny himself, or to contradict himself,[11] and nothing that he has made (including man) can be at one and the same time both Thus and Not-Thus; which means, among other things, that if we *will not* be forgiven, then, in this rational world of his, it is a mere nonsense to say that we *will* be forgiven.[12] It is impossible therefore for God to forgive one who says, 'I will not listen to the Spirit when he brings me the message of forgiveness.' It is impossible for him to save one who says, 'I will not follow the Spirit when he points me to the Saviour.' It is impossible to revolutionize one who says, 'I will not have the Spirit revolutionizing me.' That is the ultimate blasphemy; and against that not even God can do anything. The man who is determined to go to hell will certainly get there.

The readers of Luke's Gospel are thus warned against the unforgivable sin. The Spirit comes to revolutionize their lives, offering salvation in the person of the Saviour Jesus; let them not refuse. He comes to transform their lives into the image of Jesus; let them not refuse that either—for refusal is the blasphemy against the Spirit, and can never be forgiven.

Rather, let them grasp and respond to this central message of the gospel. Chapters 10 and 11 present the two sides of it, and the Lord's Prayer, which forms the hinge between them, condenses it into smaller compass. It is summed up even more briefly in the words which Luke reports as the crystallizing of the earliest message of the Christian church: 'Repent, and ... receive the gift of the Holy Spirit.'[13] They come to Christ in repentance and faith. That is chapter 10, their way to him. But as they do so, they find that he comes to them—that is chapter 11—with the gift of the Holy Spirit, and in him all the blessings of the new age.

[11] Heb. 6:18; 2 Tim. 2:13; Num. 23:19.

[12] There is a relevant and illuminating paragraph in C. S. Lewis, *The Pilgrim's Regress*[3] (Geoffrey Bles, 1943), p. 181.

[13] Acts 2:38.

12:13 – 13:21
'When he comes'

*One of the multitude. .aid to him, 'Teacher, bid my brother divide the
inheritance with me.' But he said to him, 'Man, who made me a judge or
divider over you?' (12:13–14).*

*'Do you think that I have come to give peace on earth? No, I tell you, but
rather division' (12:51).*

*He said therefore, 'What is the kingdom of God like? And to what shall I
compare it? It is like a grain of mustard seed which a man took and sowed in
his garden; and it grew and became a tree, and the birds of the air made nests
in its branches.'*
*And again he said, 'To what shall I compare the kingdom of God? It is
like leaven which a woman took and hid in three measures of meal, till it was
all leavened' (13:18–21).*

This section opens with Jesus being asked, as a person of authority
and influence, to make a ruling in a legal squabble (12:13). We tend
to read his reply as a disclaimer of any such authority: 'Who made *me*
a judge or divider over you?' If this were his meaning, he would have
the sympathy of every clergyman who finds himself asked to make
pronouncements, sign forms, join committees, and generally 'lend
his weight' to matters which have little to do with his real work! A
study of what follows, however, suggests that the disclaimer is to the
effect, not that Jesus has no such authority, but that his authority is
not to be appealed to in questions such as this one: 'Who made me a
judge or divider over *you?*' The applicant for 'legal aid' was right in
recognizing Jesus as a 'divider', or 'arbitrator' (AG), but he has come
to judge in matters far more important than that of a disputed will.
The same thought is picked up part way through this section, in

12:51–53. Jesus is truly, and ruthlessly, a divider. By reason of the message he brings, 'henceforth in one house there will be five divided, three against two and two against three'. A son will be found to be following the way of Jesus, while his father ignores the call. A mother will have received the gift of the Spirit, while her daughter rejects the offer. Matthew has the more graphic image: 'I have not come to bring peace, but a sword'.[1] But Luke's phrase, though less vivid, is perhaps deliberately chosen so as to recall the 'division' words of 12:13–14, an incident which only he records.

The section ends with Luke's version of the parables of the mustard seed and the leaven,[2] which seem to be meant as a summing up of the previous sixty-four verses: 'He said *therefore* . . .' (13:18). In other words, *because of* the instruction he has been giving from 12:13 onwards, he tells these twin stories as an apt conclusion to it. Both the mustard shrub and the leaven are pictures of the kingdom of God; and the divisions which, as we shall see, are the subject of Jesus's teaching throughout this section, are in every case between those in whose experience the kingdom has become a living reality, and those who are still, to a greater or lesser extent, unaware of it. The keen judicial eye of Jesus the Divider is distinguishing between the garden in which the mustard seed has grown into a great shrub, large enough to house nesting birds, and the garden which is still bare; between the dough in which the yeast is working, to make it rise as bread, and the dough which will turn out to be nothing but flat biscuit.

Once more, both the likeness and the unlikeness between Luke's method and John's are noticeable. Again Luke records a sequence of incidents to convey a message; again John puts over the same message, but in quite a different way—a single memorable sentence from the account of Jesus's interview with Nicodemus: 'This is the judgment, that the light has come into the world.' Jesus, the Light of the world, shines into the hearts of men and exposes their true character. They are divided, by that searching beam, into those who do evil, hate the light, and do not come to the light, lest their deeds should be exposed, and those who do what is true and come to the light, that it may be clearly seen that their deeds have been wrought in God.[3]

[1] Mt. 10:34. Conversely, it is Luke who has 'finger of God' for Matthew's 'Spirit of God (11:20 = Mt. 12:28); see above, p. 127.
[2] See Mt. 13:31–33.
[3] Jn. 3:19–21.

134

1. 'This is the judgment . . .'

Every episode in this section shows that Jesus, far from disclaiming the function of a 'judge or divider' (12:14), is in fact claiming it. He is sorting men out, according to their attitudes in a variety of matters. He does come to judge and to divide—not in a trivial legal disagreement, but in the basic characters of men. '*This* is the judgment.'

a. In practical matters (12:13–34)

The parable of the 'Rich Fool' arises naturally from the request and reply with which this section has begun. Here in the opening verses (12:13–14) is a man determined to get his share of an inheritance; and he provides a living illustration of the warning which Jesus immediately gives—'Beware of all covetousness' (12:15). To be rightly aware of the values of life will enable a man to put 'things' in the proper place. The possessions of this life belong to this life; and since this life is less important than the next, the things of this life should be valued less than the things of eternity.

The rich man in the story is sensible enough according to his own lights. He is looking 'many years' ahead, and has provided for them with 'ample goods'. The snag is that he has not taken into account the life of the world to come, where his plentiful earthly possessions will be no manner of use to him.

Only Luke records this story. By including it here he gives an apt introduction to the familiar sayings about the ravens and the lilies, and the lesson they teach concerning God's provision for his creatures, a passage more familiar perhaps in Matthew's version as part of the sermon on the mount.[4] Food and clothing are a necessary part of human life in this world, and 'your Father knows that you need them' (12:30). Your main concern, however, should not be the laying up of treasure on earth—that was the mistake of the wealthy farmer in the story—but the provision of 'a treasure in the heavens' which will ensure your wellbeing in the next world (12:33). That is what being 'rich toward God' means (*cf.* 12:21), and it is the characteristic concern of the disciples of Jesus, those who have God as their Father (12:22, 30, 32).

How then do we order the practical matters of life, as we look into the future? The keen eye of Jesus is dividing between those who are

---

[4] Mt. 6:25–33.

taken up with the needs of the immediate future and the things of this life, and those who see that the ultimate future is far more important and are chiefly concerned to provide for the next life.

b. In spiritual matters (12:35–48)

When Jesus goes on to speak in terms of a household with its master and its employees, Peter wants the metaphor explained. His question (12:41) may mean, 'Is this about people in general, or about your disciples in particular?'—since it was to the crowds that Jesus's parables were normally directed (8:9–10; Mt. 13:34). More probably, Peter sees that the parable is for the 'household' (the Lord's people) only, and his question means, 'Is this—this high honour promised to watchful servants (12:37)—for your disciples in general, or for us, the twelve, in particular?' In either case, it is upon spiritual responsibility that Jesus's searchlight of judgment is now turned. The more you have, the greater your prospect of honour—and the greater your peril.

In the parable, the master of the house is away from home and has left his servants to their various responsibilities. When he returns he expects to find them watchful (12:35–40) and faithful (12:41–48). Amid all the practical concerns of this life, do they always have an eye to his possible return, or will his coming be like that of a thief in the night, catching them unawares? Furthermore, will they occupy themselves with his business, or will they take advantage of his delay to waste and spoil their opportunities, eating and drinking and making merry, and showing themselves no better than the rich fool (12:45 and 19)? Thus he divides between those of his servants whom he will find awake, and those who will be asleep and unprepared; between those who will be found engaged in faithful service, and those who will be caught abusing their privileges.

Whether or not the first half of the parable speaks of degrees of reward in the after-life,[5] the second half certainly seems to point to degrees of punishment. Jesus does not mince his words when he describes the householder's displeasure with the employees who fail in watchfulness and faithfulness.

The fate of the servant who roundly abuses his position of trust (12:46) raises the question of the possible forfeiting of eternal life. Once the Lord's servant, always his servant? The commentaries do not help greatly; my own thought is that a punishment so severe (put

---

[5] Such a thing is clearly hinted at elsewhere (19:15ff.; cf. 1 Cor. 3:12ff.).

with the 'faithless, unbelieving',[6] or in Matthew's version 'with the hypocrites', who are 'sentenced to hell'[7]) must be for so-called church leaders whose conduct shows they were never truly Christ's servants in the first place.

c. In historical matters (12:49–59)

Next Jesus turns the attention of his hearers, disciples and multitudes alike, to a different type of question: that of his coming into the world (12:49, 51), and 'the present time' (12:56). The coming of Jesus, and the events of that 'time', were pregnant with meaning. He was not just another rabbi, not even another prophet. A baleful fire flickered around his path, a fearful baptism lay ahead of him, the even tenor of life would turn to strife and anguish on his account (12:49–53). What do these things mean?

And meaning they must have, just as clouds from the western sea mean rain, and wind from the southern desert means heat. The advent of the Carpenter of Nazareth is the most significant happening in all human history. But the majority of men, who can see meanings and connections and relationships in most of the phenomena in the world around them, and all the more so as their civilization becomes more sophisticated and rationalistic, are rank hypocrites when they look at Jesus Christ and pretend that they can make nothing of the remarkable facts of his life, death, and resurrection.

Well, a lawsuit is in progress, and a writ is being issued, and a heavy sentence is impending, and those who ignore the plain signs of the way things are going will have only themselves to blame when they are finally called to account (12:57–59).

Thus Jesus distinguishes between those who will not see his crucial place at the centre of human life and history, and those who as his disciples are beginning to glimpse, however dimly, the meaning of it all.

d. In moral matters (13:1–5)

Perhaps the mention in this paragraph of two recent disasters, one a political atrocity and the other presumably a sheer accident, arose directly out of what Jesus had just said ('There were some present *at that very time* who told him . . .', 13:1). Since Jesus had just condemned those who refused to see any significance in the 'signs of the

---

[6] AG.   [7] Mt. 24:51; 23:13–33.

times', his questioners may well have quoted to him the massacre of the Galileans in order to ask what the spiritual significance of that event was supposed to be.

From Jesus's reply, it seems that they will have jumped to the conclusion that, as there is no smoke without fire, so there is no suffering without sin. Deaths as shocking as those of the men of Galilee slaughtered during a religious service, or as pointless as those of the men of Siloam buried in the collapse of a tower, surely mean that the victims must have been very bad to deserve such a fate.

This view is precisely that of Job's friends, in the book which more than any other part of Scripture is concerned with the problem of suffering. Since you suffer, they tell Job, you must be a sinner; for if you were right with God, things would go well with you. But it is a view contradicted both by Job and by Jesus, and indeed by Christian experience. It is true that there are particular cases where God has made 'the punishment fit the crime' by an immediate come-back in the sinner's circumstances. But his basic rule, ever since the time of the flood,[8] has been that mankind in general is not treated in this world according to its deserts, and reaps the final reward of wickedness only at the judgment in the world to come.

Here, then, Jesus is dividing those who in moral matters imagine that there is a direct connection between sin and suffering—some men are better, some are worse, and it is in this life that each takes the appropriate consequences—from those who can see that man is not (fortunately) treated here and now with strict justice. 'Use every man after his desert, and who should 'scape whipping?'[9] The fact is that we are all sinners, all in need of repentance, all deserving of punishment, and all preserved from the wrath of God—at least until judgment day—purely by his mercy.

e. In religious matters (13:6–17)

Both the parable and the miracle which Luke records next (concerning the barren fig tree and the crippled woman) are about religion: not real inward religion, whose spiritual and moral aspects have been touched on already (12:35–48; 13:1–5), but religion as an institution. It is on the religious system of Judaism as it existed in the time of Jesus that we see the searchlight of his gaze now turned.

For the fig tree and the vineyard are symbols of the Jewish nation, which God had cultivated and cherished over many centuries in the

---

[8] Gn. 8:21–22.   [9] Shakespeare, *Hamlet*, II. ii. 561.

hope that it would be spiritually fruitful. But its special relationship with him had, by and large, turned into a barren religion.

Some details of the parable of 13:6–9 are debatable, but the main thrust of it is clear—that the tree is being given a last chance to prove itself. Matthew and Mark tell how Jesus later acted out this parable in real life;[10] it was the week before his crucifixion when he found by the Bethany road a fig tree which actually did have no fruit, and which he declared would never bear again. By that time the last chance had gone, and 'the fig tree withered at once'.[11]

In the same way, the sabbath day was an epitome of Jewish religion: a gift from God, full of spiritual meaning, but so fossilized and encrusted with traditions that it had become practically lifeless. To Jews such as the ruler of the synagogue, 'indignant because Jesus had healed on the sabbath' (13:14), the re-creation of the crippled woman, so far from being most appropriate to the day, was most *in*appropriate to it—a complete inversion of the truth, which in practice not even the hypocritical Jews themselves really held to (13:15–16).

Again the inexorable judgment of Jesus is dividing between those whose religion is a mere show of leaves, and those who really produce fruit; between those whose religious observance is a travesty of the 'sabbath rest' of 'the people of God',[12] and those for whom it is a matter of rejoicing and praise to the Lord (13:13, 17).

2. ' . . . That the light has come into the world'

In all these aspects of life men are shown up for what they really are, and it is very plain that what shows them up is the keen judicial eye of Jesus. He distinguishes between truth and falsehood, folly and wisdom, the blind and the seeing, the dead and the living. It is as he comes into each situation that the distinctions are revealed. He is indeed 'a judge or divider' (12:14).

a. His coming in the past

As a simple matter of history, the coming of Jesus into the world in the times of which we are reading was the coming of a judge and divider. These events from the days of his incarnation are factual examples of what happens whenever the light comes and shows up how things really are.

[10] Mt. 21:18–20; Mk. 11:12–14, 20–21.
[11] Mt. 21:19. [12] Heb. 4:9

The passage we have just considered is perhaps the clearest instance of this in the present section. Jesus is the owner of the fig tree who 'came seeking fruit'. Metaphorically, he comes into the vineyard, and by his inspection of the tree its fate is decided. Literally, he comes into the synagogue, and the result of his coming is that the crippled woman is physically 'made straight' (13:13) while the president of the synagogue is shown to be spiritually warped. There is the distinction made plain. 'As he said this, all his adversaries were put to shame; and all the people rejoiced at all the glorious things that were done by him' (13:17).

His coming into the world in the first century of our era was not, however, to be his only coming. Others are spoken of in this section. All of them, though, are comings of a judge, and the divisions made by Jesus in the days of his flesh are foretastes of the judgment he makes whenever he comes to men.

b. His coming in the future

There lies ahead for every man a final encounter with Jesus the Judge. It may be at death, when he hears the words which in the parable of 12:16–21 God speaks to the rich fool: 'This night your soul is required of you.' It may be at the return of Jesus, 'when he comes' as the householder came back unexpectedly (12:37, 43). In either case it is the end of opportunity, and one's finished life is laid open before the Judge's eye. He will then divide all whose minds have been centred on the things of this life from all whose treasure has been in heaven.

This future coming is both certain and final. From the judgment of that day there will be no appeal. It will be the 'day of wrath' of which Paul writes in Romans 2:5–8, 'when God's righteous judgment will be revealed'—when 'he will render to every man according to his works: to those who by patience in well-doing seek for glory and honour and immortality, he will give eternal life; but for those who are factious and do not obey the truth, but obey wickedness, there will be wrath and fury'. The equivalent passage in Matthew's Gospel is the description of all nations gathered before the Son of man's judgment throne, to be separated 'one from another as a shepherd separates the sheep from the goats', and to go, on the basis of that division, either into eternal punishment or into eternal life.[13]

[13] Mt. 25:31–46.

c. His coming in the present

In the meantime, he comes to men even now, day by day, with the good news of the kingdom of God. 'It is your Father's good pleasure to give you the kingdom' (12:32). While there is still time, he makes clear that, whereas some have closed with the offer and become his disciples, others have still not accepted it. Throughout the section he exposes the wisdom of the former and the need of the latter. Unspoken but implied is the urgent appeal to heed the lessons of the previous two sections, as to how man must come to seek God in penitence and emptiness, and how God will then come to meet man in salvation and blessing. Will those lessons be heeded, or not? This is the judgment.

13:22 – 14:35

The narrow door

He went on his way through towns and villages, teaching, and journeying toward Jerusalem. And some one said to him, 'Lord, will those who are saved be few?' And he said to them, 'Strive to enter by the narrow door' (13:22–24).

Jesus is 'on his way' to his crucifixion at Jerusalem. In describing various events in the context of that journey, Luke also is on his way through this central teaching section of his gospel; and we, on our way through our study of it, reach a group of seven episodes which Luke has linked together, in each of which Jesus responds to something that has been said, or that has happened, in his presence.

It may well be that Luke intends Jesus's first words in this section to be the heading for the whole of it. Certainly the picture he places before our mind's eye can refer to all seven episodes. It is the memorable picture of the 'narrow door' (13:24).

The 'narrowness' of the Christian faith is a scandal to many. But if we understand it in its proper biblical sense, we need make no apology for it. The footballer cannot score by kicking the ball just anywhere in his opponents' end of the field; he is limited to the space between the goalposts. The pilot cannot land his plane in any field that takes his fancy; he is restricted to the limits of the airfield if he is to make a safe landing. Here the issue is infinitely greater, and the restrictions correspondingly more important. It is a matter of *salvation*, Luke's constant theme: 'Will those who are *saved* be few?' It is the door to eternal life, to heaven, to the kingdom of God, which is narrow. And this whole section emphasizes that the way to salvation is only to be found within certain limits.

1. The narrow door of urgency (13:23–35)

'On his way ... toward Jerusalem' (13:22) Jesus was met by a questioner who wanted to know how numerous the company of the saved would be (13:23), and by a group of Pharisees who came to warn him of King Herod's malice towards him (13:31). Most of this half of the chapter consists of his reply to each in turn.

It seems from 13:31 that these first two episodes took place one immediately after the other, though Luke is the only evangelist to include the second of them in his Gospel. Perhaps he realized that because of the context in which he was relating the incident of 13:23–30, the incident of the following verses might also be included as an underlining of the same point.

a. To the questioner about the number of the saved (13:23–30)
In two respects Jesus's reply to the question 'Will those who are saved be few?' takes an unexpected turn. In the first place, he follows his own common practice of changing a theological debating point into a personal challenge: the questioner asked about a vague 'them', Jesus answers with a direct 'you'. But in the second place, the significant words of his little parable about the householder's locked door are really those with which it starts: '*When once* the householder has risen up and shut the door ...'. That is, to a question concerning the *number* of the saved, Jesus gives an answer concerning the *time* of salvation. At present the door is still open. But 'when once' locking-up time has arrived, the chance to get in will be past. On whatever grounds the latecomers may base their appeal to be recognized by the Lord and admitted to his kingdom—they say they have met him; they say they have listened to him—the fact remains that they did not actually take the opportunity to go in through his narrow door when it was open before them.

This point, that it is time which is limited rather than numbers, is emphasized by what apparently happened immediately afterwards, when 'some Pharisees came' and brought Jesus a warning that he was in danger from King Herod.

b. To the messengers from Herod (13:31–35)
Herod's are idle threats. Jesus's programme continues quite unaffected by them. He has two more 'days', as it were, of ministry, and on the third 'day' he will be finished, and that 'must' happen, regardless of Herod (13:32–33).

143

At this point Luke inserts the tragic words which according to Matthew were actually spoken during the week before the passion. For the Jewish people's opportunity for salvation corresponded to the same pattern. The two 'days' of Jesus's exorcizing and healing ministry are the 'days' in which he was often wanting to gather Jerusalem's children to him (13:34); and the third 'day', which ends his work, also ends their chance to respond (13:35).

Both episodes, then, stress the urgency of the message. The door is narrow in the sense that there is not unlimited *time* to enter through it. 'Behold, now is the acceptable time; behold, now is the day of salvation'[1]—tomorrow may be too late. With this solemn word Jesus begins the teaching of this section: strive *now* to enter, for the time is coming when many will seek to enter and will not be able (13:24).

Urgency is not the same as panic. The words we have just read, in Jesus's message to Herod, themselves remind us that he is the Master of time. In every case, wherever one man is honestly seeking the way in to the kingdom, wherever another is faithfully pointing it out, the Lord knows how long the process requires. Before time began, indeed, he had allowed quite as much of it as would ever be needed for the purpose of saving all who would ever want to be saved. Jesus's words about the narrow door of urgency do not entail panic preaching or stampede decisions. But they do focus on the all-important Now, and the necessity of an honest use of the present moment.

2. The narrow door of humiliation (14:1-24)

Luke indicates that the next four incidents all happened on the same occasion (compare 14:1, 7, 12, 15). At a dinner party to which Jesus has been invited, he speaks first to lawyers and Pharisees who are present, then to the guests in general, then to his host, and finally to a fellow-guest who has interjected a pious comment. It is not chronologically, however, but thematically, that Luke links the group of incidents as a whole with what has gone before ('one sabbath', 14:1). Here are four responses of Jesus to the attitudes of people at the party, and they illustrate another aspect of the narrowness of the door of salvation.

a. To the lawyers and Pharisees (14:1-6)
A sick man was present, and no doubt the Pharisees expected Jesus to

---

[1] 2 Cor. 6:2.

heal him, and thereby to discredit himself as one who flouted the law of Moses (which according to them forbade healing on the sabbath).[2] Jesus's answer to their unspoken test question was itself a question, in fact a double one. First, 'Is it lawful to heal on the sabbath, or not?' And 'they were silent', for neither answer would do: 'Yes' would brand them as law-breakers, 'No' would expose their heartlessness.

So Jesus puts a second question, which shows up their religious beliefs for the poor things they are. Arguably, Jewish law may forbid the rescue of an animal fallen into a well on the sabbath; but if it's *your* animal, says Jesus, you won't think twice about it, will you? The law of mercy (or of self-interest) will take precedence over the law of Moses. So much for the inflexible religious principles to which they pay such ardent lip-service!

The Jews of Jesus's time have no monopoly of inconsistent beliefs. Any number of people today will talk about 'One above' whom they acknowledge but ignore, will claim to be 'Christian' while denying what Christ says they ought to be, and will rest content with 'believing' in a religion which they have neither the patience nor the courage to follow through to its conclusions. The man who wishes to pass through the narrow doorway of salvation will have to discard such half-baked religious notions before he can do so.

b. To the guests (14:7–11)

It was on that particular occasion that Jesus 'marked how they chose the places of honour' (14:7), but the lesson they needed to learn is one of universal application: 'Every one who exalts himself will be humbled' (14:11). 'Recognition eludes those who demand it',[3] and this is true at the deepest level in the matter of salvation. There, more than anywhere, the man who reckons he qualifies will discover that by this very fact he does not. To claim God's approval as a right, on the grounds of one's position in the church, or one's reputation in the community, or even one's good opinion of oneself, is a positive disqualification. There is no entry through the narrow door for the one who is laden with status symbols and a sense of his own importance.

c. To the host (14:12–14)

Jesus's third word is addressed 'to the man who had invited him'. It

---

[2] See above, pp. 75f.   [3] Caird, p. 175.

is unlikely to be a personal accusation, since his host can hardly have had a return invitation in mind when he invited the poor preacher to his house, but again it is a general principle which could apply to anyone—the danger of calculating possible rewards. Real disinterested goodness is rare indeed; so much of what we do is coloured by the hope, if not the intention, that it may in some way work out to our own benefit.

Such a concern for personal advantage is another thing that will have to go if one is to get in through the narrow door. There, more than anywhere, self-interest is inadmissible. The humble aim of the would-be entrant should rather be, in the words of the old Latin hymn-writer, to seek his God

> not for the hope of winning heaven,
> Nor of escaping hell;
>
> Not with the hope of gaining aught,
> Not seeking a reward;
> But as thyself hast lovèd me,
> O ever-loving Lord.[4]

d. To the pious fellow-guest (14:15–24)

Like that of the woman in 11:27, it was a blameless sentiment— 'Blessed is he who shall eat bread in the kingdom of God!'—but also a thoughtless one. The majority of the people present could no doubt have uttered the same words in all sincerity. But how will it be, replies Jesus, when the day of the kingdom-feast actually comes?

In the parable he tells, the guests who had accepted the first invitation all found something better to do when, according to custom, the reminder arrived on the date itself. Zahn remarks on 'the diversity of their arguments and the similarity of their intention'.[5] One had a field, another some oxen, a third his new bride; but 'all alike' placed the invitation to the banquet lower down their scale of values. And to prefer anything whatever to God's invitation is to debar oneself from entry through the narrow door. All the preferences must go.

So a man may approach the doorway to the kingdom bringing his own religious ideas, his own status and reputation, his own calculated advantage, or his own scale of values. But he will have to shed

---

[4] Edward Caswall (tr.), My God, I love Thee!
[5] Quoted by Geldenhuys, p. 396.

every one of these things if he is to pass through that door. There is no room for them. Naked he came into the world, naked he will go out of it, and in the same way it is naked that he must pass from his unconverted life into the life of the kingdom of God.

So it is a narrow door of humiliation by which a man reaches salvation. The guests come to the gathering in all their finery, and Jesus strips them bare. They come to fill themselves with good things, and he sweeps the table clean. He puts down the mighty from their thrones, and the rich he sends empty away.

3. The narrow door of commitment (14:25–32)

Jesus's seventh word is spoken to the 'great multitudes' which 'accompanied him'. For much of his career he had an enthusiastic following among the ordinary people. When he spoke to them of the kingdom of God, they generally assumed that he was talking about the resurgence of their own nation in a political sense, and that he himself intended to be the new King of the Jews, overthrowing the invader Pilate and the pretender Herod. So they were eager to see the new king's triumph, and, no doubt, to benefit from it.

But, as Caird points out, Jesus was 'calling not for spectators but for recruits.'[6] When he called men to follow him, he meant them not to tag along behind him out of curiosity, but to throw in their lot with him in commitment.

In four searching statements Jesus outlines the narrow door of commitment. There is the necessity first to hate one's relatives! It sounds strange to us, perhaps, but 'to love this and to hate that' is a typical biblical way of expressing preference: 'to love this *rather than* that'. As I have suggested elsewhere, 'Love for parents . . . is to be *so far surpassed* by love for him that it will seem in comparison like hatred.'[7] Next there is the necessity to follow Jesus even in his cross-bearing—a discipleship that is prepared even to die with him. Finally there are the two pictures of the building which has to be costed, and the battle which has to be planned, as a whole. What Jesus requires is *total* service, and we have to reckon whether we have 'enough to complete it'.

In these ways Jesus shows how narrow the door is in this third respect. Total commitment means that there is no space to squeeze through the doorway into the kingdom if we are cluttered with

---

[6] Caird, p. 178.
[7] *I Saw Heaven Opened*, p. 133.

reservations and provisos, with ifs and buts.

The closing verses of the chapter (14:33–35) are a summary of all the lessons Jesus has been teaching in this section. It is only he who is prepared to 'renounce all' who will be able to enter through that narrow door. It is no use hoping for another chance, or for a less uncomfortable stripping, or for a less total yielding. You can only be a disciple if you discard all sloth, all pretensions, all reservations. That is what it means to be a disciple. That (to change the metaphor) is the distinctive saltness of the salt, the thing that makes it what it is, the discipleship which characterizes the disciples of Jesus. The time is *now*. The person concerned is *you*, just as you are. The demand is *everything*.

15:1–32
Joy in heaven

Here is a chapter full of good things. After three introductory verses, Luke begins with the story of the lost sheep (15:4–7), which Matthew also relates. [1] Alongside it he places a similar story, that of the lost silver coin (15:8–10), not recorded in any of the other Gospels. To these he adds another, longer than the first two put together and told in a rather different way, but still recognizably on the same subject. This third story, which is perhaps (along with the story of the good Samaritan) the most familiar and best loved of all the parables of Jesus, is that of the 'prodigal son' (15:11–32). Prodigal the young man was, wasteful and spendthrift with his inheritance; but as we shall see, it is even more to the point to realize his lost-ness, and to think of the three parables as being equally concerned with the finding of what is lost.

Our method here will be to consider the parables first separately, then together, and finally in the context of the preceding chapters. As we do so it will become clear that once more the great theme of salvation underlies Luke's narrative.

1. The 'who' of salvation

The three parables obviously differ in their details, and it seems unlikely that so fastidious a writer as Luke would narrate the third, or even the second, merely to underline the meaning of the first. It is true that the basic lesson is the same in all three, as we shall see when considering them together; although we are not actually told in so many words that the shepherd or the housewife or the father represents God, the plain meaning of the chapter is that, just as there is

[1] Mt. 18:12ff.

joy when any shepherd or any housewife or any father recovers a loss, so there is joy in heaven when a sinner is reunited with God. But it is improbable that Jesus (or Luke) intended to do no more than make the same point three times over; and in the context of Scripture as a whole it is arguable that the three illustrations were chosen with an eye to the different shades of meaning they would convey. Whose is the rejoicing which Jesus describes when in each case the lost one is recovered?

a. The shepherd

Unexpectedly, the actual word is not used in 15:4–7. But the description of a man owning a hundred sheep and going out to find the one which had strayed would have conjured up immediately in the minds of Jewish hearers one of the basic images of the Old Testament, that of the Shepherd of Israel. In a society which for hundreds of years had been basically agricultural, the shepherd was in every sense a familiar feature of the landscape. But for the same reason, his person and work had also acquired spiritual significance in helping Israel to understand God himself. However much the shepherd's calling might be despised by official Judaism,[2] it had been honoured by God's taking it as a picture of his own care for his people. 'He will feed his flock like a shepherd, he will gather the lambs in his arms, he will carry them in his bosom, and gently lead those that are with young', says Isaiah.[3] In the prophecy of Ezekiel, God goes further—literally: 'I myself will search for my sheep, and will seek them out. As a shepherd seeks out his flock when some of his sheep have been scattered abroad, so will I seek out my sheep; and I will rescue them from all places where they have been scattered . . . I myself will be the shepherd of my sheep . . . And you are my sheep, the sheep of my pasture, and I am your God, says the Lord God.'[4] And Psalm 23, perhaps the best-known of all the psalms, scarcely needs quoting: 'The Lord is my shepherd . . . He restores my soul.'[5]

It is no surprise that in New Testament days the title is taken over

[2] 'As a class shepherds had a bad reputation. The nature of their calling kept them from observing the ceremonial law which meant so much to religious people. More regrettable was their unfortunate habit of confusing "mine" with "thine" as they moved about the country. They were considered unreliable and were not allowed to give testimony in the law-courts' (Morris, p. 84).

[3] Is. 40:11.

[4] Ezk. 34:11–12, 15, 31; and see the whole chapter.

[5] Ps. 23:1, 3.

by the one whom Christians have learned to think of as the good Shepherd, the great Shepherd, and the chief Shepherd,[6] our Lord Jesus Christ. When we realize all that the imagery of shepherd and sheep has meant spiritually to the people of God, both before and since the time of Christ, it is perverse to suppose that the parable of these verses was told by Jesus, or recorded by Luke, simply as an example of someone—anyone—rejoicing at the recovery of a loss. There could hardly be a more apt illustration of the joyful finding of a lost sinner by the Lord himself, and, more specifically, by the Lord Jesus.

b. The father

We by-pass for the moment the parable of the lost silver, and moving on to that of the lost son, consider how its lesson may differ from the lesson of the lost sheep.

Some commentators, moving away from the traditional interpretation of the parable, have pointed out that nowhere does it state in so many words that the father whom it describes stands for God. This is true. It is also true, however, that God *is* the Father 'from whom all fatherhood, earthly or heavenly, derives its name',[7] and there is a perfectly obvious likeness, in fact, between the father in the story and our Father in heaven—namely, that there is unbounded joy in the father's house when the lost son comes home. It is the 'moral' which Luke has actually spelt out after each of the other two parables (15:7, 10), but which is so clear within this one that he will not gild the lily by adding it.

c. The woman with the lamp

Reverting now to the second parable, we have enough evidence to suggest that there may be some distinctive meaning in the picture of a woman with a lamp seeking a lost silver coin. In the first place, as we have seen, there is good reason to suppose that, while the shepherd's joy and the father's joy do represent in general 'joy in heaven over one sinner who repents' (15:7), the two figures also represent in particular the seeking Son and 'the waiting Father'.[8] It would not therefore be surprising if the woman were meant to represent something more than just a seeker of what is lost. Secondly,

---

[6] Jn. 10:11, 14; Heb. 13:20; 1 Pet. 5:4.   [7] Eph. 3:15, JBP.

[8] The title of Helmut Thielicke's fine book on this and other parables (Clarke, 1960).

151

having in mind the Christian doctrine of the Trinity (and ignoring for the moment any doubts about whether we are forcing Scripture into too tidy a pattern!), we would naturally presume that if Son and Father are portrayed in two of the parables, it would not be altogether unexpected if the remaining one portrayed the Holy Spirit. Thirdly, we are going to find a parallelism between two major sections of Luke's Gospel. Using the titles I have given to my own divisions of the text, the overall sequence of thought from 9:51 to 13:21 seems to be that when the sinner finds 'The way' to God (9:51 – 10:42), God meets him with 'The gift of the Spirit' (11:1 – 12:12), and it is Jesus, 'When he comes' (12:13 – 13:21), who brings about this critical encounter. A similar overall view of what follows, from 13:22 to 18:14, reveals a similar sequence. Again there is man's approach to God, through 'The narrow door' (13:22 – 14:35); again there is God's welcome, 'Joy in heaven' (15:1–32); again there is 'The challenge' (16:1 – 18:14) as the necessity of this encounter is brought home to Luke's readers. Now in the first of these two cycles Luke is at pains to point out an important aspect of the encounter. 'To those who ask him' the Son promises that the Father will give the Holy Spirit (11:13). The mediator of the gift is the Son; the giver of it is the Father; and the gift itself is the Spirit. Hence the title I have suggested for the section 11:1 – 12:12. Again, therefore, it would not be unexpected if, when we reached the corresponding point in the second cycle, we were to find all three Persons of the Trinity involved in the welcome to the returning sinner.

The upshot is that the symbolic meanings often attached both to 'woman' and to 'lamp' elsewhere in Scripture may well be the meanings we are intended to see in this parable. The church in Old Testament and New is the Lord's bride,[9] and as a community through which the Spirit reveals God's truth it is also a light;[10] in the picture-book of Revelation the symbols of woman and light are both used to depict the people of God.[11] If Luke 15:8–10 is meant to have this added significance, we may see in it the Spirit of God lighting the church's way as she sets about the divine work of seeking the lost.

So C. H. Spurgeon expounds the chapter in one of his sermons. 'The third parable would be likely to be misunderstood without the

[9] Is. 54:5; Ezk. 16:8; Eph. 5:23ff.
[10] Mt. 5:14ff.; Phil. 2:15.
[11] Rev. 1:20; 4:5; 12:1–17; 19:7ff.; 21:9ff.

first and the second. We have sometimes heard it said—here is the prodigal received as soon as he comes back, no mention being made of a Saviour who seeks and saves him. Is it possible to teach all truths in one single parable? Does not the first one speak of the shepherd seeking the lost sheep? Why need repeat what had been said before? It has also been said that the prodigal returned of his own free will, for there is no hint of the operation of a superior power upon his heart, it seems as if he himself spontaneously says, "I will arise, and go unto my Father." The answer is, that the Holy Spirit's work had been clearly described in the second parable, and needed not to be introduced again. If you put the three pictures in a line, they represent the whole compass of salvation . . . yet each one is distinct from the other, and by itself instructive.'[12]

We see in this chapter, then, the great scheme of the trinitarian salvation, and, viewing each parable separately, the three Persons of the Trinity as they are engaged in it. *Who* is concerned with the salvation of man? It is the triune God himself. It is his 'property' which is precious but lost, his own sheep and his own silver and his own son, and it is he who longs to have it restored and rejoices when he has recovered it.

2. The 'why' of salvation

The three parables are like three musical instruments, which, although each makes a different type of sound, are nevertheless playing the same tune. The distinctive tone-qualities we have noticed in considering each one separately. But as soon as we consider them together we can hear that their three melodies are identical. The sheep is lost, then found (15: 4, 6); the silver is lost, then found (15:8–9); the son is lost, then found (15:24, 32).

The salvation which is the fundamental theme of Luke's Gospel is here expounded from two points of view, summed up in the phrase 'lost and found'. All three parables taken together show us man's misery in being lost, and God's joy in finding him. It is on account of this misery and this joy that the great plan of salvation has been brought about.

---

[12] C. H. Spurgeon, 'The Lost Silver Piece', in *The Treasury of the New Testament*, II (Marshall Morgan & Scott, n.d.), p. 1.

a. Man's misery in being lost

If the figures of shepherd, housewife, and father are appropriate symbols for the triune God who saves, then the objects of their concern are equally symbolic of the lost-ness of man.

As the shepherd is a true picture of the Son, going to any length and making any sacrifice in order to reach and rescue the sheep,[13] so by the same token the sheep demonstrates one aspect of the human predicament: wandering on and on, from one patch of grass to the next, from hour to hour, eyes only on what lies immediately ahead, short-sightedly unaware that he is not where he should be, while all the time he is straying farther away from the flock and the fold. That is one sense in which man is lost.

We can follow out in the same way the suggestion that the woman with the lamp may correspond to the Spirit at work through the church. Since it is the Spirit who gives life, the object of his activity is most appropriately the finding of that which cannot help itself. The coin is lifeless, it cannot move, it can certainly not find its own way back like the son, it cannot even bleat for help like the sheep. Of course in some senses lost mankind is not, like the silver coin, inanimate. But spiritually—from the point of view of the Spirit—it is lifeless;[14] and the coin is an apt symbol of those who see the requirements of God and know themselves incapable of rising to them. Only the all-powerful Spirit can rescue men who in that sense are lost.

The father waits at home. That is by no means to say that he does not care whether the prodigal returns; but the Father, the heavenly Father, has sent out his Son and his Spirit to seek the lost, and he himself in the third parable represents as it were 'home base', to which in the end all will return. As on God's side the parable depicts the joyful welcome at the sinner's homecoming, so on man's side it stresses the folly of the prodigal. He deliberately made himself independent of his father, like Adam in the garden he took what would in any case have been his later, had he not short-circuited his father's plans, and he cut himself off from his father's presence. And that is a third sense in which man is lost.

In the mind and teaching of Jesus, then, men without God are not only lost, but lost in these three senses of the word. And as Jesus sees

---

[13] 'Until he finds it', 15:4; 'the good shepherd lays down his life for the sheep', Jn. 10:11; and *cf.*, *e.g.*, Phil. 2:5–8.

[14] Eph. 2:1; Col. 2:13.

them, so they need to see themselves; for not only is he Lord, so that they have a duty to accept what he says, but he is also Saviour, and their lost-ness is the very reason why he has come into the world to save them. Evangelism, now as then, must therefore include the teaching that they are astray, like the lost sheep; helpless, like the lost coin; foolish, like the lost son. Whether, and how, all three facts are to be explained to any particular hearer, is a matter for prayer and wisdom and the guidance of the Spirit. But they are all true, and to underplay them is to make nonsense of the message of salvation.

Alongside man's misery in being lost is set God's joy in finding him. When we ask 'Why salvation? Why the Saviour's coming?', this is the other aspect of the answer; this too must be proclaimed as an essential part of the good news. To it we now turn.

b. God's joy in finding the lost
'Rejoice', says the shepherd, 'for I have found my sheep which was lost'—one sheep out of a hundred—and 'even so', says the Saviour, there will be 'joy in heaven'. In the case of the woman, it is not one hundredth, but one tenth, of her precious silver which is lost and then found, and her joy must be correspondingly greater; and 'even so', says the Saviour again, 'there is joy before the angels of God over one sinner who repents'. But still we do not have an adequate picture of the delight there is in heaven over the finding of the lost, and in the third parable the celebration is for the homecoming of a son whose departure had deprived his father of half his family. That gives an even better idea of the 'music and dancing' in the heavenly home when the lost one is back where he belongs, and the prodigal has come home to his father.

In the experience of the Christian, joy is perhaps more often on the lips than it is in the heart, for it seems to be vitiated so often by the troubles of life. But however real it may become, it is still nothing compared to the joy of the angels when a sinner comes back. As the baby learns to walk, two successful steps may make it chuckle, while at the third it may take a tumble, and cry. But its parents can see what is really happening—it is *walking*—and theirs is not a momentary chuckle but an abiding delight. So it is with our Father God when the lost is found.

Why then has God set about the prolonged and painful task of saving men? The united voice of the three parables tells us: because of the misery of men in being lost, and his own joy in finding them. He pities them and loves them, and that is why he wants to save them.

155

Yet again Luke's memorable pictures are summarized in one of John's memorable sayings: 'For God so *loved* the world that he gave his only Son, that whoever believes in him should not perish but have eternal life. For God sent the Son into the world, not to condemn the world, but that the world might be *saved* through him.'[15]

3. The 'how' of salvation

The gist of chapter 15 is that it is God who saves men, and that he does so because he wishes and delights to do so. These statements are the *who* and the *why* of salvation. The practical question remains: *how* may this glorious salvation apply to me? How may I find myself in the position of the sheep and the silver which are found, and the son who is welcomed home?

To answer this question we need to place the chapter in its context, and go back to the preceding section to see why Luke arranges his material as he does.

That section, it was suggested, might be entitled 'The narrow door' (13:22 – 14:35). It described how a man may come to God, and underlined the need to strip off every pretension we have—all the things which clutter our lives, and which, often, we are loath to lose precisely because we think they will commend us to God. It is not so. There is nothing we can bring to him which is not at worst a sin and at best a hindrance. That section detailed seven words addressed by Jesus not only to Pharisees but to all sorts of men who were thus hampered. The way to God is such a narrow door that there is simply no room to bring these extras through it. Only if we are willing to shed them all can we draw near to him.

'Now', says Luke, having elaborated this point, and moving on from chapter 14 to chapter 15, 'the tax collectors and sinners *were* all drawing near' (15:1). The opening verses of the new chapter form the hinge between the two sections. For, once they admit themselves to be sinners, strip off their pride and folly and acknowledge their nakedness, they find what Luke will go on to expound in the three parables which follow—that 'this man receives sinners and eats with them' (15:2). The Pharisees and scribes uttered those words, and meant them as a complaint; but they were absolutely right, and had in fact put in a nutshell the gospel of salvation.

Thus 15:1 sums up the whole section that precedes, and 15:2

---

[15] Jn. 3:16–17.

sums up the whole section that follows. When sinners draw near, he receives them. When the prodigal returned in the frame of mind required by Jesus's 'narrow door' sayings, confessing in abject humility 'I am no longer worthy to be called your son', *then* his father 'ran and embraced him and kissed him' (15:19, 20). When I come stripped of all that I thought might commend me to his favour, it is then that he cries, 'Bring quickly the best robe, and put it on him' (15:22).

How may a man be saved? In a word, in penitence. And thus 15:7 summarizes the whole lesson. It tells us who is concerned in the salvation of mankind: the principalities and powers of *heaven*, the triune God himself, none else and none less. It tells us why: because it is God's *joy* and delight to save men from their sins. And it tells us how: by their drawing near to God as penitent, helpless *sinners*. For there is 'joy in heaven over one sinner who repents'.

16:1 – 18:14
The challenge

In the task of detecting Luke's train of thought, many find this section one of the most difficult of the whole Gospel. The majority of commentators give up the attempt, and treat these two and a half chapters as a miscellany of items which can be dealt with only piecemeal. The fact remains that Luke did claim to be writing 'an orderly account' (1:3); so an exposition which discerns some kind of order, even here, is likely to be nearer Luke's mind than one for which the passage is a rag-bag of scarcely connected episodes.

We may begin from the main themes of the last two sections. Under the title 'The narrow door', 13:22 – 14:35 showed the penitence with which the sinner must come to God; then 15:1–32 showed the 'Joy in heaven' with which God welcomes the penitent sinner. The two sections hinge on the opening verses of chapter 15. 15:1 sums up the first: 'The tax collectors and sinners were all drawing near to hear him.' 15:2 sums up the second: 'This man receives sinners and eats with them.'

The latter statement, however, is keenly ironic. It expresses a grand gospel truth; but it was uttered in fact by the Pharisees, who intended it as a complaint! In addition, therefore, to summing up the message of the two sections which hinge on them (the sinner's return, and God's welcome), these two verses also portray two kinds of people: those who accept the message and those who do not. Now these two kinds of people reappear throughout the next four chapters. Both are described in 15:1–32, where the sheep, the coin, and the son, that were lost and found, are contrasted with the ninety-nine other sheep, the nine other coins, and the elder son; and both kinds are addressed in turn in the section before us—disciples in 16:1, 17:1, 6, 22, and 18:1, and Pharisees in 16:15, 17:20 and 18:9.

Looked at in this way, this passage includes three pairs of episodes.

158

There are two parables, one for each group (16:1–31), two discourses on the coming of the kingdom, one for each group (17:20–37), and two further parables, one for each group (18:1–14). There is a short additional word spoken to disciples in 17:1–10; and that leaves a paragraph of nine verses at the heart of the section, which at first glance may seem quite out of place, a deed in the midst of all these words—the story of the healing of ten lepers (17:11–19).

What will emerge from the passage, thus considered, is the challenge which Jesus puts to his hearers. They have heard the message of 13:22 – 15:32, in which he has told them how men may come to God, and how God will welcome them. Now what will they do about it? The whole group of three sections, in fact, is parallel to the previous three sections. There we saw how we, for our part, should give ourselves to God (9:51 – 10:42), and how he, for his part, will give himself to us (11:1 – 12:12), and were then shown how confrontation with Jesus precipitates the crisis and sorts out those who will respond and those who will not (12:13 – 13:21). Here, in the same way, Jesus is confronting his hearers with the challenge to act on what they have been hearing.

1. An immediate challenge (16:1–31)

The pair of parables which constitute most of chapter 16 (often entitled 'The Dishonest Steward' and 'Dives and Lazarus') bristle with problems for the commentator, and what follows has had to be greatly simplified. But the main thrust of the two stories, in their context, seems to be a challenge to respond here and now to the message of Jesus.

a. To the disciples (16:1–13)

Luke means us to read this chapter against the background of the previous one. On the one hand, 'The tax collectors and sinners were all drawing near to hear him' (15:1), while on the other, 'the Pharisees and the scribes murmured' (15:2); 'so he told them', the latter, the three 'lost and found' parables (15:3), and then returning to the former, 'he also said to the disciples . . .' (16:1). The disciples for whom Jesus intended the parable of 'The Dishonest Steward' (16:1–9) surely included some of the aforementioned tax collectors, wealthy rogues who had themselves made a good living out of other people's financial affairs, and would have appreciated Jesus's story.

For all the difficulties which this parable poses, such listeners may well have seen in it one very plain lesson. The steward was faced, rightly or wrongly, with dismissal. The one thing that was certain in his future was that he would shortly find himself out of work (16:3). He had just one means of ensuring that when that day came he would not be stranded: his employer's books were still, for the moment, under his control. Those books he tampered with, in such a way as to reduce greatly a number of debts owed to his employer, and thus to earn the gratitude of the various debtors, who in their turn could be relied on to help him when he had to leave his present sphere of work.

In the same way, one thing is certain in every man's future: his 'dismissal' from his present sphere into the unknown regions of eternity.[1] And one means is available for ensuring *now* that he will have 'an eternal home' (16:9, NEB) to go to *then*: the right use of the opportunities of daily life. 'Unrighteous mammon' is a puzzling phrase, not so much because of the noun 'mammon', which is simply an Aramaic word meaning 'wealth', as because of the adjective 'unrighteous'; for money in itself is neither good nor bad. So Ellis suggests that the words mean 'worldly possessions', that is, possessions characteristic of this 'unrighteous' age.[2] In this passage they refer not only to money, but to all the goods of this world, and indeed to everything that we have here but shall not be able to take with us into the next life. Although these things—your property, ability, time—belong to this life only, says Jesus, yet what will happen to you then, when you pass into that life, will depend on what you are doing with them here and now. Make sure that your use of them brings you into a fellowship of friends which will survive beyond death.[3]

b. To the Pharisees (16:14–31)

Others among Jesus's hearers 'scoffed at him', and the way Luke

---

[1] 'When ye fail' (16:9, AV) would mean 'when you die'; the better reading is 'when it fails' (RSV)—*i.e.* 'when money is a thing of the past' (NEB).

[2] Ellis, p. 202.

[3] As to the paragraph which Luke adds here, perhaps it is this theme—the use of the things of this world—which links the contrasts of 16:10–12 with the sayings of 16:13, and all four verses with what has gone before. To paraphrase: 'If you serve God, you cannot at the same time serve mammon; on the contrary, you must make *it* serve *you*. In mastering the use of the things of this world, you are developing a responsible attitude which will stand you in good stead with regard to the "true riches", the things of God.'

describes them in 16:14 tells us why. These were men who lived a double life. For them the sacred and the secular were watertight compartments. In the religious compartment, they were 'Pharisees', with certain beliefs and practices by which they were assured of a good standing before God. The secular compartment was quite separate; in that, they could afford to be 'lovers of money', for their attitudes in such matters had no bearing on their religious status. That was why they ridiculed the idea that getting to heaven might be in some way connected with ordinary life.

After some introductory remarks, which again present difficulties to us, but must, one suspects, have been devastatingly clear at the time,[4] Jesus tells these men the parable often known as that of 'Dives and Lazarus'.[5] Like them, the rich man in the parable was a 'lover of money'. He had every opportunity to make something worthwhile of his secular life; but he spent his wealth on himself, and spared none for the beggar at his gate. We are not surprised therefore that in the next world he found himself 'in torment'. Once there, his conversation with Father Abraham across the great divide shows that he had had a religious department also in his life, for he and his brothers had been brought up with the teachings of Moses and the prophets. Could not those beliefs have saved him from hell? The rich man says No, obviously not, or he would not now be 'in this flame'. But Abraham says Yes, they would have saved you, had you really listened to them and let them govern your everyday affairs.

In the same way, the Pharisees both misused the opportunities of secular life, and avoided the real demands of religious law. If you must compartmentalize your life in this way, says Jesus, I have to warn you that in neither area are you going the right way to escape hell and to reach heaven. Only incidentally, we realize, does this

---

[4] It is not easy to see the train of thought in 16:15–18. The following is a possible paraphrase:

'You Pharisees claim for yourselves righteousness according to the law of Moses. But the more value you attach to outward righteousness, the less real inward value does it have in God's sight. Your attitude to the law is wrong in two respects.

'In *duration*, you regard it as *unlimited*, and hold that it is still the way to heaven. But in fact with the coming of John law was replaced by gospel. Until then you seemed the only people with a chance of reaching heaven; but now the way is open to everyone, and they come in droves!

'In *scope*, you have, by contrast, tried to *limit* the law (e.g. Mt. 19:8; Mk. 7:9–13; Lk. 10:29). But in fact its scope is unlimited, and is of the widest application; and you yourselves, for example in the matter of divorce, regularly break it.'

[5] *Dives*: Latin for 'rich', 'a rich man'.

parable deal with wealth. True, the story is garbed in simple and vivid colours by being centred on a rich man and his money; and more than that, the foil to set off this central figure will then naturally be someone poor, and poverty, as we have seen, is in Scripture a kind of code-word for piety.[6] For the rest, however, the story could equally well have featured a politician with his power, or an academic with his brains, or even a preacher with his eloquence—indeed anyone with any kind of resources or skills. Every man possesses something of the sort, be it no more than a heart and a hand and a span of life; and to every man is given some 'Lazarus at the door', a test case as to whether he will use those possessions rightly or wrongly, with love or with self-indulgence, bringing God's will into the matter or leaving it out. Will he or will he not bring into time the considerations of eternity? That is the question.

Thus 'The Dishonest Steward' and 'Dives and Lazarus' both concern the life of the world to come; but they both teach, one as an exhortation to men who are willing to hear, and the other as a warning to men who are not, that our destiny in that world depends on what we do with the 'here and now'. It is a challenge to the far-sighted use of the things of this world, the things we shall not be able to take with us, but which nonetheless constitute the raw material out of which our inner character is built.

2. An ultimate challenge (17:20–37)

By-passing for the moment the first nineteen verses of chapter 17, we come to a pair of discourses, similar to the parables of chapter 16 in that one is addressed to Pharisees and the other to disciples, though both deal with the same subject. This is the question as to when the kingdom of God is coming (17:20).

a. To the Pharisees (17:20–21)
The coming of the kingdom of God is to be understood in two senses. The Pharisees were looking for a future coming, which would be obvious and unmistakable. Such an expectation was in itself, of course, quite right; there will dawn a day when God's kingdom will come in its fullness, 'the day when the Son of man is revealed' (17:30), and of that day Jesus speaks to his disciples in the next paragraph. But every word the Pharisees utter, even when they hap-

---

[6] See above, pp. 92–94.

pen to speak the truth, betrays their wilful misunderstanding of the message of Jesus. For in another sense, the kingdom has come already: that is, God's kingly power has been revealed in the person of Jesus himself.[7] Whether 17:21 means that the kingdom is primarily an inward reality and not a political institution ('within you', RSV mg.), or that it was already present then in the person of Jesus ('in the midst of you'), the Pharisees could not see it. So, if they could not recognize the first coming of the kingdom when it was right under their noses, there was no point in telling them anything about its final coming.

b. To the disciples (17:22–37)

The disciples, on the other hand, had the discernment to see both comings. They had accepted, and indeed been sent themselves to preach, the present reality of the kingdom (9:2, 10:9), so Jesus can now go on to tell them something about 'the days of the Son of man' (17:26). This is the future event when he will return (17:30) and the kingdom will come in its fullness.[8]

As in the parallel passage in Matthew,[9] Jesus here underlines two of the facts concerning his return: that it will be unmistakable, and that it will be sudden. The cry of 'Here it is!' or 'There it is!' was inappropriate when the kingdom first appeared, because the unwilling were not able to see it anyway (17:21); when the kingdom finally comes, such a cry will still be superfluous, but for the opposite reason—no-one will be able to help seeing it (17:23f.). This, and not the suddenness of its coming, is the point of Jesus's mention of the lightning. To show how sudden, and (for most people) unexpected, the coming will be, he refers to the Old Testament stories of Noah and Lot. It will burst in upon men's ordinary life as did the flood, or the destruction of Sodom.

A third fact about the great event is brought out by Luke in an interesting way. Words of Jesus which Matthew and Mark record in connection with the sack of Jerusalem[10] are recorded by him in

[7] See, *e.g.*, 9:2; 10:9; 11:20; 16:16.

[8] Some think that the desire to see '*one of the days* of the Son of man' (17:22) means a nostalgic backward look to the time of his incarnation, since his future coming is usually the singular '*day*' (17:30–31). But it could be a forward look; that future event is called his '*days*' in 17:26, and the phrase in 17:22 could be a Hebraism for 'the first of the days' ('Number One of the days')—the day he returns will be the first day of a new age. See below, pp. 205f.

[9] Mt. 24:26ff., 37 ff.

[10] Mt. 24:15ff.; Mk. 13:14ff.

reference to 'the day when the Son of man is revealed' (17:30–32). Although in the latter case there will be no question of snatching up bag and baggage as one makes a hasty escape from coming judgment, there will still be those who are more concerned about the 'goods in the house' than about the Judge at the door. 'Remember Lot's wife', whose fatal glance over her shoulder, when safety beckoned in Zoar while destruction rained on Sodom, showed where her heart really was. These three solemn words, which only Luke records, take us back to the parables of 'The Dishonest Steward' and of 'Dives and Lazarus'. Instead of using the things of this world wisely, with an eye to the future, she had made them an end in themselves.'

So judgment came upon her.[11] And judgment will come to our world also, as the last verses of the chapter tell us. While the passages we have considered so far in this section challenge men to use present opportunities in the light of future events, the focus here is particularly on the latter, the 'days of the Son of man'.

3. A continuing challenge (18:1–14)

Two further parables, 'The Unjust Judge' and 'The Pharisee and the Publican', close the section. It is sometimes suggested that Luke puts them side by side because each deals with the subject of prayer. And so they do; but deeper than that is the spiritual reality on which true prayer must be based, namely the personal relationship which enables man to get in touch with God. To maintain that sort of contact is a challenge for every day from now till the Son of man returns.

a. To the disciples (18:1–8)

In the parable of 'The Unjust Judge', the answer to the widow's request is eventually obtained through her persistence. The judge cares neither for God nor for man; it is only 'because this widow bothers me' that after some while he at last gives her belated justice.

At a superficial reading the story might seem to make a comparison between the judge and God, teaching that God's people may, like the widow, have to 'cry to him day and night' before their prayers are answered. But Jesus surely intends a contrast, not a comparison. He says of the judge, 'For a while he refused', but of God, 'Will *he* delay?' If the widow, who had no claim that the judge

[11] Gn. 19:26.

would recognize, nevertheless succeeded in the end in getting what she wanted, through sheer pertinacity, how much more shall God's people, who are 'his chosen' (18:7, NEB), have their prayers answered by a God who is willing to 'vindicate them speedily'?

It is a mark of the disciples of Jesus that they practise constant contact with the God who they know always hears their prayer. His answer may not always be what they hope for; it may sometimes be 'No', it may often be 'Wait'. But they learn by experience that, as often as they pray, so often will they be answered speedily. 'His elect ... cry to him day and night', in fact, not because he does *not* listen, but precisely because he *does*.

Such faith has to be cultivated, even among those who understand the principle. Will it be found to be our own daily experience 'when the Son of man comes'?

b. To the Pharisees (18:9–14)

Though neither word is used, Jesus's hearers in 18:9 are as clearly Pharisees as those in 18:1 were disciples. The story he tells is more than a contrast between (as the men in the parable are often called) 'The Pharisee and the Publican'. It is their attitudes which are contrasted, and in particular their attitudes in prayer—which means, in fact, that Jesus is exposing the kinds of relationship with God which underlie the contrasting kinds of prayer.

In the words of the aphorism which Luke here quotes for the second time,[12] the two prayers show respectively the Pharisee exalting himself and the tax collector humbling himself. And 'every one who exalts himself will be humbled'; for the Pharisee's prayer is so laden with self-congratulation that it can hardly get off the ground, let alone wing its way to the listening ear of God. Meanwhile for the tax collector all that mattered was his own sin and God's mercy; and he, Jesus says, was 'justified'—his prayer of humility brought him into the relationship with God of which the first man had been deprived by his conceit.

Between the immediate call to a full use of today's opportunities with eternity in view, and the ultimate call to be ready when that last day does arrive, there is therefore the challenge to maintain a day-by-day life of humble prayer-contact with God.

[12] 18:14b = 14:11.

4. The challenge enacted (17:1–19)

We have not yet looked at the central part of this section, the first nineteen verses of chapter 17. They begin with a short address containing instruction again for disciples. Edersheim summarizes them well: 'Four things: to be careful to give no offence' (17:1–2); 'to be careful to take no offence' (17:3–4); 'to be simple and earnest in their faith, and absolutely to trust its all-prevailing power' (17:5–6); 'and yet, when they had made experience of it, not to be elated, but to remember their relation to their Master, that all was in his service, and that, after all, when everything had been done, they were but unprofitable servants' (17:7–10).[13] This, in brief, is the way forward for men who have faced and accepted the challenge.

But the remaining paragraph, 17:11–19, is the 'odd man out' in this whole series of episodes. It is different from the discourses on either side of it and from the parables at the beginning and the end of the section. The question arises, therefore, as to why Luke included a miracle at this point in a group of chapters which are generally concerned not with the deeds of Jesus but with his words. Once or twice already we have found Luke doing this (11:14ff.; 13:10ff.), and on each occasion he seems to have had a special purpose in doing so; the miracle in each case relates closely to his teaching at that point.

But on reflection it is not now so hard to see why Luke, knowing of the healing of the ten lepers, thought it an appropriate episode to insert here. For it sums up the whole of what Jesus is saying both to his disciples and to the Pharisees in the section from 16:1 to 18:14. Both groups have been given the immense privilege of hearing the word of salvation from the lips of the Saviour himself. The Pharisees, who, though privileged in this way, do not respond with acceptance and gratitude, represent the majority. But always there are some who, like the penitent sinners and tax collectors, do respond wholeheartedly. So, whether by Luke's design or by the Lord's own design, a particular miracle which took place in the course of the journey towards Jerusalem fits in here as a living illustration of what Luke has been describing. Of the ten men who are touched by the healing power of Jesus, only one realizes that what has happened deserves a personal, heartfelt response to the Saviour from whom that power has flowed; and the one thankful man is the Samaritan, the outsider. Of the nine—Jews, we infer—Jesus sees nothing more.

[13] A. Edersheim, *Life and Times of Jesus the Messiah*,[3] II (Longmans, Green & Co., 1886), p. 306.

Having been privileged to receive all this teaching, which is Luke's basic theme (the message of salvation for all men), we also face the challenge which is spelled out in the words of Jesus in this section, and illustrated by the story of one of his great deeds put into the centre of it. It is the challenge to be like the one, and not like the nine: actually to turn back, praising God with a loud voice, and to fall on our faces at Jesus's feet, giving him thanks.

18:15 – 19:44
Royal progress

Coming to the end of the central section of his Gospel, we recall the
picture of himself which Luke gave us right at the beginning of the
book. He sits down 'to compile a narrative' about Jesus (1:1); and he
has before him, as the material from which it will be put together, a
collection of accounts of Jesus's deeds and words (some of them notes
he has made himself in personal interviews with eyewitnesses), the
most important of them being, we may assume, the book we know as
the Gospel of Mark.

That book provides a basic outline, it seems, both for Luke and for
Matthew as they write their own Gospels. A 'harmony' of the Gospels, with Matthew, Mark, and Luke set out side by side, shows the
likenesses of the three. At Luke 9:51, however, there begins (as we
have already seen) a long narrative—more than eight chapters—in
which hardly anything that Luke includes has been drawn from
Mark. This is his own special part of the Gospel, the middle third of
it, which as we have noted is mainly concerned with the teaching of
Jesus, whereas his first part was generally about Jesus's deeds and
followed the other writers much more closely.

But with 18:14 Luke's special section ends, and at 18:15 he
rejoins Matthew and Mark. The last visit of Jesus to Jerusalem, and
his death and resurrection there, form a sequence of events in which
the first three Gospels (and to some extent the fourth as well) are, by
and large, telling the same story in the same order.

So although we may group the paragraphs from 18:15 to 19:44
with the previous eight or nine chapters, and reckon them to be the
conclusion of Jesus's journey to Jerusalem and of his teaching ministry, yet in one way they differ from what has gone before: most of the
incidents which Luke relates here can be found also in the corresponding place in Matthew and Mark. There are still, however, some

extras which he inserts to underline the particular points he wants to make. Both kinds of writing are instructive.

Vox populi vox dei, runs the old Latin tag—'The voice of the people is the voice of God.' This highly misleading sentiment is in fact contradicted by the passage before us. The voice of the people is saying one thing; the voice of God is saying quite another. As we conclude our reading of the Gospel's teaching section, we shall hear, in the episodes in which Luke runs closely parallel to the other writers, the voice of the people. We shall hear how they have misunderstood Jesus's message, the 'good news of the kingdom of God' (4:43). In Luke's additions to the story, it is as though the divine voice speaks in order to correct their misunderstanding and to clarify what the teaching of Jesus has really been.

1. The message misunderstood

First, then, a comparison of Matthew, Mark, and Luke will show the items which are common to all of them. Children are brought to Jesus, and he blesses them (Lk. 18:15–17 = Mt. 19:13ff. = Mk. 10:13ff.). A rich man asks how to obtain eternal life, and Jesus explains that for the wealthy such a thing is very difficult, though not of course impossible with God (Lk. 18:18–30 = Mt. 19:16ff. = Mk. 10:17ff.). He warns his disciples of the fearful events that await them when they reach Jerusalem (Lk. 18:31–33 = Mt. 20:17ff. = Mk. 10:32ff.). On the way there, at Jericho, a blind man is given his sight (Lk. 18:35–43 = Mt. 20:29ff. = Mk. 10:46ff.). The approach to the city of Jerusalem, in company with many other pilgrims going there for the Passover festival, turns into a triumphal procession (Lk. 19:28–38 = Mt. 21:1ff. = Mk. 11:1ff.). With his arrival at the capital the main teaching work of Jesus comes to an end.

a. How it came across

This sequence has one specially notable feature, like a furnishing scheme which incorporates many colours but in which one of them predominates. The children represent the attitude a person must have if he is to 'receive the *kingdom* of God' (18:17); conversely, a man preoccupied with his possessions will find it 'hard . . . to enter the *kingdom* of God' (18:24). The blind man at Jericho, as he hears the crowd passing, cries out to the 'Son of David', the descendant of Israel's greatest *king*; and Jesus responds in the same spirit, halting the procession as with a royal word of command, having the suppliant brought into the royal presence, asking his request, and granting it then and there with royal bounty (18:38–43). Some miles further on, the procession has been swollen by new crowds as it approaches David's historic capital, Jerusalem, and it becomes quite explicitly and defiantly a royal progress: 'Blessed is the *King* who comes!' (19:38).

Even in our days, when the idea of kingship means so much less, there is something stirring about the pageantry of royalty. In those days the thought that Jesus of Nazareth might be the new King of the Jews, 'great David's greater Son', must have been electrifying. That, at any rate, was how his message had come across to most people.

b. Where it came from

They were not wrong in remembering that the kingdom of God had been one of the basic ideas in the message of Jesus. It appears frequently in Luke's middle section (9:60ff.; 10:9ff.; 11:2, 20; 12:32; 13:18ff., 28f.; 14:15) and underlies Jesus's ministry in the first section (4:43; 8:10; 9:2, 11, 27), and is indeed the substance of the very first thing said about him, even before his birth—that 'the Lord God will give to him the *throne* of his father David, and he will *reign* over the house of Jacob for ever; and of his *kingdom* there will be no end' (1:32f.).

Some commentators go so far as to see the kingdom of God as the main theme of Luke's Gospel. Perhaps in the course of these studies the alternative suggestion, that Luke is chiefly concerned to present 'The Saviour of the world', will have commended itself as a more suitable title. Even so, there is no denying that the universal salvation which Luke saw so clearly at the heart of Jesus's message was very often preached by Jesus in terms of the kingdom of God. But to regard it only in that light meant that the message could be, and in fact was, easily misunderstood.

c. What it came to

The atmosphere of the Palm Sunday story, Jesus's approach to Jerusalem among the exuberant crowds, is one of euphoria. The people seem intoxicated with the prospect of the coming kingdom. They see it as an unremitting success story, with no hint of suffering on the way:

O we shall change, *but with no pangs of birth*,
To glorious heaven from this glorious earth.[1]

They see it as a political event rather than a spiritual one. They expect 'the kingdom of God . . . to appear immediately' (19:11), without any long-drawn-out struggle. They understand it, naturally, to be a Jewish kingdom, for which the Gentiles are alien forces to be overcome, and not equal candidates for admission.[2]

That was, in sum, what the message came to. Like so many religious ideas, it was a half truth, and as such even more dangerous than a lie. And it is the kind of concept which many have, especially in these days of universal education, of the message of Jesus. People who are subject to the incessant bombardment of information through the media are likely to have the illusion of being *well*-informed, when in fact they are merely (to coin a phrase) *much*-informed. They will speak positively and dogmatically on matters in which only the specialist can detect their frequent misunderstanding. This is certainly so with regard to Christianity. The Jews of Jesus's time thought they knew what was meant by the kingdom of God. People today think they know what is meant by Christianity, the church, the gospel. More often than not, however, the message has been misunderstood, and needs to be clarified. This Luke sets out to do.

2. The message clarified

Taking the basic story as it already existed in Mark's Gospel, Luke makes certain additions to it, to correct wrong impressions and to deepen shallow understanding—in other words, to *teach* what the kingdom is really about, and thus to complete his central 'teaching' section. His insertions are four, of varying lengths.

a. The kingdom must centre on the cross of Jesus (18:34)

Amid the episodes which speak of the kingdom, Matthew, Mark, and Luke all include a more sombre paragraph in which Jesus predicts the arrest, the suffering, and the death (though also the resurrection) which await him in Jerusalem. Only Luke adds that his disciples 'understood none of these things; this saying was hid from them, and they did not grasp what was said' (18:34).

[1] Frances Cornford, *The Trumpet Shall Sound* (*Messiah* 1742).
[2] See above, pp. 37f.

171

But 'these things' were quite literally the *crucial* things; and it is as if Luke is saying that, whatever people may have understood by the kingdom, when it came to the most important facts of all 'they did not grasp what was said'—their understanding of the whole was hopelessly awry *if the cross was missing from it.*

For the last act of the drama, the passion and resurrection of Jesus, was the heart of the message. This was the third explicit prediction of it which Jesus had given them[3]—indeed the seventh or eighth, if we include all his hints about it[4]—and it would in due course be seen to be, in the words of Luke's friend Paul, the fact 'of first importance' in the preaching of the gospel: 'that Christ died for our sins in accordance with the scriptures, that he was buried, that he was raised on the third day in accordance with the scriptures'.[5]

It is as possible today as it ever was, and perhaps more so, for Jesus to be claimed as a figurehead for movements which he himself would never have owned. Popular notions of what is meant by his leadership make him more than acceptable as Jesus the beautiful example, Jesus the iconoclastic rebel, Jesus the mystic guru. A variety of political, social, and religious causes may identify themselves with his 'kingdom'. But Luke supplies us with the question which has to be asked of any such movement: Are these so-called Christian soldiers 'Marching as to war, With the *cross* of Jesus Going on before'?[6] However enthusiastic may be their march on Jerusalem, if '*this* saying' is 'hid from them' their cause is not Christ's. You cannot have a crusade without a cross.

b. The kingdom must come in the hearts of men (19:1–10)

No doubt the story of Zacchaeus, being an incident dating from this very time, as Jesus 'was passing through' Jericho on his way to Jerusalem, came to Luke's mind as an apt illustration of what he had recorded a few verses back, in 18:18–30. There, Jesus had said: 'How hard it is for those who have riches to enter the kingdom of God! ... but ... what is impossible with men is possible with God' (18:24, 27). Zacchaeus was just such a rich man, for whom God had done the impossible, and brought him into the kingdom.

Even more to Luke's purpose than the events of the story is the saying of Jesus with which it ends. For the great words of 19:9–10

[3] See also 9:18ff., 43ff.
[4] See also 5:35; 12:50; 13:32f.; 14:27; 17:25.
[5] 1 Cor. 15:3–4.
[6] Sabine Baring-Gould, *Onward! Christian soldiers.*

LUKE 18:15 – 19:44

form a further corrective to wrong ideas of the kingdom. The passage in chapter 18 tells us that God can bring even the wealthy into his *kingdom*; here, that same miracle is described as *salvation* coming to the house of Zacchaeus, 'for the Son of man came to seek and to *save* the lost'. In this case, then, 'kingdom' is equated with 'salvation'.

The ultimate achievement of the message of Jesus will indeed be a social and political one, when 'the kingdom of the world has become the kingdom of our Lord and of his Christ, and he shall reign for ever and ever'.[7] But the excited crowds on the Jerusalem road who saw the kingdom first and foremost in terms of society and politics had the message back to front. Zacchaeus's entry to the kingdom is described as his salvation, and his salvation was primarily a spiritual matter. He who was universally known as a sinner (19:7) had a radical change of character (19:8). What was being changed was not first of all human institutions and policies, but the human heart. A lost soul had been saved. The description of Zacchaeus does give good hope that the other changes will follow in due course; the man is a capitalist—a collaborator—a crook—a notorious bad lot!—and when we witness the conversion of a person like that, there are two things we can hardly deny: its cause must be a power which can work miracles, and its effect will be repercussions all round in the society in which he lives. In other words, his world will begin to change. But it will be only because his heart has been changed first.

c. The kingdom must grow through the rest of history (19:11–27)
Matthew records a parable similar to this one of 'The Pounds'; his is usually known as the parable of 'The Talents'.[8] There is no reason why Jesus should not have used the same story-outline on more than one occasion, even to make rather different points. The point in Matthew is the faithful use by Christ's servants of their varying gifts; the inclusion in Luke's parable of rebellious citizens as well as more or less faithful servants is likely to indicate not that Luke is a clumsy writer (for he is not), but that he understood this parable to make a different point from Matthew's—a point for which both citizens and servants had to be included.

The story was founded on fact. At the death of Herod the Great, his son Archelaus had (like the nobleman) to undertake a long journey 'to receive kingly power' (19:12). He could not be king in Judea until his claims had been ratified by the imperial government in

[7] Rev. 11:15.   [8] Mt. 25:14–30.

Rome. And there was a deputation of his subjects, like the one in 19:14, which went to Rome to lodge a petition against his claims; the reason in his case was a deserved unpopularity.

The gist of the parable is that the nobleman is away long enough for his citizens to reveal their real enmity to him and for his servants to make full proof of their responsibilities to him. It is only after quite a long time that he returns in 'kingly power', and then he settles with both groups.

Luke in fact says expressly that this is the point being made, by stating in 19:11 that Jesus told the story 'because they supposed that the kingdom of God was to appear immediately'. On the contrary, Jesus told them, the King would return only after an unspecified, but far from negligible, period of time; and during that time, though his enemies might be plotting against him, he would expect his servants to be labouring to establish his kingdom.

Jesus's teaching in this passage corrects a whole range of misconceptions about the kingdom as it relates to human history. Is it a matter for debate whether the coming of the kingdom is present or future? No, for it is clearly both, in different senses: it is present (as in 17:20–21) from the first coming of Jesus onwards; it is yet 'to appear' in its fullness (19:11), and will do so only at his second coming. So will history as we know it, not continue indefinitely? No, for an end has been set to it. And are we ignorant of whether that end will be with a bang or with a whimper? No; we may certainly expect a bang! Does that mean the secular bang—war, plague, pollution, the exhausting of resources? No: it is 'the thunder of the Lord's appearing',[9] the return of the King, which will bring our age to its close. Should we then change our ways as that day seems to be approaching, either to withdraw from the affairs of ordinary life into an increasingly inactive piety, or to plunge into 'Christian work' with increasingly fervent activity? No, we should not need to; the same steady faithful service is what he will be looking for, whether he returns soon or late. And are we to expect that as time goes on good will gradually eliminate evil, or will the reverse be true? Neither: until he comes, with unwearied zeal his enemies will be plotting against him, and his servants working for him.

However long history may last, so long has the King decreed for the preparations for his return.

[9] F. W. H. Myers, *St Paul*, st. 142.

Let no man think that sudden in a minute
All is accomplished and the work is done; –
Though with thine earliest dawn thou shouldst begin it
Scarce were it ended in thy setting sun. [10]

d. The kingdom must reach to the ends of the earth (19:39–44)
It is 'at the descent of the Mount of Olives' (19:37), with the jubilant crowds surrounding the King who comes, as the prophet had foretold, riding on an ass, [11] that Luke makes his fourth addition to the story. After the retort to the Pharisees' shocked complaint when the disciples hail Jesus as King (19:39–40), he ends the story of the great journey with Jesus's lament over Jerusalem (19:41–44).

It comes at the travellers' first view of the city. The temple will not be sighted till a little while later; coming over the shoulder of the Mount of Olives the first glimpse of Jerusalem is the south-eastern corner of the City of David. For it is not the end of the Jewish religion which is at this stage uppermost in Jesus's mind. Rather he foresees the ruin of the nation's capital, the royal city in which his ardent supporters expect him shortly to mount the throne.

Thus again we see how Luke corrects misunderstanding about the kingship of Jesus. He is indeed 'the King who comes in the name of the Lord' (19:38); but as he comes in sight of his presumed capital, what he sees in prospect is a smoking, desolate ruin. He is King— but of what? Of this city which within a generation will be destroyed?

No; Jerusalem had failed to recognize the One who had visited her, and it was not of Jewry that he would henceforth be King. [12] For Luke's grasp of the message of the kingdom has from the beginning made him stress the universality of it. Jesus is King; but the earthly Jerusalem is too small and mean to contain his majesty. All nations are to be his. He is the Saviour of the *world*.

So the destruction of that city and people, though in one sense a tragedy, is in another sense a challenge to take seriously the call to worldwide evangelism. The kingdom is for every city, every people, that the church can reach and touch with the message of salvation.

None of these thoughts is new in Luke's Gospel. They have all appeared frequently in the central section, and nearly all were inti-

---

[10] F. W. H. Myers, *ibid.*, st. 15.
[11] Zc. 9:9.   [12] See Jn. 18:33–37.

mated in the prophetic words of men and angels which heralded Jesus's birth in chapters 1 and 2.

So Luke is reiterating and underlining the great themes of the message of Jesus. It is indeed, as Jesus had said from the beginning, 'the good news of the kingdom of God' (4:43), and the whole passage from 18:15 to 19:44 describes the King's royal progress to his capital, but Luke is concerned to bring out the real meaning of this kingdom. He turns his readers' eyes away from its ultimate glory to the suffering without which that glory will never be attained; the kingdom centres on the cross. He turns our attention away from the political transformation of society to the spiritual transformation of the soul, which must precede it; the kingdom must first come to the human heart. He conditions us to think in terms not of immediate success and quick returns, but of long delay and protracted struggle; the kingdom must grow throughout its King's extended absence. He re-focuses our gaze so that we see the King whom God has set on Zion, his holy hill, as the One who has in fact been given the nations as his heritage, and the ends of the earth for his possession;[13] the kingdom embraces the world.

These things, then, Luke would have us learn from his Gospel. God has given his only Son to die on the cross. By virtue of that death, he offers to the hearts of men salvation from sin and a new life. Then he gives them the centuries of Christian history in which to proclaim that salvation far and wide; for it is of the whole world that he will one day be Saviour and King.

[13] Ps. 2:6, 8.

The going forth of the Saviour

19:45–21:38
The temple

He entered the temple and began to drive out those who sold (19:45).

He was teaching daily in the temple (19:47).

As he was teaching the people in the temple ... *the chief priests and the scribes with the elders came up and said to him* ... (20:1–2).

As some spoke of the temple, how it was adorned with noble stones and offerings, he said, 'As for these things which you see, the days will come when there shall not be left here one stone upon another that will not be thrown down' (21:5–6).

Every day he was teaching in the temple, but at night he went out and lodged on the mount called Olivet. And early in the morning all the people came to him in the temple to hear him (21:37–38).

It would be possible to take what is often called the 'Triumphal Entry' of Jesus into Jerusalem, a week before his death, as the beginning of the last main division of Luke's Gospel (19:28ff.). In Luke even more clearly than in the other Gospels, however, it is not actually an entry, for Jesus is still approaching the city in 19:41; and for this and for a number of other reasons[1] I have linked that passage with the middle division, and taken the third division (the passion narrative) to begin not with the Palm Sunday events of 19:28ff., but here at 19:45, with the Lord's entry into the temple in Jerusalem. First we have a section just over two chapters long which, as the

---

[1] Ellis (pp. 224f., on 19:28–44) lists these, and draws from them the 'reasonable presumption that Luke regarded this episode as the conclusion of the central division'.

above quotations show, is set entirely in and around the temple in Jerusalem.[2]

1. The meaning of 'the temple'

a. The heart of the city of Jerusalem
This was one of the most splendid buildings of the ancient world. The original temple, Solomon's magnificent structure dating from the tenth century BC, had been destroyed four hundred years later, and replaced in due course by what was known as the 'second temple'; it was this one which in the time of Jesus was undergoing a prolonged and thorough renovation by King Herod,[3] who lavished immense sums of money on it. It was a complex of buildings about a quarter of a mile square, with the actual temple itself at the centre, crowning the city of Jerusalem, which itself crowned a hilltop, so that the temple—much of its exterior plated with silver or even gold, and the rest dazzling white marble—looked from a distance like the snow-capped peak of a mountain.

Its real importance, however, was not that of an imposing piece of architecture. Its religious significance, at the heart of the faith of Israel, was immensely greater.

b. The heart of the faith of Israel
It was the centre and symbol of Jewish religion. Remembering this, we can see why Luke returns to it at this stage in his narrative. For he had begun the story of Jesus in the same place. It was there that Zechariah 'was serving as priest before God' when the angel appeared to him in order to announce the coming birth of Jesus's forerunner John (1:8ff.), and there Jesus himself, as a child, was taken on two occasions, a highly significant prophetic word being uttered about him each time (2:22ff., 41ff.). In his opening chapters Luke was saying, as it were, to his non-Jewish readers, 'My story concerns the Saviour of the world; but if you are rightly to understand its message of universal salvation, you have to realize at the outset that it begins in what some may think the most unlikely surroundings—in Judaism, the religion of Israel.'

---

[2] Perhaps Luke intends a subtle extra emphasis on this setting by his omission of the fact that, when the long discourse of 21:5–36 was given, Jesus and the disciples were not actually in the temple, but on the Mount of Olives (though still of course in sight of the temple). See Mt. 24:1–3; Mk. 13:1–4.

[3] Cf. Jn. 2:20.

From this root had grown the new plant, the religion of Christ. Through nineteen chapters Luke has chronicled its growth and development. And now, as the life of Jesus nears its climax, Malachi's prediction (already quoted more than once in the Gospel) is fulfilled again: the Lord comes to his temple.[4] Luke returns to the place from which the new 'faith of Israel' has sprung; as if to say, 'And now what is to happen to the old faith, the faith for which this temple stands?'

c. The heart of the spiritual experience of mankind

As I have said, we are not here concerned with Middle Eastern archaeology; but neither are we concerned only with comparative religion. For 'the temple' has a deeper meaning even than that of the symbol of Judaism. It represents, in both Old Testament and New, the place where God meets with man. Such an encounter is not necessarily restricted to one particular place, and in his second volume Luke will explain this both to Jewish and to non-Jewish readers, in the words of Stephen for the one and of Paul for the other.[5] For Judaism, the promised place of encounter was indeed, for many years, the Jerusalem temple; for Christianity, it is within[6] or among[7] God's people, wherever they may be, since they are themselves his temple.

According to this deepest significance, then, all of us have our own 'temple', the place in our innermost being where we confront God. The 'temple' stands for our relationship with him. It may not be a very good relationship. It may be a sham, or an illusion. But it is our religion, our faith, our way of life: 'me and God'—whatever sort of God I may believe in.

2. The criticism of 'the temple'

Now Jesus returns to the temple. What is to be done with it—the old inherited religion of his people? What happens to men's beliefs and ideas when Jesus comes to inspect them?

'He entered the temple and began to drive out those who sold' (19:45). The title traditionally given to this passage is 'The Cleansing of the Temple'; and that is exactly what happens. Jesus comes to cast a critical eye over what the Jews have made of their very special

---

[4] Mal. 3:1; Lk. 1:17, 76; 7:27.   [5] Acts 7:48; 17:24.
[6] 1 Cor. 6:19.   [7] 1 Cor. 3:16.

relationship with God.[8] He finds much that needs cleaning up, much grime and rubbish that needs removing. Most of the episodes that follow in chapter 20 are, on the surface, attempts by the Jews to entrap Jesus. But each is turned by him into an exposure of them. The faults and evils of their traditional, distorted, religion are mercilessly revealed.

The evils which had accumulated in Judaism in the time of Jesus are not peculiar to the Jerusalem temple. We may all find, as Jesus enters our own 'temple' and inspects our faith and life, things that need to be thoroughly cleaned out from it.

a. Man-centred religion (20:1–18)

'Tell us by what authority you do these things', Jesus is asked by the Jewish leaders (20:2). The point at issue both in the argument in 20:1–8 and in Jesus's parable in 20:9–18 is, What right does Jesus have to speak and act as he does?

The argument turns back from the question of the Lord's own authority to that of the authority of the herald who had preceded him, John the Baptist. John's prestige was as high as ever, though it was now two or three years since his death, and the chief priests dared not disparage it. The trouble was that his authority and his Lord's would stand or fall together; the chief priests could not give the impression of allowing John's claims without seeming to allow Jesus's also. Thus their attack along that line was frustrated. Jewish malice raged unabated, however, and provoked Jesus's parable about the wicked tenants in the vineyard.

The Jewish leaders may not have known how to answer the argument, but they certainly did not fail to understand the parable (20:19). It replied to their original question (What right had Jesus to speak and act as he did?), and told them plainly that he had every right. The vineyard in the parable is Israel;[9] and whereas the Jewish leaders are the tenants whose responsibility is to care for it, Jesus is the last of a long line of messengers sent by the owner to call the tenants to account. He is, indeed, the most important of all the messengers, for he is the owner's own son. Jesus has every right to criticize the temple. In fact he is himself (to change the metaphor) the most important stone in the temple (20:17).

[8] Note that instead of particular groups within Judaism, such as the Pharisees, it is 'the chief priests and the scribes with the elders' (20:1), in other words the Jewish leaders themselves, 'the principal men of the people' (19:47), who now confront Jesus.

[9] Is. 5:1–7.

LUKE 19:45 − 21:38

It is not hard to see, in the way that they try to call him to account when in fact it is he who challenges them, the common attitude in which we reserve to ourselves the right to have the last word. This (we say) I can believe; that I will even obey; but the other I am not prepared to accept. In the last analysis it is I who decide what does and what does not belong in my temple. I am ready to challenge even the right of Jesus to the final authority there.

It is not 'clever' people alone who think like this, though they perhaps stand in particular danger of doing so. The 'I know best' attitude is the result not of education, nor of intellect, nor of commonsense, nor of intuition (although any of these may foster it), but simply of the basic pride of the human heart.

This kind of religion must be swept right out. We cannot afford a man-centred, 'I'-centred faith. We must 'respect *him*' (20:13), for the temple from which the chief corner-stone is 'rejected' (20:17) cannot be far from collapse. He must always have the central place and the last word.

b. 'Religious' religion (20:19–26)
The question about Roman taxes was another attempt to discredit Jesus, which like the first one rebounded on the questioners. They wanted him either to endorse the paying of tribute, which would make him a traitor to patriotic Judaism, or to condemn it, which would make him a traitor to the occupation forces of Rome.

But the answer of Jesus did three things. It evaded their trap; it established the principle of the Christian attitude to the state, which has been normative for the Christian church ever since; and (most important from our point of view, in the context of Luke's Gospel) it exposed another evil in the temple.

For the Jews' assumption was that you must be either loyal to the Jewish faith, or loyal to the Roman state. Their narrow view could not take in both at once. But Jesus's reply is that we must 'render to Caesar the things that are Caesar's, *and* to God the things that are God's' (20:25). His kind of religion is one which embraces all of life, the secular as well as the sacred, and has something to say about every part of it.

Thus he repudiates 'religious' religion, which divides life into a number of watertight compartments, and confines its thoughts of God to those areas it thinks appropriate—Sundays, church buildings, co-religionists—while Caesar's world is something totally unrelated. This area belongs to God, that one belongs to Caesar. Now I

183

too speak in terms of these different areas, says Jesus; but the way I see them is not the way you see them. You must learn to live in *both* areas, and relate each to the other, and realize, indeed, that true faith in God will spill over into Caesar's area, and into every other besides. Compartmentalized religion must go.

c. Unbiblical religion (20:27–40)

Next comes a question based on Scripture. 'Moses wrote' (20:28, quoting Dt. 25:5) that a childless widow should marry her late husband's brother, in order to bear children, if possible, so as to preserve the family name; and the Sadducees, 'who say that there is no resurrection' (20:27), concoct the ridiculous story of the seven brothers who each in turn married the same woman, and would thus cause problems in the resurrection life—if there ever were such a thing.

It is noteworthy that the query which has a 'biblical' basis is the one which receives (according to the first two Gospels) Jesus's sharpest rebuke: 'You are wrong, precisely because you do *not* know your Bible.'[10] And he proceeds to demonstrate, by a type of argument which we might think unusual but which was to them very familiar, that the resurrection was clearly implied in the Scripture which they were claiming to have read.[11]

Their religion is full of half-baked notions of what the Scripture says. But it is no use your quoting the Bible at me, retorts Jesus, when you have obviously not studied what it really does say. A religion which sits so loose to Scripture, for all its pretensions to the contrary, has no place in the temple. Like man-centred religion and 'religious' religion, unbiblical religion must be swept out.

d. Thoughtless religion (20:41–44)

Now it is Jesus's turn to ask a question. He holds up before his audience a theological belief of the Jewish leaders: namely, the view that the Christ, the long-awaited Messiah, will, when he eventually comes into the world, be a descendant of King David. For, as against that, the Scripture says (again he turns to the Scripture) that the

[10] Mt. 22:29; Mk. 12:24.

[11] Jesus attaches the fullest possible meaning to the actual words of Ex. 3:6, and his argument is: 'If in the time of Moses, when Abraham is long since dead, the Lord can still say that he "is" the God of Abraham, then there must still be an Abraham for him to be the God of! A man with whom the living God has a living relationship must himself be alive, even though he may physically have died.'

Christ is David's *Lord*. As David's descendant, the Christ will be in a sense his inferior; as his Lord, he is obviously his superior.

'What?' they might have said; 'Do you mean our leaders are wrong in that also?'

'By no means', Jesus would have replied; 'that is not at all what I intend. My question is, *How can they say* that the Christ is both David's descendant and David's Lord? It happens that they are quite right to say it; but *why*? On what basis do they hold that view?'

And 'no one was able to answer him a word', recounts Matthew (Mt. 22:46); while Luke simply ends his paragraph with Jesus's unanswered question!

This really will not do either. After three exposures of their perversions of true religion, Jesus brings up one thing, at any rate, in which they are right, only to show that they have no idea why they believe it. [12] And how much religion is of that kind! Among a mass of sub-Christian, non-Christian, or even anti-Christian beliefs, a man suddenly reveals that at least he has *something* right—and then gives the game away by being quite unable to give any grounds for believing it. 'Always be prepared to make a defence to any one who calls you to account for the hope that is in you.'[13] A thoughtless religion is as unworthy of the temple as any of the distorted kinds we have seen hitherto. It is no use accepting truth without thinking it through—swallowing it without digesting it.

e. Showy religion (20:45–21:4)

Lastly Jesus denounces the kind of religion which is merely outward show. The scribes like to be noticed and honoured, while in fact, beneath the religious trappings, their morality will not bear examination: they are quite prepared to use their influence to satisfy their greed, and 'devour widows' houses' (20:47).

Some commentators think that the story inserted next by Luke, that of the poor widow and her tiny gift to the temple treasury (21:1–4), has no connection with 20:45–47 apart from the fact that they both mention the word 'widow'. But it is not hard to see in this woman an instructive contrast with the scribes Jesus has just condemned. For he, who knows the hearts of all men, perceives that the two coins she has put into the temple offering are actually 'all the living that she had'. Her total devotion, which no-one but Jesus

---

[12] The answer, of course, lies in the double nature of Christ: as man he is David's descendant, while as God he is David's Lord. *Cf.* Rom. 1:4.

[13] 1 Pet. 3:15.

would have realized, is the exact opposite of the Jewish leaders' religion, all show and no heart.

Theirs is the fifth type of religious rubbish which 'will receive . . . condemnation' (20:47) and be cleared out of the temple. Such is the kind of thing which Jesus found defiling old-style Jewish worship, and which spoils the beliefs of thousands of people even today.

3. The destiny of 'the temple'

Luke began this section by describing how Jesus came to the temple to cleanse it. But it soon became clear that the Jewish leaders were not prepared to let it be cleansed. It was their cherished system of faith and life, and they would not let it go. Jesus, on the other hand, would not let it remain; and he and they were thenceforward engaged in a conflict to the death. For their part, 'the chief priests and the scribes and the principal men of the people sought to destroy him' (19:47). Conversely, when some of his hearers, oblivious of the gist of what he had been saying, referred to the glories of the temple (21:5), he for his part gave an answer which applied not only to the building but to the whole religious system which it symbolized: 'As for these things which you see, the days will come when there shall not be left here one stone upon another that will not be thrown down' (21:6). Jesus versus unrepentant Judaism: each envisages the destruction of the other.

The rest of chapter 21 is Luke's version of what is sometimes called the 'synoptic apocalypse', an unveiling by Jesus of the events of the future, which is found in each of the first three Gospels. It contains much of great interest, and of great difficulty, and there is no space here to go into it in detail. But in the context (the criticism which Jesus is making of the temple and all for which it stands), his discourse concerning the future makes two points very plainly.

a. The destiny of the Jerusalem temple
In the conflict between the two systems, the perverted religion of Israel and the new faith of Jesus, neither will give way. And at first, as we shall see in the next two chapters, the Jews apparently emerge victorious. They succeed in destroying Jesus. But he has already said in John's account of the cleansing of the temple, 'Destroy this temple, and in three days I will raise it up'. As John explains, 'he spoke of the temple of his body'.[14] The body in both its senses, the physical

[14] Jn. 2:19, 21.

body of Jesus and his mystical body which is the church, is to begin a new life: the new temple will come into being. In the long term, it is Jesus who wins the battle, and he foretells in 21:20–24 that it is the old temple, Judaism as it has become in his day, which is in fact going to be finally destroyed.

We are left in no doubt concerning how and when these prophecies come true. What Jesus says about the appearing of the new body (or temple) is fulfilled in one respect at the resurrection, and in another at Pentecost. The shell of the old survives for another forty years, but in AD 70 come the 'days of vengeance, to fulfil all that is written' (21:22), and the 'desolation' of Jerusalem by the armies of Rome (21:20) makes the end of the old system a public and historic fact.

b. The destiny of every man's 'temple'

In his unveiling of the future Jesus looks on beyond the destruction of the Jerusalem temple and the Jewish system. He speaks of the coming of the Son of man 'in a cloud with power and great glory', of the coming of 'the kingdom of God', of 'that day' which will come upon 'all who dwell upon the face of the whole earth' (21:27, 31, 34, 35). He looks forward, in other words, to the time when he will return to the universal temple, the place where every man has in the end to confront his God.

Before his warnings about the two coming judgments, the Jewish one (21:20ff.) and the universal one (21:25ff.), Jesus has given a warning of another kind. His disciples have asked, 'What will be the sign when this is about to take place?' (21:7). And although Jesus's long reply is really all about signs, it is helpful to distinguish, as Ellis does,[15] between 'signs of the age' and 'signs of the end'.

The disciples are told what to look for as signs of the end: these will be plainly visible. 'When you *see* Jerusalem surrounded by armies' (21:20), that will be the end of Jewry; 'they will *see* the Son of man coming in a cloud with power and great glory' (21:27), and that will be the end of the world.

Jesus discourages a 'countdown' interpretation of prophecy, by which current events can be plotted in sequence to show how far we have yet to go to judgment day. Like those who saw Jerusalem besieged, those who see the Son of man coming in glory will know that judgment is not simply on its way, but has actually arrived. These, and these only, are the end-signs. All other signs indicate,

[15] Ellis, pp. 241f.

not the end we look towards, but the age we live in. Periodically throughout the time between Jesus's first and second comings there will be upheavals in the world at large (21:8–11), and persecution for the church (21:12–19). The disciples are told 'to reject the usual apocalyptic interpretation of political distress. It is a sign of the age, not of the end.'[16] 'This will be a time for you', not to calculate the nearness of the Lord's return, but 'to bear testimony' (21:13).

The call of Jesus's closing words, therefore, is to be watchful and prayerful, ready at any time for his return to his temple. On that day the Holy of Holies, the place where God and man meet face to face, will no longer be a dark room in an ancient building in an eastern city; it will have expanded to the limits of the whole human world. On that day all religions, and all substitutes for religion, will pass under the critical eye of Christ. All our beliefs and ideas about God and the world and life and ourselves—he will see whether they are worthy of the temple. Will they 'stand before the Son of man' (21:36), or will they be swept away?

[16] Ellis, p.242.

22:1 – 23:25

Satan's hour

'This is your hour, and the power of darkness' (22:53)

The full moon of Passover rises over Jerusalem, and the last night of Jesus's earthly life begins. His ministry has throughout been a running battle with the powers of darkness, but this night finds

> principalities and powers
> Mustering their unseen array[1]

as they had not done since the first confrontation with Jesus, in the desert, at the beginning of the ministry. It was Luke who told us that after that trial of strength 'the devil . . . departed from him until an opportune time' (4:13). Now it is Luke who tells us that the opportune time has come.

Our passage describes the last supper, the walk to the Mount of Olives, the agony in the garden of Gethsemane, the midnight arrest, and the trials, of varying legality, which occupied the early hours of the following morning. It is a complicated story, and presents a number of problems, chiefly about the supper[2] and the trials.[3] But

[1] Charlotte Elliott, *Christian, seek not yet repose.*

[2] There has been much debate as to whether or not the last supper coincided with Passover. John says that the supper took place *before* Passover (Jn. 13:1ff.; 18:28); the other Gospels say that it *was* the Passover (*e.g.* Lk. 22:7–8). It may well be that John is right in placing the official Passover meal on the later date (so that while the Passover lambs were being slaughtered in the temple, Jesus was himself, significantly, being put to death on the cross); but that the others, equally rightly, show Jesus and his disciples celebrating it earlier, according to an unofficial calendar used at that time by some minority groups within Judaism. This suggestion was first elaborated by Mlle. A. Jaubert, *The Date of the Last Supper* (New York, 1965), and the argument is summarized in most recent commentaries. Whatever the facts about its date, the supper is rich in Passover symbolism.

we shall try to see what are the ruling themes in Luke's mind as he selects and depicts various incidents, highlighting this rather than that, so as to bring out what is to him of greatest importance.

1. Evening: the two plans revealed (22:1–38)

In his description of the Passover meal shared by Jesus and his friends, and of what preceded it, Luke makes us very conscious of the undercurrents beneath the surface of events. Two fateful plans were afoot, in counterpoint with each other, a plan of destruction and a plan of salvation.

a. The plan of destruction (22:1–6)

The destruction of Jesus is the object of this plot. His enemies are scheming, as they have had in mind to do for some time already (19:47; 20:19f.), to eliminate the trouble-maker from Nazareth.

The first item in their plan is 'the feast of Unleavened Bread, ... the Passover' (22:1). They would have preferred to get rid of Jesus at a time when there were fewer of his possible supporters about; but it cannot be helped, and the deed cannot be postponed, so they will use the occasion as best they may. Passover commemorates Israel's departure from Egypt; and if a connection between that exodus and the one being organized for Jesus occurs to any of them, it will seem, one presumes, no more than a grimly ironic pun—though Jesus himself knows better.[4]

---

[3] Contrary to the opinion of some, it is by no means impossible to reconstruct a sequence of events such as might underlie the four Gospel accounts. The following references show where each episode is recorded at greatest length:
1. A trial before Annas; Peter's first denial (Jn. 18:12–24)
2. Peter's second and third denials (Lk. 22:58–62)
3. An unofficial trial before the Sanhedrin (Mt. 26:59–68; Mk. 14:55–65)
4. An official trial before the Sanhedrin (Lk. 22:66–71; = Mk. 15:1a)
5. The death of Judas (Mt. 27:3–10)
6. A first trial before Pilate (Jn. 18:28–38a)
7. A trial before Herod (Lk. 23:7–12)
8. A second trial before Pilate (Lk. 23:13–22)
9. The scourging (Mk. 15:16–20)
10. The condemnation (Jn. 19:4–16).

[4] See below, p. 192 n. 7.

The next point in the scheme is that there should be someone to engineer the arrest of Jesus, a friend who is prepared to betray him. Judas is to hand, one 'of the number of the twelve' (22:3). Whatever his motives may have been for the treachery he planned, the fact remains that he was willing to be implicated in the plot.

Its sponsors were 'the chief priests and the scribes' (22:2). We have seen how the Pharisees, the sect within Judaism which had been particularly opposed to Jesus, have now handed over the role of his bitterest enemies to the chief priests, scribes, and elders, the leaders of the Jewish people. They are the official representatives of the old Israel, Judaism as it had become, a religious system unwilling to accept God's chosen Messiah when he came to claim its allegiance. We note in these verses their malice towards Jesus, their fear of the ordinary people who might support him, and their unholy glee at finding a traitor in Judas.

But behind them loomed an even more sinister power. We are reminded of the cosmic view which Luke so often evidences. Just as he is concerned not with one nation only, but with the world, so he is concerned not with this world only, but with the 'super-world', what Paul calls the 'heavenly places' where spiritual forces are locked in the ultimate conflict between good and evil.[5] So alone among the evangelists Luke mentions the activity of Satan (22:3, 31), describes Jesus's agony[6] and bloody sweat in Gethsemane (22:44), and records his words in 22:53, 'This is your hour, and the power of darkness.'

Thus with Passover the occasion, Judas the catspaw, the leaders of Jewry the plotters, and Satan the moving spirit, Luke describes the plan to destroy Jesus. But is Jesus the helpless victim of these machinations? Nothing could be further from the truth. And Luke tells his story in such a way as to show that Jesus also is pursuing a plan, which keeps pace step by step with Satan's.

b. The plan of salvation (22:7–38)

'Jesus sent Peter and John, saying, "Go and prepare the passover" ' (22:8). The strange thing was that as they went they found the way had already been prepared for them (22:10–13). And what happened with the preparations for the meal was happening also on the broader scale. A divine plan was being unfolded, as a counter-plot to that of Satan. In order to make this clear, Luke brings together into his

[5] Cf. Eph. 6:11-13.
[6] 'Agony' is related to the Greek words for 'struggle, contest'.

account of the last supper a group of the sayings of Jesus which are in various places, or indeed are not recorded at all, in other Gospels.

First he shows how the Passover fits in (22:14–20). It is part of that old Jewish religion which has become twisted and distorted, and whose leaders are even now plotting to kill Jesus. But the Passover, which will be the occasion of the success of their plot, is already a part of his. It is going to be *'fulfilled* in the kingdom of God' (22:16). For the Jews, it meant the deliverance from Egypt into Canaan. But now it is to be *filled* with its *full* meaning, and from this year onwards will signify to the people of God a deliverance of the profoundest kind, from sin and death into eternal life. Moses' exodus will be fulfilled in Jesus's exodus. [7]

Next, what will Jesus make of Judas? He too is a part not only of Satan's plan but of God's counter-plan (22:21–23): already the betrayal of the Son of man 'has been *determined*' (22:22). Judas is known; his treachery is known; his fate is known—'woe to that man'; all these things are already known, allowed for, and woven into the divine scheme.

And what of the chief priests? Jesus looks round at his disciples (22:24–30); they still understand very little about the community he is forming out of them (22:24), but he tries to explain something of what is happening. Out there in the city, he seems to say, are the leaders of the old Israel, made God's people by the old covenant; but they have rebelled against God. So 'I *covenant* to give you' (for that is the word 'appoint'), 'as my Father *has covenanted* to give me, a Kingdom';[8] and under the terms of that new covenant, it is you who henceforth will be the twelve rulers of the new Israel (22:30).

And Satan, the master-plotter, who has already entered into Judas Iscariot—what of him? Listen, says Jesus to his apostles (22:31–34): it was not only Judas that Satan wanted; he demanded to have you all.[9] Judas I have abandoned to him. But for the rest of you, although Simon is going to deny me, yet I can restore even one who sinks as low as that, and through him I shall restore all of you. So much for Satan's power! He has met his match. When the Son prays to the Father, a power is released which checks all Satan's demands.

So Jesus has already allowed for all the elements in the plot against him. He is fulfilling the Passover, predicting his betrayal, covenant-

---

[7] Luke has described how, at the transfiguration of Jesus, 'Moses and Elijah' also 'appeared in glory and spoke of his departure, which he was to accomplish at Jerusalem' (9:31–32). Luke's word for 'departure' is *exodos*.

[8] 22:29 (Weymouth).   [9] 'You' in 22:31 is plural (in 22:32 it is singular).

ing to replace the old Israel with a new one, and praying effectively against the schemes of Satan. His powerful counter-plan is in operation. This is no longer a mere rehearsal, like the evangelistic tour of 10:1–12 (22:35). This is the real thing, the 'fulfilment' (22:37) of the plan.

2. Night: the two plans interwoven (22:39–71)

Four episodes take Jesus through the lonely hours of the night and into the dawn of Good Friday.

a. The agony (22:39–46)

As has been mentioned, only Luke tells of the spiritual conflict in Gethsemane.[10] Why is it so appropriate in his account of the passion? Because as he has been revealing Satan's plan of destruction and God's plan of salvation, it has become apparent that they are *both driving towards the same object*. Jesus's enemies are bending all their efforts and their ingenuity to bring him to the cross; yet that is the very 'cup' which the Father has given him to drink (22:42). His Father's will converges with 'their will' (23:25). No wonder he is 'in an agony', with 'his sweat ... like great drops of blood' (22:44).

b. The arrest (22:47–53)

The lights twinkle across the Kidron valley towards the garden, and Jesus's enemies 'come out as against a robber, with swords and clubs'; it is their 'hour' (22:52–53).

Yet Jesus has gone to the garden 'as was his custom' (22:39), and has made no effort to avoid capture. He forbids his disciples to defend him, though they are able and willing to do so (22:49). There is no question but that he has gone deliberately into a trap from which he could have escaped with ease. His enemies are carrying out their plans, but he is altogether in control.

c. The denial (22:54–62)

The shame and remorse of Peter, following his denial of Jesus, focus our immediate attention in this episode. Is it not a triumph for Satan, that with Jesus practically destroyed, this is the sort of leadership to which his disciples are going to be entrusted?

[10] See above, p. 191.

Yet, while 'Peter remembered the word of the Lord, how he had said to him, "Before the cock crows today, you will deny me three times" ' (22:61), we may also remember the other word Jesus had spoken: 'I have prayed for you that your faith may not fail' (22:32). Even here at the defection of his chief disciple Jesus is still in control.

d. The decision (22:63–71)

Day has come; but we may be sure it was the merest glimmer of dawn when the council was convened, as early as it legally could be, so we may count its meeting as one of the events of the night. The council members sit in judgment on Jesus, and from the crucial words he speaks in these verses he is condemned.

But notice exactly what he does say: 'From now on the Son of man shall be seated at the right hand of the power of God' (22:69). From now on it is Jesus who will occupy the throne of judgment. By rejecting God's Christ, they forfeit their right to be leaders of God's people. In the act of judging him, they themselves are judged by him. From this point onwards the old Israel is replaced by the new, whose rightful ruler he shall be for evermore.

Thus as their plans mature his own are brought to fruition. The Jews' decision in 22:71 is the crucial one. From thereon, it is downhill all the way, as the two plans hasten to their common conclusion.

3. Morning: the two plans carried through (23:1–25)

It is simply a question of getting the council's decision ratified. In fact, a mortifying series of complications ensues before Jesus is satisfactorily nailed to the cross, as will be realized if the four Gospel accounts are read in combination. But Luke simplifies the story, and shows us the responsibility of the various authorities as the morning of Good Friday proceeds to its inevitable climax.

a. Pilate's reponsibility (23:1–7)

If there is one thing clearer than another in the accounts of the trial of Jesus, it is the innocence of the prisoner. 'I find no crime in this man' (23:4). The famous Roman justice should therefore have dismissed the charges against him, and stopped the whole ghastly affair. But Pilate was a weak man, and there were many pressures upon him, which succeeded in diverting the course of justice. As Caird says, 'Pilate does everything in his power to secure the discharge of Jesus, sho t of discharging him.'[11] That was what he could and should have done. And though Luke is careful to lay the chief blame elsewhere than on the Roman authorities, he is by no means prepared to whitewash Pilate and absolve him from responsibility in the condemnation of Jesus.

b. Herod's responsibility (23:8–12)

Herod 'had long desired' to see Jesus, and 'questioned him at some length' (23:8–9). But however prolonged his interest and his talk, they evince nothing whatever of serious concern about Jesus. Herod is a man of intolerable frivolity. All he wants is to see some magic; and when Jesus refuses to play, Herod's curiosity turns to contempt (23:11). But the man who shows that attitude towards Jesus, and cannot treat him seriously even at such a critical juncture, is himself the most comtemptible of all the characters on the stage of Good Friday, and Luke takes no pains to conceal the fact. Herod is as responsible as Pilate for the death of Jesus, for he found him 'not guilty' (23:15), yet apparently it did not occur to him to release the prisoner himself, as he could well have done, and as no doubt Pilate hoped he might have done.

c. Israel's responsibility (23:13–25)

Jesus is sent back from Herod to Pilate; but in this second trial before Pilate it is the chief priests who are spotlighted. Three times Pilate proposes to release Jesus, and three times the Jews shout him down. They have their way; and on them Luke lays the chief blame.[12]

We must not think that he is showing some kind of anti-semitism in this. It is not Israel as such on whom he fastens the responsibility. 'He is not a real Jew who is one outwardly, nor is true circumcision something external and physical. He is a real Jew who is one inwardly, and real circumcision is a matter of the heart, spiritual and not literal.'[13] The false, external Israel, the perverted Judaism which rejects its Messiah, is the villain of the piece, and it is itself to be rejected in favour of the new, true Israel which, though based upon the faithful remnant of old Israel, is to be drawn from men of all nations. That is one of Luke's favourite themes: the sloughing off of

[11] Caird, p. 248.
[12] *Cf.* Acts 2:23; 3:13; 4:10; 5:30.
[13] Rom. 2:28–29.

195

the old nationalistic husk of Judaism so that the new living 'people of God' may emerge.

Nevertheless all are guilty, not only the Jews. Frivolous Herod and feeble Pilate are guilty too, and so is treacherous Judas. And so is Peter. And so are the rest of the disciples. All are sucked into the vortex of Satan's cosmic plan for the destruction of the Son of God. We may be, in the most literal sense, eternally grateful to God that the fate to which they all helped to send Jesus was in fact the cross which God himself had planned as the means of our redemption. But that is no excuse. *Felix culpa* maybe, but still *culpa*.[14] As Peter says afterwards, in words reported by Luke in Acts 2:23, Jesus was 'delivered up according to the definite plan and foreknowledge of God,' but even so he was 'crucified and killed by the hands of lawless men.'

The two plans converge at Calvary. But the difference between them is all-important, and men must choose on whose side they will be: either beneficiaries of the plan by which God brought Jesus to the cross, or accomplices in the plan by which Satan brought him there. We are back with the stark contrast of 11:14–23, and the challenge of its last verse: 'He who is not with me is against me.'

The aim of an exposition is to re-state what the Bible said when it was first written so that it can be heard speaking still today, in the terms of today, to the needs of today. If the expositor has his feet firmly on the ground, in our case the late twentieth-century ground, the message he brings from Scripture for our generation may often be different from that which was needed by an earlier one; and, by the same token, the relevance of such a message may not last very long, because the needs of our successors will be different again.

But the nearer we come to the heart of the gospel, the deeper we penetrate beneath the changeable surface of human life, and the closer we get to matters in which our needs are indistinguishable from the needs of men in any other period of history. Of course good exposition will not deal with timeless truths only, to the exclusion of contemporary truths; but neither will it be always contemporary and never timeless. For example, the story of the cross, to which we come in our next section, is to be 'applied' by today's preachers just as it must be 'applied' by the preachers of every age: namely, to the basic need of sinful men, which is the need to know how God can save them from their sin.

[14] From the Roman Missal: *O felix culpa, quae talem ac tantum meruit habere Redemptorem* ('O happy fault, which has deserved to have such and so mighty a Redeemer').

The section we have just been studying is in many respects similar. We have seen how, as Good Friday dawns, all the human actors in the drama, from the humblest to the most powerful, are caught up in a superhuman contest. 'Clashing systems gather for a fall', and the clash is between principalities and powers in the heavenly places; its consequences are inconceivably great. The unseen conflict dwarfs even the Herods and the Pilates of this world, and along with them all the contemporary problems to which contemporary preachers have ever applied their expositions! In face of such immensities, individual Christians feel themselves to be very small units in a very big war; and the lesson of that is now what it always has been—to thank God that we have been 'chosen to be soldiers . . . for our Captain's band',[15] that the conduct of affairs is his responsibility, that the crucial battle has already been fought and won by him, and that the eventual result is not in doubt. Meanwhile our orders are simply to trust and obey.

And yet, having said that this is a truth needed equally by Christians in every age, there is nevertheless a peculiar aptness about it today. In the global village which our world has become, all of us are going to suffer unless the potential evils of misapplied science, runaway technology, limited resources, and political imperialism both of the right and of the left, can be kept in check. And the outcome is so manifestly not in *our* hands, that we, more than any previous generation, need desperately to know that *someone* is in control.

To our times in particular, then, the account which Luke gives of the last hours of Jesus's earthly life brings a much-needed assurance. The most diabolical of all the schemes of Satan was not only countered at every point by a superior plan of God's devising. It was actually woven into that plan, and made to serve its ends. And if that was what God could do with the master-plot of hell, then there can be no evil which he cannot in the end turn to blessing.

[15] Frances Ridley Havergal, *Who is on the Lord's side?*

23:26–56
The cross

Only once in this passage, in its first verse, does Luke mention the actual word; but it is 'the cross' which is central here—not only central to Luke's description of 'the place which is called The Skull' (23:33), but central to his Gospel, to the Christian faith, and to the whole of history. The cross was the wooden gibbet to which, in Roman times, a condemned criminal was fastened, until he died of exposure, asphyxia, and loss of blood. Of all the tens of thousands of crosses on which men died during the years in which that system of law prevailed, one towers above the rest: the cross on which Jesus of Nazareth was crucified. Christians use this image as a metaphor of what happened on it, and when we say 'the cross', we mean the death of Jesus. On the cross, then, we focus our attention now.

Commentators noting the differences between the various Bible writers sometimes assert that Luke, unlike the other evangelists, 'has no theology of the cross'.[1] We have to look elsewhere, they say, for explicit statements that the death of Jesus saves men from sin and death; we shall not find them in Luke.

It is true that Luke does not spell out such a statement in his description of the crucifixion, and that he omits some of the most important passages in which the other evangelists make it clear.[2] But let us see what he does say about the cross.

---

[1] Morris, p. 42. It should be noted that Morris is mentioning this assertion in order to refute it.

[2] *E.g.* Mt. 20:28 = Mk. 10:45; Mt. 26:28 = Mk. 14:24 (if, as many hold, Lk. 22:19b–20 does not really belong to Luke).

1. The road to the cross

They led him away . . . to the place which is called The Skull (23:26, 33).

From Pilate's judgment hall to the place called Calvaria, 'The Skull', is a few hundred yards in distance. But the road to the cross is a long, long one measured in time. We can trace it, and see the cross at the end of it, through the whole of Luke's Gospel.

Early in his first main section, in the stories of Jesus's infancy, he records the words of the aged Simeon spoken to Jesus's mother concerning her baby boy: he will be 'a sign that is spoken against', and a sword will pierce through her own soul also (2:34–35). It is thirty years ahead; but there already on the horizon looms the cross. Much later, when his ministry has begun and he has gathered around him a band of disciples whom he is instructing, he tells them that 'the Son of man must suffer many things, and be rejected by the elders and chief priests and scribes, *and be killed*, and on the third day be raised' (9:22): there too is the cross. Transfigured in glory on the hilltop, he talks, in the hearing of his amazed followers, with Moses and Elijah; and their subject is 'his departure, which he was to accomplish at Jerusalem' (9:31): there again is the cross.

In the great central section of his Gospel, concerned largely with the teaching of Jesus, Luke touches on the same subject again and again. 'The days drew near for him to be received up', and 'he set his face to go to Jerusalem' (9:51), to the cross. He has 'a baptism to be baptized with' (12:50), and that, as we may deduce from the other Gospels,[3] means the cross. To those who warn him that Herod wants to kill him, he replies, 'Go and tell that fox, "Behold, I cast out demons and perform cures today and tomorrow, and the third day I finish my course . . . It cannot be that a prophet should perish away from Jerusalem' (13:32–33); there the cross awaits him. Speaking about his final return at the end of time, he reiterates that 'first he must suffer many things and be rejected by this generation' (17:25): they will send him to the cross. As the Gospel's central section draws to a close he repeats his earlier plain teaching: 'We are going up to Jerusalem, and everything that is written of the Son of man by the prophets will be accomplished. For he will be delivered to the Gentiles, and will be mocked and shamefully treated and spit upon; they will scourge him and kill him' (18:31–33), by nailing him to a cross.

---

[3] Mk. 10:38–39; Jn. 18:11.

The passion story, Luke's third main section, opens under the very shadow of Calvary: 'the chief priests and the scribes and the principal men of the people sought to destroy him' (19:47). As before, it is the sayings of Jesus himself, as Luke records them, which recognize that looming shadow, and show that he knows himself to be deliberately walking the road to the cross. He tells the parable of the vineyard, whose tenant-farmers, having ill-treated all the owner's previous messengers, eventually kill his son (20:9–15): there is the cross. 'The Son of man goes as it has been determined', he declares (22:22)—goes to the cross. 'This scripture must be fulfilled in me, "And he was reckoned with transgressors"' (22:37)—ranged alongside thieves on the cross.

The cross dominates the prospect for Jesus. It is like a landmark on the skyline, on which his eyes are fixed, and towards which, however winding the road, he constantly moves. And in the same way it dominates Luke's scheme of relating the Gospel. He has no need to underline the fact of the crucifixion when he comes to it, no need to focus a blinding spotlight on it; we find simply the quiet statement that 'when they came to the place which is called The Skull, there they crucified him' (23:33). For ever since the childhood episode with Simeon (2:34–35)—in the temple, at a distance of thirty years though a mere half-mile away—the Jesus whom Luke has been describing has been travelling the road to the cross.

In the same way, let no reader imagine that he has begun to understand the Christ of the gospel—or indeed the gospel of the Christ—unless the cross has come to dominate his horizon also. Only when he has sought it, and reached it, and let it fill his vision, as it filled the vision of the Lord and of his evangelist, can he say that he is beginning to see what the Christian faith is about.

But to understand how this applies to us personally, we need to hear more of what Luke's Gospel has to tell us about the matter.

2. The Man on the cross

'This man has done nothing wrong' ... *'Certainly this man was innocent'* (23: 41, 47).

Luke does not simply thread his story on to the theme of a prophesied cross. He is very much concerned also to show us the Man who hangs on it. There is one thing in particular about this Man, as Luke depicts him, which will help to bring out the meaning of the crucifixion.

Already he has made it plain, before he reaches the description of how the sentence is carried out. Jesus is still on trial when Pilate addresses the Jewish leaders in these words: 'You brought me this man as one who was perverting the people; and after examining him before you, behold, I did not find this man guilty of any of your charges against him; neither did Herod, for he sent him back to us' (23:14–15). The Roman governor and the Idumaean king both pronounce the prisoner guiltless. Even his accusers have, in effect, done the same. 'They began to accuse him, saying, "We found this man perverting our nation, and forbidding us to give tribute to Caesar, and saying that he himself is Christ a king" ' (23:2). So impossible is it even for them to find anything of which he is guilty, that they are reduced to inventing charges which are almost the precise opposite of the truth.

This same delineation of the character of Jesus is continued in our present passage. Luke alone reports the words of the thief concerning Jesus: 'This man has done nothing wrong'—or, as Plummer interprets the Greek word *atopon*, ' "nothing unbecoming," still less anything criminal'.[4] The comment of the centurion, who according to Matthew and Mark calls Jesus a 'son of God' (Mt. 27:54; Mk. 15:39), is recorded by Luke as: 'Certainly this man was innocent' (23:47). Here also Plummer's note is illuminating: 'Probably the two expressions represent one and the same thought: "He was a good man, and quite right in calling God His Father." '[5] Even among the Jewish leaders the same opinion about Jesus is maintained: Joseph of Arimathaea, 'a member of the council, a good and righteous man, ... had not consented to their purpose and deed' (23:50–51); in other words, *righteous* men should have agreed that Jesus too was righteous.

There is no mistaking the fact that Luke wants us to see the innocence of this Man. When we consider the road to the cross, it is as if we hear Luke proclaiming, from the very beginning of his Gospel, that 'Jesus has come into the world *to die*;' and the words echo down the arches of the years, through the length of the Gospel story, 'to die—to die—to die'. Then when we consider the Man himself, now that he hangs dying on the cross, Luke declares: 'And

4 Plummer, p. 534.
5 Plummer, p. 539.

201

his death is *undeserved*;' and again the words echo around that claustrophobic Good Friday scene, 'undeserved—undeserved—undeserved'.

No doubt Luke has an eye to his readers, both Roman and Jewish, and wishes to show that Jesus is not at all the disreputable character they might have assumed from the fact that he died a criminal's death. But there is in Luke's mind a more compelling motive than that, as we shall realize when we consider another metaphor. If we can speak of the cross, and mean more than rough timber, we may be permitted to speak of the nails, and mean more than sharp iron. What might we understand by them?

3. The nails in the cross

'Father, forgive them; for they know not what they do' (23:34)

'Truly, I say to you, today you will be with me in Paradise' (23:43)

The question that arises from what Luke has shown us so far is a portentous one. He has emphasized, not by crude underlinings at the crucifixion itself but by the whole tenor of his story, that its great aim is accomplished when Jesus dies on the cross. But he has also made it quite clear that that death was not the penalty of the sins of Jesus; for he had none. And the question is this: If it was not his own sins which nailed him to the cross, *then what did*?

To see Luke's answer to that question, we must remind ourselves of two leading characteristics of his Gospel. We have seen the importance he attaches to sayings—words of prophecy, messages from God, particularly the teachings of Jesus. We have also seen that one of his main themes, perhaps the main one, is salvation: the saving of men, by Jesus the Saviour. So it is not surprising that Luke includes in his account of the crucifixion, the climax of his story, certain sayings of the Man on the cross; nor is it surprising that they should concern the subject of salvation.

All four of the sayings of Jesus in this passage are recorded only by Luke. For the moment we look at the second and third of them. There is a prayer for those who crucify him, and a promise for one who is crucified with him: 'Father, forgive them; for they know not what they do'; 'Truly, I say to you, today you will be with me in Paradise'. Both these sayings provide a good deal of material for discussion, and have been variously interpreted. What cannot be denied, however, is that the former claims forgiveness of sin, and the latter offers eternal life. Between them they speak of the doing away of the old and the coming of the new, the replacement of the life of sin by the life of the Spirit, which is the double-sided coin of *salvation*. At the cross, therefore, as throughout his Gospel, Luke presents Jesus as the Saviour.

Now, if I am shown Jesus suffering the penalty of sin, and if I am assured nevertheless that in him there is no sin, and if I find him offering me salvation from sin, it takes no great effort of the intellect to grasp that what nails him to the cross is the sin from which he promises to save me—*my* sin. Its effects have been diverted from me to him. And there, not (it is true) in so many words, but in the whole scheme of his story-telling, is Luke's theology of the cross. It is no less definite than Peter's—'He himself bore our sins in his body on the tree'—or Paul's—'For our sake he made him to be sin who knew no sin'.[6]

4. The people round the cross

'There followed him a great multitude of the people' (23:27).

Luke, interested (as always) less in one narrow group of people than in humanity in general, depicts around the cross a grandly comprehensive array of characters. By doing so, he adds to his description of a Saviour who dies on the cross not for his own sins but for those of others, an indication of who may, and who may not, benefit from that offer of salvation.

Extra to the traditional list of 'Seven Words from the Cross' which can be compiled from all four evangelists is another saying of Jesus, uttered on the way to the cross. Like the others in our present passage, this earlier one is peculiar to Luke: 'Daughters of Jerusalem, do not weep for me, but weep for yourselves and for your children ... The days are coming when they will say, "Blessed are the barren, and the wombs that never bore, and the breasts that never gave suck!" ... For if they do this when the wood is green, what will happen when it is dry?' (23:28–31).

His words about the 'daughters of Jerusalem' raise problems,[7] as

---

[6] 1 Pet. 2:24; 2 Cor. 5:21.

[7] The most obvious problem is the meaning of 23:31 (green wood and dry). Since in 23:28 Jesus is contrasting his own fate on this occasion, in (say) AD 30, with that of the inhabitants of Jerusalem who will be involved in the sack of the city in AD 70, then

do those about the soldiers and those about the thief (23:34, 43). But what is unmistakable is that the outlook for the city which these women represent, the old Jerusalem, is in one sense much worse than his own prospect of crucifixion. To bring salvation was the object of Jesus's coming; but again and again he has warned that there will be *no* salvation for those who reject God's chosen Saviour. This is the seventh and last of his prophecies of the doom of Jerusalem, the city which represents all who refuse the saving gospel.[8]

But for the rest—for the thief, for the soldiers, for the friends, for the bystanders, even for Joseph (member of the Jewish Sanhedrin though he was!)—the offer of salvation stands open. It is for all who are not fatally determined to make their own way without Jesus. It is at the cross that they hear the prayer of the Son to his Father, a prayer which cannot fail to be answered: 'Father, forgive them: forgive them for all the sins which stand between them and salvation.' It is at the cross that they hear the promise of the Saviour: 'Today you shall enter eternal life with me.'

This is what Luke's Gospel is all about. In fact, this *is* the gospel. When this point has been reached, the earthly life of Jesus can come to an end; and so it does, with the last of the seven words from the cross: ' "Father, into thy hands I commit my spirit!" And having said this he breathed his last' (23:46). The body is taken down from the cross, wrapped in a shroud, and buried. There is yet to come the glorious resurrection, by which Jesus will be 'designated Son of God in power according to the Spirit of holiness',[9] and after which his own new life will be made available to all his people. But by mid-afternoon on the first Good Friday the salvation of the world was accomplished, at the cross of Christ.

---

presumably 'what is done to green wood' corresponds to the former, and 'what is done to dry wood' corresponds to the latter. This would point towards the kind of interpretation well expressed by Caird (pp. 249f.): 'Israel's intransigence has already kindled the flames of Roman impatience, and if the fire is now hot enough to destroy one whom Roman justice has pronounced innocent, what must the guilty expect?'

[8] See 11:49–51; 13:6–9; 13:34–35; 19: 41–44; 20:16; 21:20–24; and the present passage, 23:28–31.

[9] Rom. 1:4.

24:1–53

The first day of the week

The young man reading the Gospel at his ordination service forgot the usual form. When he reached the last verse, he added a sentence like that which had followed the Epistle: 'Here endeth the Gospel.' The bishop was heard to growl: 'Heaven forbid!'

With chapter 24, Luke brings us to the end of his Gospel; but heaven forbid that the gospel of Christ should ever come to an end. The first verse of the chapter, which together with its last verse forms a kind of frame for Luke's picture of the resurrection, indicates that he is in fact describing a beginning. It is 'the first day of the week'. All the events of the chapter are chronicled as if they happened on that one day, even if (as some believe) he is combining several incidents which were in fact spread over the six weeks between the resurrection and the ascension.[1]

Both in Genesis and in Revelation we find the pattern of the working week, with the work completed on the sixth day and with a

---

[1] Luke was quite well aware that forty days elapsed between these two events (Acts 1:3). So the chronology of chapter 24 may be explained in one of two ways.

(a) He is telescoping into one 'day' a number of incidents which took place at various times during those forty days, and 'intends to present a theme rather than a chronicle' (Ellis, p. 271). In this case, 24:51 describes the ascension, and includes the words 'and was carried up into heaven' (RV, RSV mg.).

(b) Alternatively, everything in chapter 24 happened on Easter Day. Luke, having changed from the intentionally vague chronology of his account of Passion Week to a close-knit, timed, account of the actual crucifixion and resurrection, extends the same close chronology throughout the whole of his last chapter (23:44, 54, 56; 24:1, 13, 33, 36). Omitting, as some manuscripts do, the second half of 24:51, we understand the end of the night walk to Bethany to be Jesus's leave-taking at the end of Easter Day, a disappearance like that of 24:31, and *not* his ascension.

If, as I think, this second explanation is correct, it means that Acts 1:9 is the only account of the ascension in Scripture (apart from the mention in the unreliable longer ending of Mark).

rest on the seventh, and the same pattern is clearly discernible here at the centre of history.[2] On the sixth day, Friday, the work of redemption is accomplished (23:54; cf. Jn. 19:30). On the seventh day 'they rested according to the commandment' (23:56). But then 'on the first day' (24:1) a new week began. It was the first day of a new era, a new creation. A whole new world was coming into being on that first Christian Sunday. Thus Luke ends his Gospel with an account of that first day which was to begin the new age. In three episodes he sets the new age on its course.

1. Morning: the garden tomb (24:1–12)

The tomb belonged to Joseph of Arimathea,[3] and it was situated in a garden close by Calvary.[4] The traditional site (now the Church of the Holy Sepulchre) is within the present walls of Jerusalem, although in the time of Jesus it was probably outside the city. The other site pointed out to visitors is the 'garden tomb', beside what is known as Gordon's Calvary.[5] Archaeologists think little of it, but it is at any rate still outside the city wall, and in it one can recapture to some extent the atmosphere of that far-off Sunday morning when 'the women who had come with him from Galilee' (23:55) came with spices for the embalming of his body.

a. The need of the human soul

They did not find the body . . . They were perplexed (24:3–4)

As the women arrive at the tomb, they find the stone rolled away from its entrance, and the body gone. They are 'perplexed' by what is not there, and 'frightened' by what is there (24:4–5)—two men whose appearance outshines the pale light of early morning, and who greet them with the angelic proclamation of the resurrection message.

So far as their perplexity is concerned, it is not only the empty tomb which they cannot understand. To judge from what the angels

---

[2] See my *I Saw Heaven Opened*, p. 202.
[3] Mt. 28:60.   [4] Jn. 19:41.
[5] General Gordon visited Jerusalem in 1883, shortly before his death at the siege of Khartoum, and was impressed by the appearance of this site, first noted by others some years earlier. See André Parrot, *Golgotha and the Church of the Holy Sepulchre* (SCM Press, 1957), pp. 59-65.

say to them (24:6–7), they can make nothing of the betrayal of Jesus either, nor of his crucifixion, nor, it is implied, of all he has said about these things beforehand. Whatever has happened at the tomb, they can see no meaning in the event, and it is just one of a whole series of events that are all equally meaningless.

So most men live through the events of this life without any awareness of their meaning. 'Like brute beasts that have no understanding',[6] like the dog which, when you point at a bone, sniffs not at the bone but at your finger, they cannot see what all these things point to. Their physical and emotional need is sufficient to occupy them fully; food, clothing, security, these are the things that 'the nations of the world seek' (12:30), and the deeper need—to understand what it is all *about*—remains unsatisfied.

Yet on the other hand the offer of a supernatural answer makes them 'frightened'. For this is the genuine article. It is not a voice at a séance which says what they want it to say, with the bonus of a pleasurable tingling of the spine. It is a real message from the world beyond, which 'bows their faces to the ground' in awe. That kind of fearsome intervention they are not eager to court. It is nevertheless what they need, and we notice next how exactly that need is met.

b. The word of the divine Saviour

'Remember how he told you' ... And they remembered his words (24:6, 8)

For it is a *word* which the angels bring. Compare Luke's report with those of the first two Gospels. Mark has, 'He has risen'; Matthew, 'He has risen, as he said';[7] Luke, true to this special emphasis of his, goes further—'Remember *how he told you* ... that the Son of man must be delivered into the hands of sinful men, and be crucified, and on the third day rise'; and then, he adds, '*they remembered his words*'.

No deed of Jesus, and certainly not this last and greatest, has been without its accompanying word. No event has been left unexplained. Nor has any part of God's creation or man's life. The disciples know the words of Jesus, and need to be reminded of them. The world at large has the words of Jesus available to it, and needs the church to preach them and apply them to its condition. Yet both church and world are often quite unnecessarily ignorant of these words, a system

---

[6] From the 1662 Prayer Book Marriage Service!
[7] Mk. 16:6; Mt. 28:6.

of faith which takes everything into account and interprets all of life as one connected and meaningful whole.

The first step in the way of salvation is to begin to see that life does make sense, and it is the teaching of Jesus which enables men to see this. The prime responsibility placed, therefore, on those who have the opportunity to speak either to the church or to the world outside, is to go back to the plain words of Jesus and to remind men of those: 'Remember how he told you'.

2. Afternoon: the Emmaus road (24:13–32)

Of the four evangelists, only Luke has preserved for us the story of the walk to Emmaus. With his typically human touch, his unfailing concern about the human condition, he has chosen as so often before to record an episode about ordinary people and their needs, and about how those needs are met by the message of salvation in Jesus.

A seven-mile walk which ended at Emmaus 'toward evening' (24:13, 29) must have occupied the last two hours of Easter afternoon. More, perhaps, if (as some have suggested) Cleopas's companion was his wife;[8] and their step may have been slower still in view of their state of mind as they left Jerusalem.

a. The need of the human soul

Jesus himself drew near and went with them. But their eyes were kept from recognizing him (24:15–16)

The conversation of the two disciples was heavy with sorrow (24:17), disappointment (24:21), and bewilderment (24:22–24). As he tells how a stranger overtook them, and asked why they were so sad, Luke shows us the greatness of their need, and pinpoints the cause of it.

For the stranger's enquiry elicited from them (wonderful to relate) nothing less than *a full rehearsal of the facts about Jesus*. Read again the Gospel according to Cleopas, in 24:19–24! There is the ministry of Jesus in word and deed, the crucifixion which completed it, and the hope of redemption which filled it with meaning. There is the conquered grave, and there is the apostolic witness to that. There is

---

[8] 'Foolish *men*' (24:25) does not represent exactly what Luke wrote; there is no noun (NEB is more accurate: 'How dull you are!'), and one of the two could have been a woman.

everything—everything except a personal word from the living Christ which would in turn make the facts live also.

Yet for the greater part of their journey[9] Jesus had actually been walking with them! Somehow 'their eyes were kept from recognizing him'.[10] An experience of the living God was what they wanted; but though he came to them, and paced alongside them, yet still their hearts were cold.

b. The word of the divine Saviour
'Did not our hearts burn within us while he talked to us on the road, while he opened to us the scriptures?' (24:32).

The first step towards salvation is to see that life does have a meaning, and is not

> a tale
> Told by an idiot, full of sound and fury,
> Signifying nothing.[11]

The second step is to see that that meaning is to be found only in Christ. Just as his words alone could make sense of what to the women at the tomb seemed a meaningless jigsaw of events, so his words alone could reveal to the couple on the Emmaus road his own living self as the key to the jigsaw. See, by their own confession, what it was that warmed them into new life: 'Did not our hearts burn within us while he talked to us on the road, while he opened to us the scriptures?'

Again it is the word which brings life. 'The word' here means two things, yet the two things are one. First, it is Jesus who speaks. This is something even better than the word of his earthly ministry. It is

---

[9] Jesus joined them soon enough after they set out for them to assume that he too was coming from Jerusalem (24:18).

[10] A paradox in this and other episodes of the forty days following Easter highlights one unique feature of the appearances of the risen Christ. He was so 'ordinary' that they had at first no suspicion of his being anything other than a flesh-and-blood mortal like themselves; yet in some extraordinary way they could walk and talk with him for two hours or more without recognizing the well-known, well-loved, features and voice of Jesus of Nazareth. Experiences so unlike what they might have expected, even if they had been looking for a resurrection appearance, are hardly likely to be hallucinations.

[11] Shakespeare, *Macbeth*, V.v.16.

the word of his risen power, for he has been 'designated Son of God in power according to the Spirit of holiness by his resurrection from the dead'.[12] And in the power of the Spirit he is living yet. That is why still today we can turn to his words, written and preached, and our own dead hearts come to life; still today we can tell others with delight what 'Jesus says', and they come to life in their turn.

Secondly, the Scripture speaks also—the Old Testament which Jesus was expounding, in which, on his own authority, we find everywhere 'things concerning himself' (24:27), and to which we add the apostolic witness of the New Testament. To the Scripture also we turn eagerly, for it is a living testimony to the living Christ.

John Wesley found his 'Emmaus road' in London, on May 24, 1738. 'In the evening', he tells us in his Journal, 'I went very unwillingly to a society in Aldersgate street, where one was reading Luther's preface to the Epistle to the Romans. About a quarter before nine, while he was describing the change which God works in the heart through faith in Christ, I felt my heart strangely warmed. I felt I did trust in Christ, Christ alone, for salvation; and an assurance was given me that He had taken away my sins, even mine, and saved me from the law of sin and death.' It was William Holland's reading of Luther's commentary on Paul's epistle, but even at those three removes Wesley heard the voice of the living Christ and found in it salvation.

3. Evening: the upper room (24:33–53)

Although the Gospels nowhere say so, it is quite likely that the house in Jerusalem to which these two disciples returned that evening, knowing that the others would be there, was the same house in which the last supper had taken place three days before, and was to be the central meeting place of the Jerusalem church in the days to come—the home of Mary, the mother of John Mark.[13] If so, we can picture the large upper room of 22:12 as the scene of this third episode also.

a. The need of the human soul

They found the eleven gathered together and those who were with them (24:33).

---

[12] Rom. 1:4.   [13] Acts 1:13; 12:12.

The first Easter must have been a day of conflicting emotion. First the women had reported the tomb empty. 'Just like women,' said the men (just like men!), till some of them went there too and found the women were right after all. Then the body which had disappeared, reappeared—a corpse no more, but alive and well; at least Mary Magdalene claimed to have seen it,[14] and so did some of the other women,[15] and when in due course it appeared to Simon Peter also (by this time, surely, no longer 'it' but 'he'), that seems to have convinced the company gathered in the upper room that Jesus had risen indeed. Into this gathering burst the two from Emmaus, with the detailed account of their own experience; and while yet his living presence was the subject of their tale, suddenly it became once more the reality in their midst.

His coming found them believing and unbelieving, startled and joyful and afraid all at once (24:34, 36, 41). Emotionally, they were thoroughly confused. Furthermore, they were not a group which was tidily representative of the infant church: at least two of the apostles were absent,[16] and a number who were not apostles were present. And as to what this collection of disoriented individuals was *for*, as to what the church was *about*, confusion reigned supreme. When we consider the matters which the risen Lord duly 'opened their minds to understand' (24:45), it is clear that until then the nature and purpose of the church, which they themselves constituted, were to them a closed book.

For the third time, therefore, Luke chooses to convey the glorious message of Easter to his readers by starting with man and his need, and then showing God and his answer.

b. The word of the divine Saviour

He opened their minds to understand the scriptures, and said to them, 'Thus it is written, that the Christ should suffer and on the third day rise from the dead, and that repentance and forgiveness of sins should be preached in his name to all nations' (24:45–47).

What is God's answer to the need of man? He meets the morning's perplexity at the garden tomb with the words of his Son. He meets

[14] Jn. 20:11ff. [15] Mt. 28:9f.

[16] They were no longer twelve, because of Judas's death; and although they were now officially called 'the eleven' (24:33), only ten of them, at most, were actually there (Jn. 20:24).

the afternoon's misery on the Emmaus road with his Son's exposition of Scripture in the power of the Spirit. And now he meets the evening's confusion in the upper room with the words of the Son, the expounding of Scripture, and an unfolding of the future as well as of the past. Jesus speaks not only of his crucifixion and resurrection but of the coming gift of the Spirit and the subsequent career of the gospel. Having brought coherence into human life, and Christ into the human heart, the word of salvation now brings a plan and a purpose before Christ's people.

Four guiding lights show them the direction in which they are expected to go. They are given a biblical theology (24:46), an evangelistic programme (24:47), an apostolic authority (24:48), and a spiritual dynamic (24:49).

During the centuries since, God's people have often found themselves again in the same state of uncertainty in which they were at the start of that memorable evening. For many Christians, today is such a time, and they are feeling similar doubts about the role and objectives of the church. Where are we supposed to be going? What are we meant to be doing? What are we *about*? What are we *for*? In circumstances like these our course needs to be set once more according to the same four guiding lights. We consider them now in the reverse order.

The sighting again of the fourth of them, the necessity of a *spiritual dynamic* (24:49), has become one of the most widespread and noteworthy features of the Christian world today. Movements of spiritual renewal may be given various names; they may appear in unlikely quarters; they may express themselves sometimes in regrettable ways, and even sit loose to scriptural norms; but they have certainly recalled much of Christendom to a truth too easily forgotten—that unless the church possesses the 'promise of the Father', the miracle-working power of the Holy Spirit, it is *nothing*. C. S. Lewis, a prophet in this as in much else, used to insist that far more important than most other dividing lines within the Christian world was the one between supernaturalists and the rest. Thirty or forty years ago that might have seemed the opinion of an odd minority, with 'humanist' Christianity a much more widely acceptable alternative. But those days, surely, are past; and to us it must be clear that we shall get nowhere unless we have been clothed with power from on high, and are expecting supernatural deeds from the Spirit of God.

A thing which is still not always seen, however, even by some who have been powerfully touched by spiritual renewal, is the third guiding light, the need for *apostolic authority* (24:48). What we believe and what we proclaim must be only those truths which we are authorized to believe and proclaim by the teaching of the twelve. They and they alone 'are witnesses of these things.' No doubt later generations of the church have produced many a bigger brain and many a sharper wit than Peter's or John's; but these men had the unsurpassed advantage of being able to say, 'It was so; so I heard and saw',[17] and of having been divinely commissioned to speak in this way. As we have already seen,[18] 'the teaching of the twelve' means for us the contents of the New Testament, corroborated by the twelve even where written by others, and to this we refer every question. We are not at liberty to say that we feel 'led by the Spirit' along paths which have not been mapped by the twelve. To learn of Jesus, and so of his way forward for his church, we look to their witness alongside the witness of the Spirit: neither without the other.[19]

Moving back through these four verses, we come to the second of the principles laid down by Jesus for his people's understanding of what they are. The nature of the church is spiritual; the basis of the church is apostolic; and the purpose of the church is evangelistic. There is a higher purpose, which the church shares with the rest of God's creation: all that he has made exists ultimately to worship and glorify him. But the church, as the church, is given the particular objective of bringing glory to his name by preaching the gospel to his world. So Jesus sets before the apostles their *evangelistic programme* (24:47). They are to preach 'repentance and forgiveness . . . to all nations'. The first half of that phrase (God's offer of a new start, and man's turning to accept it) says 'Salvation'; the second half says 'for the world'. How clearly these words reiterate Luke's chief theme! We heard it at the outset of his 'symphony';[20] he has since given us a full-length exposition of the deeds and words of the One who embodies it; now he fines it down again to this simple re-statement; and in due course the second part of his great work will consist of the development of the same theme, though with a subtle and marvellous change of orchestration, as the voice of God's Son gives place to

[17] Robert Browning, *A Death in the Desert*. Browning's poem pictures the last days of the last surviving member of that apostolic band, and is, in the view of William Temple, 'the most penetrating interpretation of St John that exists in the English language' (*Readings in St John's Gospel*, Macmillan, 1961, p.xx).

[18] See above, pp. 24f.   [19] Jn. 15:34f.

[20] See above, p. 38 n. 15.

213

the voice of his Spirit speaking through his people. But the theme throughout is that of the Saviour of the world.

Before all these things, however, the nascent church has been shown that it must have a *biblical theology* (24:46). Its spiritual dynamic is inseparable from this, for when the Son tells us that the power of the Spirit is 'the promise of my Father', he is speaking of a promise made not only through his own lips but also through those of his predecessors the prophets.[21] Its apostolic authority is underpinned by this: while its doctrine is, as the rest of the New Testament will show us, built solidly upon the teaching of the apostles, they in turn are deeply grounded in what for them is already Scripture, that is, the Old Testament.[22] Its evangelistic programme is derived from this: *'it is written* . . . that repentance and forgiveness of sins should be preached in his name to all nations'; indeed, Jesus says that all these great New Testament matters are to be found 'written' in the Old Testament, not in proof texts in its obscure corners, but as the very warp and woof of it.[23] Christ and his gospel are the new hope promised in Genesis,[24] the new life typified in Exodus,[25] and the new law foreshadowed there and in the books that follow;[26] they are the ideal which all the judges, all the kings, either felt towards or rebelled against;[27] they put flesh on the insights of David,[28] they bring to life the pattern of Jonah,[29] they fulfil the visions of Isaiah.[30] The two Testaments are one, and the theology which is the sap of the church can rise only from roots which run thus deep and wide through the whole of Scripture.

In this way the new people of God is commissioned. For as the Son came into the world bringing the message of salvation, so his people are now to go out into the world bearing the same message. For the last time, we transpose Luke into the key of John, and hear in the words of the fourth Gospel the direction of the Lord to his church: 'As the Father has sent me, even so I send you.'[31]

With keen insight, therefore, Luke ends his first volume where he began it: God's people praising him in his temple. For 'the temple'

---

[21] Nu. 11:24–29; Is. 61:1ff.; Ezk. 36:26f.; Joel 2:28f.
[22] Acts 1:16; 2:16, 25, 30, 31, 34, 39; 3:22, 24, 25; *etc., etc.*
[23] See above, pp. 77ff.
[24] See above, pp. 56–58, 60.   [25] See above, pp. 79, 129, 192.
[26] See above, pp. 78f., 85ff.   [27] See above, p. 79.
[28] See above, pp. 79, 110, 150, 176.   [29] See above, p. 129f.
[30] See above, pp. 35, 61, 110, 150.   [31] Jn. 20:21.

means, as we have seen, the place where God meets man. The Gospel began there, at the heart of the old Jewish faith, for if in those days God and man were ever to come together, that was the place where the meeting would be—in the religion of the ancient Israelites: 'to them belong the sonship, the glory, the covenants, the giving of the law, the worship, and the promises'.[32] What has been achieved in the course of the gospel story is that a new way has been opened by which man and God can be reunited. There is a new temple. So it is in the temple that Luke not only begins but also ends his Gospel (24:53); the important thing now, however, is not the old building, which is doomed to destruction, but the community of Jesus's people gathered there. Henceforth it is they who 'are God's temple',[33] and among them God is to be met with. For them, and for them alone, life is a meaningful thing, God's word is a living reality, and the proclamation of the good news is a consuming passion. They know the Saviour, and they want the world to know him too.

Whether or not Luke had planned from the outset that his Gospel should have a sequel, he has written it in such a way that its twenty-fourth chapter certainly does not come to a 'full close'. This is simply the end of the overture, with the music poised on a great chord of the dominant, ready to surge forward into the next movement of the work. That will be the Book of Acts, the account of how, in the power of the Spirit, the good news of the Saviour is taken out into the world. But then Acts too, in its turn, is open-ended. Below the last verse of his second volume also, Luke might well have written the words 'To Be Continued'. And if we have understood him rightly, we shall realize that the story continues even today, and in the making of it we ourselves are enlisted as co-authors.

[32] Rom. 9:4.
[33] 1 Cor. 3:16; cf. 1 Pet. 2:5; and see above, pp. 180f.